# Connecting in College

# Connecting in College

## How Friendship Networks Matter for Academic and Social Success

JANICE M. McCABE

The University of Chicago Press
Chicago and London

The University of Chicago Press, Chicago 60637
The University of Chicago Press, Ltd., London
© 2016 by The University of Chicago
All rights reserved. Published 2016.
Printed in the United States of America

25  24  23  22  21  20  19  18  17  16       1  2  3  4  5

ISBN-13: 978-0-226-40949-8 (cloth)
ISBN-13: 978-0-226-40952-8 (paper)
ISBN-13: 978-0-226-40966-5 (e-book)
DOI: 10.7208/chicago/9780226409665.001.0001

Library of Congress Cataloging-in-Publication Data

Names: McCabe, Janice M., author.
Title: Connecting in college : how friendship networks matter for academic
    and social success / Janice M. McCabe.
Description: Chicago ; London : The University of Chicago Press, 2016. |
    Includes bibliographical references and index.
Identifiers: LCCN 2016012481 | ISBN 9780226409498 (cloth : alk. paper) |
    ISBN 9780226409528 (pbk. : alk. paper) | ISBN 9780226409665 (e-book)
Subjects: LCSH: College students—Social networks—United States.
Classification: LCC LB3607 .M33 2016 | DDC 378.1/980973—dc23 LC record
    available at http://lccn.loc.gov/2016012481

# CONTENTS

ILLUSTRATIONS

# Introduction

Some friends were beneficial to my career. Other ones were just troublemakers and totally discouraged me from studying. But my really close friends were really good motivators and were like, "Hey, let's go to the library" [or] "Hey, we have to get up early and study."

—Betsy

Like Betsy, many college students rely on their friends for more than just having fun. But surprisingly, we know very little about what college students' friendships look like, or how they might benefit from these friendships, socially and academically, in the short and the long term. At a time when only four out of 10 students graduate from four-year colleges within four years (DeAngelo et al. 2011), understanding friendships may assist students and institutions in drawing on friends' benefits and avoiding their pitfalls.[1] In this book, I explore how friendship networks matter for college students' lives both during and after college. In doing so, I identify different types of friendship networks—for instance, the extent to which young people have tight, cohesive friendship groups or move effortlessly among different social circles—and how these networks are associated with social and academic success for students from different race, gender, and class backgrounds. As we see with Betsy, the benefits of friendship are not the same for all friends. These benefits also are not the same for all students. I find instead that friendship network type influences how friends matter for students' academic and social successes and failures. Consider the following three students whom I met during my research for the book.

Alberto was a fifth-year college student at a public four-year university in the midwestern United States, which I will refer to as "MU" (Midwest University).[2] When Alberto arrived on campus after a year at another college, he was excited about an academic program at MU. Despite his enthusiasm, he felt lonely at first. He also felt marginal as a Latino[3] man on a predominantly white campus. He joined several campus organizations, including a Latino fraternity. Alberto formed a tight-knit friendship group that brought together friends from home with those he met at MU, and he referred to them as a "family." This group provided a range of academic support to Alberto and to each other: they studied together, provided emotional support regarding academics, and engaged in stimulating intellectual conversations. His friends also helped him cope with the race-based marginality he experienced on campus, talking about incidents when professors and peers made what Alberto called "derogatory" and "offensive" comments about Latinos. Alberto received tremendous academic and social support from his tight-knit group of friends. Four years after he graduated, Alberto was still close to many of these friends and remained convinced that they had played an important role in his academic success.

I met Mary at the stately sorority house where she had moved earlier that year, at the beginning of her sophomore year. Mary, a white middle-class[4] woman, described her first year at MU, especially the first semester, as a time when she had "a lot of problems just adjusting to everything." The presence of thirty thousand undergraduates at MU was overwhelming for her, coming as she did from a high school with about fifteen hundred students. At first, Mary did not feel that she fit in on campus or could make friends in her dorm. For her, joining a sorority was a pivotal moment: she found a sense of belonging within her sorority and felt that it connected her to MU. Most of the friends she made on campus were members of this historically white sorority. Mary also maintained a large group of friends from home whom she had known since high school, junior high school, or even elementary school. While Mary's friends from home were strictly social friends, friends in her sorority also provided some emotional support regarding academics. Her main source of academic support, however, came from acquaintances, not friends; she studied with acquaintances she met in class and they shared notes and quizzed each other before exams. The second time I interviewed her, Mary was starting her third year in a PhD program in a nearby state. While most of her friends were not those she had had five years earlier, she still described having different groups of friends: she received social support from friends from home and from a few friends from her MU sorority, and she received academic emotional support from her graduate school friends.

Martin was working, checking out video cameras and recorders to students, when I met him. He is a black man from a lower-class background and was in his fourth and final year at MU. He described himself as making friends effortlessly regardless of the setting. At MU, Martin made friends in many places, including his first-year dorm, the campus newspaper, and a theater group. He also remained in close contact with two friends from his hometown church and three family members, counting them among his list of friends. Like Alberto, he experienced race-based isolation. Martin often felt hypervisible as the only black man in his classes, campus organizations, and social events. Yet at events with other black students, he also described feeling as if he did not fit in. Several times during the interview, he rhetorically asked, "Where do I belong?" But unlike Alberto, Martin rarely discussed this isolation with his friends, and Martin also felt lonesome in his academic pursuits. Thus, despite having many friends and being involved on campus in a range of student organizations, Martin felt alone socially and academically at MU. When I interviewed him five years later, he had maintained friendships with only two of the people he had mentioned during college, but despite moving to four different states, he had crafted a tight-knit friendship network and no longer felt isolated.

Drawing on the experiences of young adults, such as Alberto, Mary, and Martin, this book shows how friendship networks are an important, yet often-overlooked, factor influencing social and academic success. Given national trends of increasing tuition and declining subsidies for higher education (Delbanco 2012), coupled with high dropout rates (DeAngelo et al. 2011; NCES 2014), understanding the potential benefits that friends can provide would be an economical way to maximize student success. The average college student spends only 15 hours a week in class but 86 hours a week with his or her friends (Arum and Roksa 2011, 97).[5] But who are these friends, and how much of a role do they play in college students' success?

Although Alberto, Mary, and Martin all had friends, the ways in which their friends were connected to each other resulted in different types of network structures: Alberto had a "tight-knit" network with one densely woven friendship group; Mary "compartmentalized" her friends into two clusters (friends from home and friends from MU); and Martin "sampled" friends from a variety of places, with the result that his friends were less connected to one another. Figures I.1–I.3 illustrate these three network types, showing the typical shape of each type; Alberto's, Mary's, and Martin's networks appear later, in chapters 3–5. All three students experienced loneliness when they first arrived, and they all made friends at MU, joined several campus organizations, graduated from MU, and went on to pursue graduate degrees. But not all of them felt equally supported by their friends in this

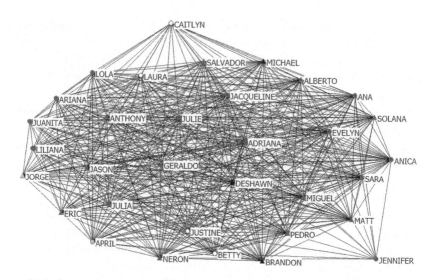

I.1. Sociogram representing the tight-knitter network type (Adriana). In all sociograms, the student I interviewed is near the center of the network, connected by a line to each of his or her friends. Each person is represented by a shape—a circle for women and a triangle for men—and colors correspond to racial/ethnic background. Friends are connected by a line when they know each other, according to the student I interviewed.

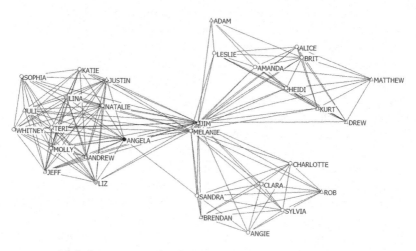

I.2. Sociogram representing the compartmentalizer network type (Jim)

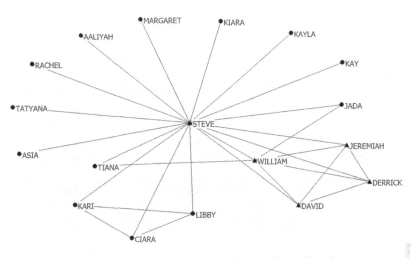

I.3. Sociogram representing the sampler network type (Steve)

journey or were able to overcome the loneliness they felt to thrive socially and academically at MU. Table I.1 summarizes the three network types and the experiences associated with them. In this book, I consider how these experiences are shaped not only by the college itself and the students' own behavior and background but also by their friends and the connections among their friends.

I examine how friendships matter for college students' social and academic success and isolation.[6] The story I tell is not focused on individual friendships but on the structure of students' friendship networks—that is, the connections among students' friends. Using multiple research methods, I examine numerous aspects of students' friendship networks and demonstrate how both the structure and the content of networks matter for students' success. I also demonstrate how friendship networks positively and negatively influence students' academic performance, social experiences, and life after college. In short, *Connecting in College* examines the types of friendship networks students form, who forms which type, what academic and social outcomes are attached to each type, and how they affect students after college. These are some of the issues this book considers as it follows Alberto, Mary, Martin, and their peers over a five-year period from their undergraduate years at MU into life after college.

While readers may identify with one of the network types and reflect on their personal experiences, I hope that thinking about the types closely, as I do in this book, will also generate more recognition of the importance of

**Table I.1 Typology of network types**

|  | Tight-knitters | Compartmentalizers | Samplers |
|---|---|---|---|
| Key elements | One cohesive friend-ship group | Two to four friendship clusters; few con-nections between clusters | Disconnected col-lection of friends; most friends do not know each other |
| Who has this network type | Black and Latina/o students | Middle- and upper-class white students, especially women | Diverse in terms of race, class, and gender |
| Social benefits | High levels of social support from friends; friends helped combat race-based marginality | Moderate levels of social support from friends, often from one cluster | Limited social support from one-on-one friendships |
| Social costs | Difficult to exit friend-ship network | Time and identity pressures from managing multiple friendship groups | Lonely or isolated socially |
| Academic benefits | Success with academic multiplex ties and those that provide academic emotional support | Successful students of color and lower-class students have academic involve-ment from *both* (*a*) one cluster and (*b*) academic multiplex ties; more privileged students find success with *either* | Successful without friends; friends do not distract students from academic success |
| Academic costs | Friends with lower academic focus and outcomes can distract students and lack skills and knowledge to help | Time and identity pressures from managing multiple friendship groups | Lonely or isolated academically |
| Networks after college | Kept the most friends, especially those who provided academic emotional support and academic multi-plex ties | Mostly new friends but kept compart-mentalized network structure | Mostly new friends; became tight-knitters and found social support |

friendship and the support that friends can provide. Throughout the book, I provide suggestions for students, parents, faculty, and administrators who seek to help students thrive academically and socially. Rather than be taken as one-size-fits-all solutions, I hope that these suggestions encourage conversations about what will improve students' experiences, taking into account the particular challenges and strengths of the student and the institution.

## Higher Education in the United States

This study is embedded in a particular moment in higher education. Headlines bemoan the many ways higher education is failing our youth: stagnant graduation rates, soaring college prices, record levels of student loan debt, and gaps by socioeconomic class and race in who attends and graduates from college. Social scientists have revealed a range of important explanations for students' college success, including the differential preparation students receive from earlier levels of schooling (Massey et al. 2003), the value institutions place on undergraduate learning (Armstrong and Hamilton 2013; Arum and Roksa 2011), and the appeal of college social life (Armstrong and Hamilton 2013; Holland and Eisenhart 1990). To this list of explanations, I add the structure and content of undergraduates' friendship networks: I find that the connections (or lack of connections) between students' friends and what happens in the interactions among friends matter for young adults' success in college and beyond.

### A Network Approach

Sociologists have long considered network explanations for social phenomenon; for example, Georg Simmel (1955, 163) argued, "Society arises from the individual and the individual arises out of association." Put differently, interactions between people are the basic building blocks of society. Social network analysis involves mapping these connections to measure network structure. Sociologists have found many ways that network structure matters for individuals' life chances, arguing, for example, that "weak ties" (i.e., acquaintances) lead to more productive job searches (Granovetter 1973), people who connect across groups have more good ideas (Burt 2004), and adolescents' delinquency is shaped by the delinquency of their friends and how tightly their friends are connected to each other (Haynie 2001). Nicholas Christakis and James Fowler's (2009) book *Connected: The Surprising Power of Our Social Networks and How They Shape Our Lives* nicely summarizes the effects that network structure has on a range of outcomes, including health, happiness, wealth, weight, and emotions. Networks, however, do not always provide benefits. Alejandro Portes (1998), for example, reviews the negative consequences of the social capital embedded in networks, including demands on group members, limits on individuals' freedoms, and enforcement of norms that keep individuals from rising out of the group's social position. Networks, thus, can not only help people but also constrain them.

## The Importance of Peers

Since at least the 1950s, when James Coleman performed his research, sociologists who study education have acknowledged the importance of peers for students' academic achievement. Research tends to focus on peers— that is, young people of a similar age, who may or may not be friends— rather than the more specific ties of friendship. Coleman (1961) argued that high school students strive for social, rather than academic, success because that is what they believe their peers value. More contemporary researchers have investigated how high school peer cultures and friendship groups shape students' experiences and attitudes in school and how they do so differently according to students' race, class, and gender. Some of this research shows how friendship groups collectively resist success in school, such as the lower-class students who shirk schoolwork to spend time with friends (Bettie 2003; Willis 1977). In contrast, other research shows friendship groups supporting academic achievement, particularly for black and Latino students who help each other succeed academically (Akom 2003; Bettie 2003; Datnow and Cooper 1997; Flores-Gonzalez 2002; Horvat and Lewis 2003; Mehan, Hubbard, and Villanueva 1994; Valenzuela 1999). In other words, many researchers view "friendship through rose-colored glasses" (Crosnoe 2000, 378), while others focus on friends' and peers' negative impact. Overall, this body of work shows that peers and friends have an academic impact but does not go so far as to use the insights of network analysis to map students' friendships and consider connections among friends. This research also focuses on *either* the benefits *or* the costs of friends.

Researchers applying the insights of network analysis have revealed important characteristics of high school students' friendships, including their racial composition (Kao and Joyner 2004; Moody 2001), the academic resources of best friends (Cherng, McCrory Calarco, and Kao 2013), and the potential of academically oriented friendships to be academically beneficial (Crosnoe, Cavanagh, and Elder 2003; Riegle-Crumb and Callahan 2009). These researchers focus on measuring the academic impact, often using representative samples that tell us much about large-scale patterns, rather than on showing the process through which this impact occurs. And, like the previous body of work, this research does not consider connections among students' friends. This gap was highlighted over thirty years ago by Joyce Epstein (1983, 244), who argued, "More complete research on students' multiple friendship and peer groups may be the single most important new direction for studies of peer and friendship selection and influence." *Connecting in College* takes up this call, using the tools of network analysis to visualize students' friendship networks, paired with rich descriptions of students' experiences, to show for the first time how students form different types of friendship networks and use them in different ways to manage their academic and social lives.

## College Friendships

While our understandings of friendships are incomplete for the high school years, even less research exists at the college level. Reviewing this limited literature on college friendships across sociology, anthropology, history, education, and economics, however, points to friends' importance for students' experiences and outcomes. In general, we know that friends matter, but we do not know the types of networks students form, who forms which type, and what academic and social costs and benefits are associated with them in both the short and the long term.

Given the importance of friends to high school students and the even greater time residential-college students spend with peers, it is not surprising that peers' influence does not wane in college. In fact, scholars studying emerging adulthood assert that it is during these years (ages 18–25) that "friendships may reach their peak of functional significance" (Arnett et al. 2011, 27; also see Kimmel 2008; Rawlins 1992). Large bodies of research in economics and education document how much college peers matter. Economists refer to this as "peer effects," and they have established the positive and negative impacts that peers have on a range of behaviors, such as crime, drinking, career choices, and educational outcomes. Several studies of college students demonstrate that roommates' grades or SAT scores affect students' own academic performance (Sacerdote 2001; Stinebrickner and Stinebrickner 2006; Zimmerman 2003). Rather than focusing on how—that is, the process through which—peers matter, economists have focused on quantifying *how much* they matter and grappling with measurement and modeling issues, particularly that friendships are not randomly formed.

In contrast, education researchers tend to see peers as positive, overlooking the potential *costs* of friendships for academic and social life. For example, education theorists stress the value of peer involvement, which has also been studied using terms such as "social involvement" (Astin 1993), "social integration" (Tinto 1993, 2012), "social engagement" (Kuh et al. 2005; Pascarella and Terenzini 2005), or "sense of belonging" (Hurtado and Carter 1997). While most of this research focuses more generally on peers, research that focuses specifically on friends also views them positively, as academic resources. This research shows that friends can be involved in academics through talking about workloads and deadlines (Brooks 2007), trying out ideas with each other (Martinez Alemán 1997, 2000), having intellectual conversations about social issues (antonio 2001; Martinez Alemán 2000), and increasing intellectual self-confidence (antonio 2004). Though it is clear from this research that college peers matter and that friends can provide academic benefits, both economists and education researchers overlook the ways that friends are connected to each other.

Researchers employing some aspects of network analysis have revealed considerable variation in network content and academic benefits of college friendships. One line of research focuses on who is in the network, particularly in terms of establishing that homophily (social similarities in terms of race, gender, and academic orientation) and propinquity (being in close proximity in classrooms and dorms) shape undergraduates' choice of friends (M. Fischer 2008; Flashman 2012, 2014; Moffatt 1989; Newcomb 1961, 1967; Newcomb and Wilson 1966; Stearns, Buchmann, and Bonneau 2009). Like the analyses of high school students' networks, this research often uses representative samples to provide important insights into large-scale patterns in students' friendships, but it leaves unanswered many questions about mechanisms and does not measure connections among students' friends. A second line of research, which is more focused on students' experiences, overlooks the structure of students' networks but tells us more about their value. For example, in their book *How College Works,* Daniel Chambliss and Christopher Takacs (2014) argue for the importance of the people students encounter in college, but they ignore friendship structure, instead focusing on individual relationships. Notably, they assert that students get more out of college when they find "*two or three good friends, and one or two great professors*" (2014, 21, emphasis in original).[7] As a whole, this research suggests there is considerable variation in college students' networks. I argue that we could better understand this variation in students' friendships and their importance by investigating network structure.

In line with sociologists' identification of the negative consequences of networks, some have argued that college friendships are largely irrelevant or even damaging to academic life. Those who assert that friends negatively affect academic life do so as part of a more general argument about how undergraduates tend to be focused on social life at the cost of their academics, echoing James Coleman's (1961) research on high school students. This can be seen in the titles alone of several books on college culture, including *Party School* (Weiss 2013), *Paying for the Party* (Armstrong and Hamilton 2013), *Beer and Circus* (Sperber 2000), and *Educated in Romance* (Holland and Eisenhart 1990). These and other books by historians, anthropologists, and sociologists offer rich descriptions of friends who participate together in college social life but who rarely discuss or engage together in academics (e.g., Horowitz 1987; Moffatt 1989; Stuber 2011). Another book, aptly titled *Academically Adrift*, documents how studying with peers has a negative effect on undergraduates' learning, specifically critical thinking, complex reasoning, and writing skills (Arum and Roksa 2011). This research, however, focuses narrowly on cognitive outcomes, does not differentiate between friends and other peers, and overlooks what peers are doing when they study together (Arum and Roksa 2011). Building on existing research, I use insights from network analysis, along with rich descriptions of students' experiences, to consider how friendship network structure and content might positively and negatively affect undergraduates. In other words, I contribute to this debate about whether peers are positive or negative by showing how friends come with both costs *and* benefits.

I focus on how friends matter not only academically but also socially. Many studies show that friendships can provide social support to counter loneliness and isolation, experiences that are far too common among college students. For example, a large survey of over ninety-five thousand students at 139 colleges finds that over half of students reported feeling "very lonely" in the past 12 months (ACHA 2010). It might be surprising that students with friends would end up feeling socially marginal or isolated, especially since a large body of research, particularly in psychology, has shown that friends can provide social support. The main focus of this research, however, is on measuring perceived social support from friends and other ties and suggests that not all friendships provide social support.[8] In fact, previous research finds that loneliness is contagious in networks and extends beyond direct friendships to include friends' friends' friends

(Cacioppo, Fowler, and Christakis 2009). I ask whether the structure of friendship networks might also influence people's experiences of social marginality and isolation.

## Inequalities in Higher Education

Experiences of isolation on college campuses, however, are not random but are tied to students' social class and racial backgrounds. Mitchell Stevens and colleagues (2008) describe college as a sieve where not all who enter college reap the same rewards. For example, lower-class students who are the first in their families to attend college report greater loneliness and less ease on campus than do more-privileged students (Stuber 2011). For many students of color, isolation occurs because of race-based experiences. Students of color experience racial jokes, loneliness, and invisibility, which often are accompanied by mental anguish and academic costs (e.g., W. Allen et al. 1991; Beasley 2011; Feagin, Vera, and Imani 1996; Hurtado and Carter 1997; Wilkins 2014; Willie 2003). More recent scholarship has termed these experiences "microaggressions" and tied them to campus experiences of marginality, isolation, hypervisibility, and discrimination among Latino and black men and women (e.g., McCabe 2009; Smith, Allen, and Danley 2007; Solórzano, Ceja, and Yosso 2000).[9] The racism that students of color face on college campuses refutes dominant beliefs that universities are open, tolerant, and meritocratic (Feagin, Vera, and Imani 1996), and this racism has consequences for these students' persistence and achievement in college (Charles et al. 2009). I uncover how students' experiences of race- and class-based isolation and their responses to them differ by type of friendship network.

Students' race, gender, and class backgrounds are tied to their success entering and graduating from college. Graduation rates are lower (1) for black, Latina/o, and Native American students than for white and Asian students, (2) for first-generation students than for those whose parents attended college, and (3) for men than for women (DeAngelo et al. 2011; DiPrete and Buchmann 2013; NCES 2014; Roksa et al. 2007).[10] These same patterns appear when we consider who enters college. As mentioned earlier, scholars have put forth a range of reasons for these inequalities in who enters and leaves higher education, including features of schools and of students' backgrounds (see, e.g., the review in Stevens, Armstrong, and Arum 2008). To this list, I add the structure and content of students' friendship networks as another feature that may influence the college experiences of students of diverse race, gender, and class backgrounds.

Although scholars argue that inequalities, such as those generated by gender and race, cannot be understood separately (e.g., Collins 1990), our understanding of how these inequalities are reproduced within higher education has been hampered by the lack of data enabling comparisons along multiple axes of inequality.[11] As a whole, research provides insightful glimpses of how undergraduates' friends support one another on the basis of racial, ethnic, and gender similarities (Martinez Alemán 1997, 2000, 2010; McCabe 2015) and across racial and ethnic lines (antonio 2004; McCabe 2011, 2015), suggesting that multiple inequalities matter. My unique approach allows new insights into why such differences are consequential and how they happen across multiple axes of race, class, and gender.

In sum, given that sociologists have long accepted that networks matter and peers matter for a variety of outcomes, it may be surprising how many questions remain about college students' friendship networks. How do college students experience friendship? In what ways are friends involved in students' academic and social lives? How are their friends connected as a network? How are these networks associated with students' success during and after college? And how do friendships differ for students of different backgrounds? In this book, I answer these questions, providing a unique contribution to the scholarly conversation on education and friendship. I take up the call in a recent review of higher education that noted the need for "further inquiries into network dynamics at the experiential core of college" (Stevens, Armstrong, and Arum 2008, 134). By expanding into higher education network researchers' arguments about the value of network structure, I demonstrate how friendship networks matter for academic and social success during and after college.

## The Study

This is a case study of "MU," a large public research university located in the midwestern United States. *US News and World Report* categorizes MU as "more selective" in admissions, with MU admitting about 75 percent of applicants. Many students whom I interviewed noted that they aspired to attend MU because of its vibrant social scene, sports teams, well-known traditions, beautiful campus, and position as the flagship university in the state. MU has several academic programs ranked in the top tier, but only a few participants mentioned specific programs as influencing their decision to attend the college. Because research shows that organizational arrangements on campus shape student experience, I paid particular attention to this in my selection of the institution and the students in the study.

While one university cannot represent the experiences of all students in US higher education, I chose MU because it is typical in many ways of the type of institution attended by most students at four-year campuses—6.8 million students in 2005 (NCES 2014).[12] Table I.2 presents key characteristics of other large public midwestern campuses (specifically the 11 schools

Table I.2 Characteristics of my participants and students at MU and peer institutions

| | Big Ten Schools* | MU | Sample |
|---|---|---|---|
| Background: | | | |
| Race: | | | |
| White (%) | 77 | 85 | 51 |
| Black (%) | 5 | 5 | 28 |
| Latina/o (%) | 3 | 2 | 16 |
| Asian and other (%)[†] | 14 | 7 | 4 |
| Gender (% female) | 50 | 52 | 73 |
| Age (years) | — | — | 20 |
| Year in college | — | — | 2.8 |
| In-state resident (%) | 73 | 70 | 76 |
| First-generation college student (%)[‡] | — | 20–25 | 46 |
| Class:[§] | | | |
| Lower (%) | 19 | 16 | 28 |
| Middle (%) | — | — | 34 |
| Upper (%) | — | — | 28 |
| Employed (%) | — | — | 50 |
| Hours/week, if employed | — | — | 18 |
| Academic characteristics: | | | |
| ACT score** | 26 | 24 | 24 |
| GPA at first interview | — | — | 3.2 |
| Campus activities: | | | |
| Academic club (%) | — | — | 44 |
| Identity-based club (%) | — | — | 17 |
| Living-learning center (%) | — | — | 16 |
| Greek affiliated (in sorority or fraternity) (%) | 16 | 20 | 45 |
| No MU clubs or organizations (%) | — | — | 5 |
| Living on campus (%) | 36 | 35 | 48 |
| N | 31,000 | 30,000 | 82 |

* Figures are from 2005 Common Data Set for the 11 schools in the 2005 Big Ten Conference.
† This category includes Asian, international, Native American, and race "unknown."
‡ Students are considered first-generation college students if their parents, stepparents, or guardians did not graduate from a four-year college or university.
§ Data for the institutions are based on the percentage of students receiving a Pell Grant, which is an indicator of students from low-income backgrounds. See n. 4 in the introduction for details about my sample.
** ACT scores presented here include those converted from SAT scores using the guidelines developed from a concordance study conducted by the ACT and the College Board (see http://www.act .org/solutions/college-career-readiness/compare-act-sat/). MU accepted both SAT and ACT scores. Average SAT and ACT scores at MU rose slightly most years from 2002 to 2009 and then leveled off. Scores for my sample are based on self-reports.

that made up the Big Ten Conference in 2005, which over three hundred thousand undergraduates attend at any one point in time), MU, and my sample.[13] Focusing on a public university is also a corrective to sociological literature on higher education, which concentrates on highly selective institutions (see discussion in Armstrong and Massé 2014).

Like many other large public universities, MU is predominantly white, attracts students from a range of class backgrounds, and hosts many types of clubs and organizations, including sororities and fraternities. Among the thirty thousand undergraduates at MU, about 85 percent are white, 5 percent are black, 2 percent are Latino, and 7 percent are "other" (mostly Asian and international students). Because I was interested in exploring how race affects students' experiences, black and Latino students make up about half my sample, a much greater proportion than their presence on campus. Students were divided along racial lines in terms of whether they felt that MU was racially diverse. Similar to what Allison Hurst (2010) found on another midwestern campus, most white students I interviewed noted that the campus was diverse, often without my directly asking, while most black and Latino students brought up how there were few people who "looked like them." Some black and Latino students stated that MU's mailings and other recruitment materials often showed "people diversity," which distorted their expectations about who would be on campus. While MU differs from some four-year public schools in terms of racial diversity—for example, many public schools in California have larger proportions of Asian and Latino students, and many public schools in the South have larger proportions of black students—the percentages of black and Latino students are similar to most institutions in the Northeast and Midwest, including those in the Big Ten Conference, as shown in table I.2.[14] Higher education institutions—including large public four-year institutions like MU—have become slightly more diverse since I collected the original data in 2004–5,[15] suggesting that the racial issues discussed here are even more relevant today.

While many students commented on the racial diversity on campus, few commented on socioeconomic class diversity (or lack thereof) among students. In other words, class diversity was more hidden on campus than racial diversity. Indeed, statistics on the class backgrounds of students were not publically available at MU or at many other universities. Without information on parents' income or education, researchers and policymakers have often turned to measures of grants, scholarships, and federal loans, particularly Pell Grants. I find that the proportion of students at MU receiving such aid is similar to the proportions at selective public institutions,

suggesting that students at MU may be from more socioeconomically advantaged backgrounds than students at some other institutions, but their
class backgrounds are not atypical among selective public institutions or
those in the Big Ten Conference, as shown in table I.2.[16] My participants
represent a range of class backgrounds, with approximately 40 percent self-
identifying as middle class, 30 percent as lower class, and 30 percent as upper class. The class diversity at MU and among my sample is important to
examine because previous research shows that class influences whether undergraduates feel at ease on campus and whether they graduate (Armstrong
and Hamilton 2013; Hurst 2010; Mullen 2010; Stuber 2011).

Greek life—that is, sororities and fraternities—is a central aspect of the
social scene at many colleges. At MU, their parties and their members are
highly visible on campus, and about 20 percent of students join sororities
or fraternities. MU resembles some other large public universities, including about half of the Big Ten schools, where approximately 20 percent of
students are Greek.[17] While this rate is higher than that at some schools,
it is much lower than others, including Dartmouth College, where half of
students join, and DePauw University, where more than two-thirds of students join.[18] Students in sororities and fraternities make up 45 percent of
my sample so that I could explore the experiences not only of students
in historically white organizations (Armstrong and Hamilton 2013; Stuber
2011) but also of those in historically Latino, black, and multicultural organizations. Previous research has documented a number of differences between historically white and minority Greek organizations, including their
orientation to academics, traditional gender beliefs, and focus on career
goals (Berkowitz and Padavic 1999; Ray and Rosow 2012; Torbenson and
Parks 2009). Greek organizations were central to social life for many students at MU, but so were some of the over four hundred campus clubs and
organizations, along with off-campus bars and late-night coffee shops. MU
had alternative social scenes.

By focusing on one university, I am able to explore the diversity at one
institution in more depth than a comparative study would allow, since the
latter type of study tends to focus on only one or two groups of students.
To best capture the range of student experiences at MU, I reached out to
students through four types of campus organizations: identity-based clubs
for women and students of color, living-learning centers, academic clubs,
and four types of Greek organizations (i.e., historically white, Latino, black,
and multicultural organizations). I also sought students who were not part
of any campus organizations. Table I.2 shows students' participation in
these campus activities. Of the 82 students in my study, about half were

students of color and about half were the first in their families to attend college, referred to as "first-generation college students." Although I was able to capture much variation in student background and experiences, there are other groups of students for whom we need to know much more about their experiences, including Native American, Asian, international, immigrant, and LGBT (lesbian, gay, bisexual, and transgender) students.

I employed several techniques to learn about the campus, taking a mixed-methods and longitudinal approach in that I combined multiple methods of data collection and analysis and tracked participants over time. In 2004–5 I conducted interviews and focus groups, made ethnographic observations, and collected friendship networks and surveys from 82 undergraduates. In 2009 I conducted follow-up interviews and collected surveys and friendship networks from many participants. I collected archival information about MU from newspapers, websites, and reports throughout this whole period. Connecting rich descriptions of students' experiences with detailed maps of their friendships over time provides a unique lens with which to study the lasting academic and social benefits and disadvantages of friends. Whereas most research on college students is primarily quantitative (e.g., Arum and Roksa 2011, 2014) or qualitative (e.g., Armstrong and Hamilton 2013; Holland and Eisenhart 1990), *Connecting in College* draws on the strengths of *both* traditions.

Most stories in this book come from the one-on-one interviews that I conducted with MU students. I used a semistructured design that covered predetermined topics but in a more conversational manner, with the goal that students would feel comfortable sharing their experiences with me while ensuring comparability across interviews. Each interview covered their decisions to attend college in general and MU in particular; perceptions of their college social and academic experiences; making friends at MU; the relationships among their friends; friends' involvement in their academic, intellectual, and social lives; involvement in campus organizations; and ideas and goals for the future. In addition to the interviews, I observed meetings and events of many of the clubs and organizations where I recruited students. This enabled me to see relationships within the organizations and between them and the rest of campus. It also enabled me to recruit participants and to informally follow up with students I had already interviewed. I conducted focus groups with students in some of these organizations—a living-learning center for students interested in African American culture, a historically white sorority, a multicultural sorority, and an academic organization. At the individual and focus group interviews, students completed a survey of demographic information (such as age, race, and parents' occupation) and identity scales (such as the academic-social scale discussed in chapter 2). Because I was interested in how students' friendships and college experiences affected their lives beyond college, I contacted participants four to five years later, presumably after they would have graduated. Anticipating that their lives would be busy, I set up a web-based survey to collect as much information as I could, then followed up with a telephone interview to delve more deeply into their experiences and gain more detail about their survey answers. I also used archival data to find out if and when participants graduated and to construct a portrait of MU, relying on newspaper articles, statewide reports, websites, pamphlets, and institutional records. I discuss and reflect on these methods in more detail in the methodological appendix.

Through these multiple research methods, I developed rich descriptions of young adults' experiences and explored the meanings they attached to these experiences. All accounts, however, are partial, capturing slices of their lives. I read, reread, and analyzed the hundreds of pages of field notes and thousands of pages of interview transcripts. I also constructed sociograms—visual diagrams of friendships, such as those in figures I.1–I.3—and tabulated numbers in the network and survey data. In this book, I present the key findings regarding how friends are involved in students' academic and social lives. The individuals profiled in this book and the quotations presented illustrate general patterns in the data in a way that engages the reader. I discuss how these individuals may be unique and I also present insights from other individuals when they provide additional dimensions to the patterns that are not captured by the highlighted students' experiences.

## Organization of This Book

Chapter 1 focuses on friendship, examining what friendship means to participants and the composition of their networks. In contrast to popular representations of college friendships as superficial, this chapter shows that most students—men and women—developed meaningful friendships in college. It concludes by describing the three types of friendship networks illustrated in figures I.1–I.3: tight-knitters, compartmentalizers, and samplers.

In chapter 2, I examine students' discussions of how their friends are involved in their academic lives. I find that nearly all students engage in "testimonies of balance," describing themselves as balancing academic and social life, while also engaging in "cautionary tale testimonies of imbalance," where they describe students who fail to achieve this balance. I also identify ways that students separated friends from academics to deal with the potential distraction of friends and ways that their friends were involved academically. Contrary to conventional wisdom, students are quite savvy in recognizing that friends can distract them and in strategically using friends to help them improve their academics.

Chapters 3–5 discuss how students' strategies of integration and separation differ for tight-knitters, compartmentalizers, and samplers, respectively. In chapter 3, I show that students with tight-knit networks typically have social support but that academic success varies according to the academic involvement of their friends. In chapter 4, I show that students with compartmentalized networks attain academic and social success often by segmenting academic and social support so that they receive academic support from one cluster of friends and social support from another cluster. Although this enables them to balance academic and social life, managing these multiple friendship groups can exert time and identity pressures. In chapter 5, I show that students who sampled friendships lacked crucial social support and did not rely on friends for much academic help. They ended up with high academic outcomes but felt socially and academically isolated.

Chapter 6 returns to the three students highlighted above—Alberto, Mary, and Martin—focusing on their lives after graduation. I reflect on similarities and differences in the three network types, arguing that they not only affect students during the college years but have lasting, postcollege effects (see the bottom row of table I.1). In each chapter, I discuss how race, gender, and class influence students' friendships, and I offer concrete suggestions for improving students' experiences. Chapter 7 reviews the implications of this study for research as well as practice. In a time of limited resources, I provide concrete and powerful solutions for students, parents, college administrators, and professors.

# ONE

# Friendship

JM: Can you tell me a little bit about your friends and your friendships?
MOLLY: Yeah. I'm smiling just thinking [*laughs*] about my best friends.

Friendship is a fun topic to discuss with college students. As this quotation from Molly suggests, most students get enormous joy from their friendships. College students also devote a good deal of time, energy, and effort to their friendships. Indeed, lay advice—such as "you make your lifelong friends in college" and "college is the best time of your life"—encourages this focus on friendships. So does the structure of college. At residential colleges, such as MU, students find themselves surrounded by same-age peers where they live, eat, attend classes, and walk around campus. At no time before or after will individuals spend more time with friends than they do during the college years. We know anecdotally and from related research that friends play an important role in students' lives, but rarely has research focused explicitly on this topic. Consequently, despite the obvious centrality of friendships in students' lives, there is much we do not know about the meanings, experiences, and structure of undergraduates' friendships.

In this chapter, I seek to expand our knowledge of college students' friendships. I first discuss where students draw the line between friends and nonfriends, while also explaining how I measure friendship in this study. Second, I focus on the structure of students' friendships, examining ties among students' friends and identifying three network types: tight-knitters, compartmentalizers, and samplers. Examining the patterns of connections between people allows us to understand what networks look like and what happens inside them. I expand on these three network types in chapters 3–5. Third, I describe race, class, and gender differences in students' friendships, drawing on the diversity of my sample. In the final section of the chapter, I briefly discuss nonfriend relationships that played important roles in students' college experiences, particularly those with professors, significant others, and parents. As a whole, this chapter provides important context for the arguments that follow, laying the groundwork for what friendships look like in a college setting.

## Where to Draw the Line? Measuring Friendship

What does friendship mean? Who is a friend? Writers and researchers often lament the vague definition of "friendship" and note that people use the term "friend" in a variety of ways (e.g., C. Fischer 1982; Flora 2013; Rubin 1985; Spencer and Pahl 2006). Researchers have come up with various ways to categorize the term; for example, Liz Spencer and Ray Pahl (2006, 60) organize people's ties into four kinds of "friendship repertoires" that include eight levels from simple friendship (associate) to complex friendship (soul mate). Like academics, the students I interviewed also gave a range of definitions and used a range of terms. In this study, I sought to both acknowledge this messiness and find meaningful patterns in it.

During the interviews, therefore, I let participants use their own definition of "friend," but I asked them about their definition and how they decided where to draw the line between those they considered a friend and those they did not. I wanted to improve upon the vague definition of "friend" used in most previous friendship research as well as attempt to understand participants' own meanings of the term. Some students talked of "best friends," others of "best guy friends" and "best girl friends." Others used terms like "closest friends," "inner circle," "crew," or "family." Most distinguished between "true friends," "real friends," "close friends," "closer friends," "good friends," or "really good friends" and others whom they termed "acquaintances," "associates," "kind-of friends," "other friends," "Facebook friends," or "cool people." Some even characterized their friendships on a spectrum: for example, Riyad summarized his friendships by saying, "I have a ton of acquaintances, a few friends, and maybe one or two best friends."

I am glad that I left the definition and number of friends so open because it led to rich discussions about what friendship meant to my participants. Although not everyone had the same definition, trust and closeness came up most frequently; for example, students would often comment that their friends knew things about them that acquaintances did not. Other frequently mentioned features that distinguished friends from nonfriends were that friends shared a "connection," spent time together, and "know me well" (or "understand me") and that these relationships were characterized by honesty, similar interests, shared experiences, and duration. Molly's discussion of her friends includes several of these features: "I feel like it's just about being yourself—at this age. College is about finding yourself and what you wanna do and where you wanna go. And I feel like your friends, who will most likely be in the same boat as you trying to find themselves and everything, should most definitely be the people that will help you and not hold you back and motivate you and just remind yourself to have fun but take things seriously—work hard, play hard [*laughs*]." Molly explained the closeness of her friendships as primarily resulting from her friends' sharing her interests ("being yourself" and "finding yourself") and mind-set ("work hard, play hard"). As Molly's discussion shows, students' stories of friends construct not only their friendships but also their self-identities—"who they are." They construct self-identities not only by drawing similarities with friends, as Molly does, but also by distancing themselves from specific traits of friends (A. Anthony and McCabe 2015). Some respondents had quite-casual definitions of friendship—for example, describing friends as people who are "a lot of fun to hang out with"—while others had incredibly coherent and complex definitions, yet all respondents drew a line as to whom they characterized as a friend.

Students named 18 friends, on average.[1] On the one hand, this average hides a great deal of variation since students named between three and 60 friends. On the other hand, having 50–60 friends was not the norm. In fact, the vast majority of students reported between six and 25 friends, as shown in figure 1.1.[2] I also found some differences in number of friends by participants' race, class, and gender background and by network type, which I discuss below. Because researchers have used different definitions of friendship, no data are available to compare friendships across colleges or the life course. For example, two rigorous studies of interracial friendships during college restrict the number and type of friends students can name: in a study of a highly selective private research university, Elizabeth Stearns and colleagues (2009) use data that limit students to eight friends and exclude family members, and in a study of UCLA students, anthony antonio (2004) limits students to seven UCLA friends.[3] Such arbitrary restrictions on who and how many can be named as friends have greatly limited our knowledge about college friendships. Given that the average in my study was 18 friends, asking about only seven or eight friends does not adequately capture the range of friendships that are meaningful to stu-

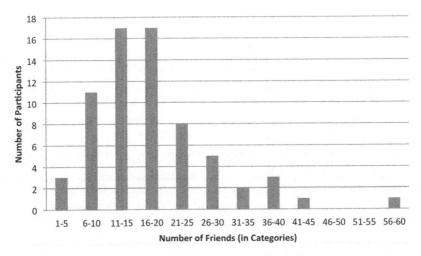

1.1. Number of friends in students' networks

dents. Although these researchers were able to capture information for a larger number of students—antonio (2004) for 677 students and Stearns, Buchmann, and Bonneau (2009) for 800 students—their survey methodology did not permit students to explain what friendship in general or any specific relationships meant to them. My approach, using an interview to gain much more context about students' friends and their relationships, as well as leaving open the number of friends students could name, provides definitions of friendship that are more grounded in students' own meanings and experiences.

Along with friend lists and definitions, I also asked participants for demographic details about each friend and systematically went through their friend list asking whether each friend knew each other friend. I include a detailed description of this process in the appendix. From the demographic information, I was able to contextualize students' friendships and provide measures of the similarity of students' friends along these dimensions. The information about connections among their friends allowed me to look at factors that social network researchers often use to understand network dynamics, particularly network density, betweenness centrality, and modularity. These measures are discussed later in this chapter. With all these data, I looked for meaningful patterns in students' networks and how their friends connected to one another.

Most students' networks included a mix of friends from home and friends they met at MU. On average, 53 percent of students' networks were composed of friends they met at MU, 12 percent were friends from home who attended MU, another 26 percent were friends from home, and 9 percent were from other settings, such as people they met at a job or summer camp. This means that if a student had 18 friends, on average, he or she would have met 10 of them at MU, two would be friends from home who also attended MU, five would be from home, and one would be from outside MU or home. The proportion of students' friends whom they met at MU grew slightly as they spent more time on campus. While the difference from year to year is not always significant, the difference over the first three years is sizable: first-year students report meeting 40 percent of their friends on campus; this increases to 46 percent for second-year students and increases again, to 57 percent, for third-year students and beyond.[4]

At MU, students most frequently made friends in their dorms (especially first-year dorms), in student organizations, and through other friends. They also made friends in classes, in their on-campus jobs, and at other campus events, such as festivals and orientations. Network researchers have long focused on the importance of proximity—that is, with whom one regularly comes into contact—in shaping whom college students befriend (e.g., Marmaros and Sacerdote 2006; Newcomb 1961). Network researchers have also pointed to homophily—that is, similarity based on race, gender, or other characteristics—as another important basis of friendship (e.g., Marmaros and Sacerdote 2006; McPherson, Smith-Lovin, and Cook 2001; Stearns, Buchmann, and Bonneau 2009). Therefore, it is not surprising that many MU students frequently formed friendships with those who shared their dorm or other spaces on campus (such as Greek houses or clubs) and with those who shared their racial or ethnic identity.

Most students spent a lot of time with friends and a lot of time staying connected with them when they were not physically together. For example, students' closest friends were typically other MU students, whom they would see several times a week and stay in touch with more frequently electronically or on the phone. With people they had just met and friends from home, electronic communication played a bigger role; students commented that Facebook helped them to stay in touch with people whom they had recently met and to keep track of what was happening with friends from home. They used instant messaging much more than e-mail with friends, which is probably similar to students' use today of text messaging rather than e-mail with friends. Although the types of social media have changed since this study began in 2004, research on youth's use of social media suggests that youth's practices remain the same when specific types of social media change (boyd 2014). The frequency of face-to-face contact, however, may be higher at residential colleges like MU than at commuter schools or community colleges, where students lack or have limited access to the peer-centered worlds of the dorms and apartments on or near campus. In this way, context likely influences how friends stay in touch; however, it is not clear that it changes the patterns of friendships that I focus on in this book.

## How Are Friends Connected to Each Other? Network Types

Students do not just have individual friendships; they are embedded in a larger social structure. Social network analysis enables the systematic study of social structure and social integration. In this way, it allows for a more complete understanding of the structure of friendships. The collection of network data permits this information to be systematically analyzed and presented visually and numerically (Marsden 1990, 2000). Network researchers refer to the visual maps of friendships as "sociograms" and the individuals represented in them as "nodes." In these maps, the shape and color of nodes can indicate attributes of individuals, such as gender and race. Researchers also compare networks using numeric measures of network concepts, including density, betweenness centrality, and modularity.

The density of a network refers to the connections among an individual's friends. In a sociogram a connection between two of an individual's friends is indicated by a line connecting the symbols that represent them. Mathematically, density is the proportion of ties (connections) present out of possible ties, ranging from zero (where no one in the network is connected) to one (where everyone is tied to each other) (Marsden 1990).

In my study students' friendship networks spanned from 0.08 to 1.00 in density, with an average of 0.56, which suggests that, on average, just over half of students' friends knew each other. More interesting than the average, however, is that three types of network structures emerged among my respondents. These correspond to thirds of the density distribution.[5] Figures I.1–I.3, in the introduction, visually show these three types. *Tight-knitters* are students with highly dense networks (0.67–1.0 density); their friends form one cohesive group because they all or almost all know each other. *Compartmentalizers* are students with middle-density networks (0.34–0.64 density); they compartmentalize their friends into two to four clusters. *Samplers* are students with low-density networks (0.08–0.32 density); their friends are less tied to one another because samplers "sample" friendships. As with the friendship research discussed earlier, no data are available to compare density across colleges or the life course. Relatively few studies examine friendship network density and the factors associated with it in detail, probably because collecting these data is quite labor intensive for both the participant and the researcher.[6] Even incredibly rich sources of network data, such as Claude Fischer's (1982), Barry Wellman's (1979), and the National Longitudinal Study of Adolescent Health (Add Health) data sets, limit the number of relationships measured. For example, Fischer (1982) measures the relationships between three and five members of respondents' networks; Wellman (1979) allows respondents to report a maximum of six "intimates"; Add Health limits friendship nominations to five friends of each gender from the same school attended by the participant. In general, however, this research concludes that dense networks are not the norm (C. Fischer and Shavit 1995; Haynie 2001; Schreck, Fisher, and Miller 2004; Wellman et al. 1997). Dana Haynie (2001, 1014) put it most clearly: "Most adolescents do not belong to a single, densely knit, isolated friendship clique, but instead are affiliated with many loosely bounded friendship groups with varying degrees of cohesion and permeability." My findings confirm that dense networks are not the norm for white students, but they are the norm for black and Latino students, as described below and in more detail in chapters 3–5.

In addition to density, two other network measures—betweenness centrality and modularity—help to distinguish between these three network types. Betweenness centrality is a measure of how central a person is in a network in terms of how many members are connected only through that person. I focus on the centrality of the students I interviewed. I use a normalized centrality measure so that it varies from zero to one, with higher scores indicating that the person is more central in connecting others in the network.[7] Betweenness centrality scores differed for all three groups: when looking at the overall data, tight-knitters' average score is 0.04, whereas it is 0.25 for compartmentalizers and 0.62 for samplers. Lower betweenness centrality scores suggest that fewer people in the network are connected principally through the focal student—the "ego," to use a sociological term. It makes sense that tight-knitters would have the lowest score, since most people in their network are connected to each other, and that samplers would have the highest score, since their friends are least likely to know each other.

Modularity is a measure of communities in a network. It is calculated by comparing the number of edges—that is, connections between friends—present with the number expected by chance (Newman 2006); scores range from –0.5 to one, with positive numbers indicating that there are more edges than are expected by chance, meaning that there are multiple communities. Tight-knitters' average modularity score is 0.02, whereas it is 0.19

for compartmentalizers and 0.25 for samplers. Modularity distinguishes tight-knitters from the other two types but does not distinguish compartmentalizers from samplers. This occurs because tight-knitters' networks do not fall into clusters as do the other types. Overall, because betweenness centrality and modularity scores differ across network types, they confirm that there are meaningful differences between tight-knitters, compartmentalizers, and samplers.

I found a few differences in the characteristics of students with each of these three network types. Tight-knitters' networks were smaller, with 13 friends, than those of compartmentalizers and samplers, with 20 friends.[8] Compartmentalizers also differed somewhat in gender and class background, with more women and more middle-class students than the other network types. Samplers were more likely to live on campus (three-quarters of samplers vs. one-half of the other network types) and less likely to be in a romantic relationship (only one sampler vs. 40%–50% of the other network types). Tight-knitters were more likely to work (68% vs. 36%–42%); however, samplers who were employed worked longer hours (24.5 vs. 18–19 hours per week). The network types also differed in ACT scores, GPAs (grade point averages), and graduation rates: tight-knitters scored lowest in each category.[9] The final and most important way they differed was in terms of race: most students of color were tight-knitters and most white students were compartmentalizers. I discuss these racial differences below and expand on the role of friendship groups in coping with racial experiences on campus in chapters 3–5. See table A.1 in the appendix for overviews of these differences. In chapter 6, I discuss changes in these networks after college, which suggest that these network types are driven not by stable personality traits or friendship preferences but by the college setting.

## Gender

Overall, there were far more gender similarities than differences in terms of students' friendships. I find this somewhat surprising given the focus in existing literature on gender differences in friendship among people in general (Rubin 1985) and specifically among college-age youth (Felmlee, Sweet, and Sinclair 2012; Martinez Alemán 1997, 2000; Sheets and Lugar 2005). For example, despite claims of the value of college women's friendships on learning (Martinez Alemán 1997, 2000), I found few differences in friends' academic involvement. The gender differences in friendships also do not appear to contribute to women's advantage over men in college grades or completion (DiPrete and Buchmann 2013). Qualitative research discussing gender differences in friendship among college students, however, tends to focus only on one gender (e.g., Armstrong and Hamilton 2013; Holland and Eisenhart 1990; Kimmel 2008; Martinez Alemán 1997, 2000), which may overemphasize gender differences. In my study, women reported slightly fewer friends than men (17 vs. 20); however, they have similar density scores[10] and proportions of friends who are MU students, from home, from home who attend MU, and family members. This suggests that the structure and composition of women's and men's networks are largely the same.

In my sample, the primary difference in women's and men's networks was that women had more women friends. On average, 72 percent of women's friends were other women, whereas only 59 percent of men's friends were other men. Overall, these rates are similar to those reported by Rutgers undergraduates, where one-third of friendships were cross-gender (Moffatt 1989). These differences between women and men seemed to stem from women's beliefs that men may seek sexual or romantic ties rather than just friendship and from students' beliefs that women were often more willing to listen. As psychologist William Pollack (Pollack and Shuster 2000, 249) put it, "When they feel ashamed to turn to their parents and male friends for support, female peers are frequently there to listen, understand, and help them stay the course. Boys feel at ease in sharing their fears, sadness, and disappointments with close female peers."

This gender difference, however, is even more pronounced for men who were in fraternities. Joining a fraternity increased the number of ties men had with other men. The eight affiliated men in my sample had, on average, 69 percent same-gender friends, and the 14 unaffiliated men had 54 percent same-gender friends.[11] While unaffiliated men made female friends from many places on campus (e.g., dorms, academic clubs, intramural sports), fraternity men's friendships with women were frequently formed with members of the sororities with whom their fraternities organized mixers or other events. Coed fraternities would provide an interesting comparison, but they did not exist on MU's campus.

In contrast with popular conceptions of college men's friendships as being more superficial than those of college women, I find that both genders had deep and meaningful relationships. On the basis of 20 years of research with early to late adolescents, Niobe Way (2013) argues that boys have some supportive and emotionally satisfying friendships with other boys, but that these relationships dissolve when they transition into late adolescence. Way does not follow youth into the college years, although research on college-age men describes their same-gender friendships as grounded in having fun together, often tied to alcohol and "based on suppression of emotion, false bravado and toughness," rather than as "genuine" or "real" friendships (Kimmel 2008, 278). Among the college men in my study, I find evidence for both. Some men had satisfying and supportive same-gender friendships, such as Daniel. Daniel's friendship network had 81 percent same-gender friends, and he described close and supportive relationships with at least three men, all of whom were in his fraternity. When I asked Daniel about his friends, I was surprised by how quickly he opened up. He described his relationship with these friends as "just really close. I mean, there's nothing that we're worried to tell each other about. . . . We can really legitimately talk about anything at all and none of us feel awkward about it or anything." In contrast, other men felt more easily able to connect with women, such as Steve and Martin, who are discussed in chapter 5. Steve wanted to connect with other men, but found that they rarely shared his interests and that he had more in common with most women. Martin similarly connected better with women but did not seek out relationships with other men, explaining: "Up until this point, I have had a hard time maintaining friendships with men just because I always thought men were stupid . . . , really thickheaded, stupid individuals that follow a group mentality. It wasn't until college that I actually got to see there were other male figures around that actually weren't that way." Martin credits his strong relationships with women to growing up in a household with his mother and grandmother. While some students, like Martin and Steve, discussed difficulties forming close friendships with other men, some, like Daniel, described meaningful and close relationships with men, both those they grew up with and those they met at college, including in fraternities.

Overall, the gender differences and similarities in students' friendships should provide hope against claims that our culture stunts young men's ability to form meaningful friendships, especially with other men (Kimmel 2008; Pollack and Shuster 2000). Many men and women alike formed supportive friendships.

## Race and Ethnicity

While I expected to find many gender differences in students' friendships and found few, I discovered more racial and ethnic differences than I expected. Most research on race and college friendships focuses on their racial composition, specifically the high levels of same-race friendships among black youth (antonio 2001, 2004; M. Fischer 2008; Stearns, Buch-mann, and Bonneau 2009). Racial composition is just one of the race-based patterns in friendship that I focus on in this book. More important to the experiences of students of color are the race-based marginality that they experience and how differing friendship network structures help (or do not help) them cope academically and socially.

As far as composition, white students report higher percentages of same-race friends (84%) than do black (76%) or Latino (61%) students. In their study of first-year students at a highly selective private research university, Stearns and colleagues (2009) also find that white students have the high-est percentages of same-race friends (84%), followed by black (69%), Asian (48%), and Latino (20%) students.[12] On the one hand, these numbers sug-gest that whites have the most racially homogeneous—or "homophilous," to use a sociological term—friendships and that students of color have more diverse friendships. This stands in contrast to perceptions that "all the black kids sit together in the cafeteria," for example (see discussion in Tatum 1997). On the other hand, these numbers suggest that students of color are friends with same-race others at rates higher than would be ran-domly expected, while whites are not. If we consider friendships relative to racial representation on campus, white students are friends with other white students at about the rate expected by chance (since they make up 85% of the MU population), whereas blacks and Latinos have same-race friends at a much higher rate than expected by chance (since they make up 5% and 2% of the MU population, respectively). White students rarely commented that they desired same-race friendships. Instead, most claimed a color-blind ideology, in which they did not notice race in their friend-ships (McCabe 2011). White students, however, frequently commented on how diverse MU's campus was, whereas students of color frequently noted a lack of diversity. This is consistent with Mary Grigsby's (2009) findings at another large public midwestern university. White students typically saw MU as a friendly place where it was easy to make friends because "everyone was in the same boat," as one student put it. In contrast to white students' general ease on campus, most students of color experienced race-based iso-lation and microaggressions (McCabe 2009, 2015), often seeking support from friends to deal with these experiences. My findings suggest that it is not that students of color wish to segregate themselves but that they are of-ten seeking (and receiving) support from those with common experiences, which they often find in same-race friends.

I interviewed white, black, and Latino students with racially diverse friendship networks and those with little racial diversity. In fact, students fell along the full range, with 0–100 percent same-race friends. Most friendship networks, however, contained a high proportion of same-race friends. Almost one-fourth of students had 100 percent same-race friends, while only one student had no same-race friends. When breaking this down by race, nearly one-third of white and black students had solely same-race friends, while no Latino students had solely same-race friends. Thus, many students had homophilous networks. Two examples are Keisha, discussed in chapter 3, a black woman with 100 percent black friends, and Mary, discussed in chapter 4, a white woman with 88 percent white friends. Still, there were students in each racial group who had more diverse friendships. Diverse networks were least common among whites. While only one in 34 white students had half or fewer same-race friends, one in 10 black students and one in four Latino students had half or fewer same-race friends. Two examples are Julia, discussed in chapter 4, a Latina with 42 percent Latino friends, and Martin, discussed in chapter 5, a black man with 50 percent black friends. Some students with diverse friendships discussed growing up in diverse areas or having diverse friendship groups in high school, while others explained that their diverse friendships in college marked a huge change from their previous friendships, neighborhoods, or schools. The same was true among students with homophilous friendship networks. These patterns fit with some previous studies (Hall, Cabrera, and Milem 2011)—but not with others (M. Fischer 2008; Harper and Yeung 2013)— that explored whether racially diverse interactions before college predicted racially diverse interactions during college. I find that network type— whether students were tight-knitters, compartmentalizers, or samplers—was more strongly associated with academic and social success than was network composition. Both same-race and racially diverse friendships can support academic and social success among students of color (McCabe 2015).

Definitions of friendship also varied across racial groups. White students more frequently described friends as fun or cool people, while students of color more frequently provided more thorough definitions centered on levels of closeness. For example, compare Mya's description of friendship with Krystal's. Mya, a black student, told me: "Friendship to me is very, very close and personal. . . . I have acquaintances, which means that they're friendly and they're nice people. And then I have people that really are my friends and that I let into my life. . . . Most people would be like, 'That's my friend,' and then the next minute they're talking about them. I don't consider that friendship." Mya reiterated the adage: "If you have a friend, it should be your friend for life. That's how I look at it." In contrast, when I asked Krystal, a white student, to describe what friendship meant to her, she paused, then said, "I have no idea why I'm friends with these people. We just kind of hit it off. We have a good time." For Krystal and many other white students, enjoying time spent together, rather than trust or duration, is the primary reason someone is labeled a friend. As will be shown in later chapters, students of color less frequently experienced the transition to college as easy, instead describing isolation and obstacles to success. As they worked to overcome these obstacles, they discovered their "true friends."

The largest racial differences in friendship appear in the network types. Given the isolating campus climate for some students of color, black and Latino students formed different types of networks for social support than did white students. Most white students (82%) were compartmentaliz-ers, who segmented their friendship network into different groups, each of which served as a place where they belonged. Most black and Latino students (63%) were tight-knitters, who crafted dense networks of friends who provided comfort and support to them given the racial composition of and the racial climate at the university. Across racial groups, a smaller number of students (around 20%) were samplers, with sparse networks that provided little support and only from one-on-one friendships rather than from groups. The racial differences in network type are shown in table 1.1.[13] Students of color often sought support from friends in deal-ing with the race-based isolation and microaggressions they experienced (McCabe 2009, 2015). Students in all three network types had these experi-ences. Tight-knit networks, however, provided the most consistent social support for race-based isolation. Although there were not many compart-mentalizers who were students of color, they were typically able to find social support among one cluster of friends. In contrast, students of color who were samplers continued to feel isolated and alone. The one-on-one friendships common among samplers did not provide the same level of

Table 1.1  Patterns in network density by racial identity

|  | Total (%) | White (%) | Students of Color (%) | | | |
|---|---|---|---|---|---|---|
|  |  |  | Overall | Black | Latina/o | Asian (%) |
| Tight-knitters | 33 (22) | 6 (2) | 63 (19) | 67 (12) | 58 (7) | — (1) |
| Compartmentalizers | 49 (33) | 82 (28) | 17 (5) | 11 (2) | 25 (3) | 0 |
| Samplers | 18 (12) | 12 (4) | 20 (6) | 22 (4) | 17 (2) | — (2) |

Note: Numbers in parentheses are the number of students in that group, out of 67 students. Percent-ages are not provided for Asian students because of the small sample size.

social support. See table I.1 for a summary of these differences and chapters 3–5 for more detail on each network type.

## Social Class

Class also affects students' friendships in specific ways. First, students' definitions of friendship varied across class. Lower-class students more frequently offered descriptions of friendship that appeared well thought out and involved multiple levels of closeness. For example, Jason, a lower-class and first-generation student, described "different degrees of friends" and deeper relationships with "the friends that I hold dear," while Caitlin, an upper-class and non-first-generation student, described friendship through mentioning how her friends bonded over "going out and having fun." As with the racial differences described above, when students find ease in the college environment, which was more common for middle- and upper-class respondents, their definitions of friendship appear less serious and seem to be based primarily on having fun together. Second, lower-class students' networks contained fewer friends from home. Similar patterns appeared when I examined whether students were employed or first-generation college students, both of which are highly correlated with self-reported social class.[14]

Finding class differences is not surprising, since several recent books have documented class differences in students' college experiences (Armstrong and Hamilton 2013; Mullen 2010; Stuber 2011). However, I do not find as many class differences as this research would predict. For example, in contrast to Jenny Stuber (2011), who found that working-class students had smaller friendship networks and more friends from home and family in their networks than upper-middle-class students, I found little difference in network size (lower-class students had 20 friends vs. 18 among others), but lower-class students' networks contained *fewer* friends from home. Perhaps this difference is due to the precision of the network data used. Stuber relied on general discussions of friendship, whereas I systematically collected and analyzed friendship network data. Thus, students' talk about friends might differ more by class than their actual friendship networks do.

## Intersections of Gender, Race, and Class

Race intersects with gender and class to shape some more nuanced differences in friendship patterns. Although these patterns are complex, they are important to analyze because people are affected not only by their gender, race, *or* class but also by their position in all three dimensions (see Collins 1990). For example, although network size did not differ among white men and women (who reported 19–20 friends, on average), there were differences among other groups. Latino and black men reported 21 friends, on average, whereas Latinas reported 17 friends and black women reported only 12 friends. Similarly, students of color from lower-class backgrounds named 21 friends, on average, whereas students of color from middle- or upper-class backgrounds named 13.[15] At 24, the number of friends is even higher, on average, among the nine black and Latino men from lower-class backgrounds.[16] As mentioned above, students' definitions of friendship differ by both race and class. Students of color from lower-class backgrounds were even more likely than those with one of these background characteristics to discuss specific levels of closeness among friends and how overcoming obstacles revealed their true friends. Similarly, those from more privileged race and class backgrounds often provided friendship definitions based primarily on having fun together, which was tied to the relative ease they experienced on campus. This shows how broader structural inequalities have an impact on the way students experience college and friendships.

## Other Relationships: Professors, Significant Others, and Parents

While friends are the focus of this book, it would be limiting to completely leave out a discussion of other people who matter in students' lives. Other works have more closely examined students' relationships with professors, finding that one or two professors can make a difference in students' college experiences (Chambliss and Takacs 2014). I found that professors can indeed make a difference, but that meaningful relationships with professors were unusual. When I asked about professors, most students noted how frequently they met with professors during office hours or whether they had a professor who was "really funny," "really crazy," or the like. Professors also came up when I asked students about a favorite and least favorite class they had taken at MU; most often, it was the professor who made it more or less enjoyable or interesting.

Professors, however, did make a big impact in a few students' lives as mentors. For example, students named specific professors who encouraged them to attend graduate school, served as role models for the type of person they hoped to become, and gave them a "second chance" when they had missed a deadline for an assignment or an application for a special program. For example, Keisha described a professor as her mentor, explaining that "she was one of the main advocates for me, like she would talk to my teachers for me and let them know that I seriously had something going on. . . . She really helped me a lot and she was one of the people I'll remember out of everyone here." Overall, most students did not leave MU with a meaningful or deep relationship with even one professor or adviser, in contrast to what Chambliss and Takacs (2014) found at a small liberal arts college. My findings are consistent with theirs, however, in two other areas. First, the students who did find such relationships appeared grateful for them and found them quite rewarding. Second, developing such relationships occurred, not in a systematic way, but through chance meetings and serendipitous encounters.

While professors and advisers were very rarely named as friends, significant others were included in about half the networks where students were in relationships. The number of students reporting a romantic relationship increased throughout their college career.[17] And students' descriptions of how significant others affected academics were more interesting than these numbers. Nearly every student mentioned romantic relationships as a possible academic distraction in the abstract. However, when I asked students how *their* boyfriend or girlfriend affected their academics, the answers were divided. Significant others helped in multiple ways, providing instrumental assistance, emotional support, and intellectual engagement (as discussed in depth in the next chapter). For example, Ruth described how Chuck, whom she had been dating for three years, reinforced her academic focus and aspirations: "When we started dating, I started being a little more academic because we had that in common—we knew what our goals were." In addition to that emotional support, they helped each other instrumentally; for example, as they ate lunch on the day of our interview, she quizzed him on his Spanish test and they discussed the presidential candidates and what they expected to happen in the upcoming debate. Like Ruth, Julio discussed a range of ways that his girlfriend helped him academically: "I talk to my girlfriend a lot about my academics because she understands like everything I'm going through. She's been on the dean's list every semester." Julio believed that he modeled his girlfriend's behavior in striving to do well academically. They also read each other's papers, studied together, and discussed intellectual matters, such as "race issues, discrimination issues, racism issues; we talk about a lot of different issues, not just academics."

Both men and women discussed their significant others as taking time and energy away from academics but as also helping them academically. However, women seemed to help their boyfriends more than the men helped them. For example, Ruth gave several examples of helping Chuck study for tests, but none of her examples included him quizzing her. Some women were aware of this gender inequality. Mary commented about her ex-boyfriend, "I help[ed] him more than he really helped me with my classes." Betsy made a similar point about her current boyfriend: "I'll put Adam's homework before mine, which is totally wrong because he can do it, he's just lazy." This is a trend that Betsy saw not only in herself but also in her friends, including Libby: "I'm like, 'Libby, you yell at me for caving in to Adam and then you cave in to Josh, so shut up.' She's like, 'I know.' [*laughs*] Oh man!" This gender difference in the academic benefits of romantic relationships fits with research on first-generation white men, which finds that off-campus girlfriends encouraged men's academic goals (Wilkins 2014), and with research that finds that romantic relationships can limit college women's friendships, since they require time and effort (Armstrong and Hamilton 2013; Chambliss and Takacs 2014; Holland and Eisenhart 1990). I find that significant others can be academic distractions and they also can help academically, but it seems that men get more of a boost from significant others than do women.

More often than professors or significant others, students mentioned family members as helping them academically. While only 2 percent of the friends students mentioned were family members, nearly every student brought up family in his or her interview. Frequently, it came up in their discussion of whom they talk to about academics—sometimes it was to say that they talk in great detail about academic events and decisions with a member of their family, whereas other times it was more superficial. As an example of the latter, Gina was typical when she said that her mom and dad "pretty much just ask how I'm doing. . . . They're like, 'Oh, so how are your classes? How are your grades?' That's pretty much what they're concerned about. And I'm like, 'They're fine.' And they're like, 'Are you getting all your homework done?' And I'm like, 'Yes.' [They say,] 'That's great!' [I ask,] 'Are we done?'" Some of the parents who were more involved are the type of helicopter parents we often hear about, as Kathryn explained:

I talk to my parents a lot about school, and about how I've been finding a really good balance, how I have a quiz coming up Saturday so I'm a little nervous about that, and telling them that I'm studying really hard. . . . My parents always want to know what classes I'm going to take. They always [ask], "Is that the class you actually need right now?" Yeah, so my parents are really involved. . . . They always want my schedule so they know [*laughs*] where I'm going to be at what time if they need to get ahold of me.

Both Kathryn's parents have graduate degrees, and her dad is employed in the field she hoped to enter after graduation.

Parents without college degrees are sometimes as involved, but rather than giving advice, they discuss academics in more limited ways. First-generation students often described a relationship like Angela's, who said, "I talk to my parents a little bit about it [academics], but they don't really understand so much," or Sean's, who commented, "My mom's supportive. She doesn't tell me what to do and she doesn't tell me exactly the moves I should make. She'll let me make my own decisions and she'll support them." First-generation students discussed more academic relationships with family members other than parents (such as siblings, cousins, aunts, uncles, and grandmothers) than students whose parents had attended college. First-generation students with younger siblings frequently mentioned giving advice on topics ranging from financial aid applications to college selection to college major choices. Even students who were not close with their parents described talking to their parents about academics, but in a "limited" or "basic" way, such as what Jenny, who spoke to her parents on the phone about once a month, described: "[They ask] 'How's your classes?' [I say,] 'They're fine.' [They say,] 'Oh, okay. What are you taking?' [I say,] 'Um, I don't know.'"

In sum, students discussed family members', especially parents', involvement—ranging from financial support to general encouragement to attend college and get good grades to day-to-day advice on papers and assignments, course schedules, or majors and careers—yet most students' relationships with parents "fade into the background" (Clydesdale 2007, 93), unlike those with friends. As students discussed their academic and social lives at college, friends were more often in the foreground.

## Conclusion

Friendships are a central element of college life. Faculty, parents, administrators, and students themselves could support social ties simply by recognizing that students spend much time with their friends and by not devaluing this social time. These relationships are meaningful in students' eyes, yet they are also consequential in reflecting broader structural inequalities in race, gender, and class. I found the biggest differences in friendship structure and composition for race and the smallest for gender. In general, the patterns I found reflect differences in whether students experienced comfort and ease in the college environment (finding college filled with people "like them") or whether they experienced hardships and isolation (finding college a place where they "feel like a minority" in terms of race, class, or both). Importantly, rather than assuming that friendships work in the same way for all students, we should recognize how structural inequalities may be reflected in the shape of students' friendship networks, as well as in the purposes those networks serve for students.

Context affects students' friendships as well. In his study of the first year after high school, Tim Clydesdale (2007, 96) observes that "the main difference was that teens residing at home had fewer casual friendships. They did not make acquaintances through residence halls or through involvement in on-campus organizations," but they still had "as many significant friendships to navigate as residential college students do." By attending a large residential college, MU students may have more casual friendships than students at nonresidential colleges. Although this may not influence the number of friends they have, because students' friend lists typically include only closer friendships, it might influence the structure of their networks. In other words, it may affect the connections among their friends. For example, it is possible that smaller schools, particularly those in rural areas, have fewer samplers, commuter campuses have more samplers, less affluent schools have more tight-knitters, and campuses with fewer nontraditional-aged students have more compartmentalizers. In general, campuses where students spend more time together, and less time off campus, may have fewer samplers. Future research could test these possibilities.

Exploring the patterns among friendship structure and composition lays the groundwork for understanding how friends are central to students' college experiences. Friends also play important roles—both positively and negatively—in students' academic success, which is the topic of the next chapter.

# TWO

# Balance

Many scholars argue that friends distract college students from academic success. Although theories assert the value of social integration for success, the rich descriptions available of college life show friends hanging out together in dorms or parties rather than encouraging each other to spend time on their classes or intellectual development (Armstrong and Hamilton 2013; Holland and Eisenhart 1990; Moffatt 1989).[1] Parents of college-age children make similar arguments about friends as academic distractions. My examination of students' accounts and experiences shows that friends can indeed be distractions, but that the picture is much more complex. In this chapter, I highlight two important tensions in students' narratives of how their friends influence academic life, and I make suggestions for improving students' experiences.

The first tension is between "testimonies of balance" and "cautionary tale testimonies of imbalance." Using narrative analysis, I describe these two types of testimony—firsthand accounts from students—which appear in nearly all my interviews. In "testimonies of balance," students discussed the importance of "doing well" by balancing academic and social life and presented themselves as balancing the two. Yet, nearly all students also used "testimonies of imbalance" to provide cautionary tales of students who were "too social" or "too academic." A clear disconnect thus appears between how students view themselves as balancing academic and social life and how they present students in general as imbalanced. Both of these testimonies, however, highlight shared understandings among college students about the desirability of balance, the dangers of being imbalanced, and the potential of friends to distract from academic success.

The second tension I introduce is the way students often vehemently claimed that they separated friends from academics as a way to deal with the potential distraction of friends, yet they also described their friends as involved academically in a range of ways. Students' initial response to questions about how they balance academic and social life is that they "keep them very, very separate" (as more than one student told me). A closer examination of how students described their time with friends, however, uncovers that friends are not always uninvolved in academics. In fact, nearly all students described multiple ways that their friends were academically integrated. I identify the strategies students enact to both integrate and separate their friends from academics, revealing both the positive and the negative roles of college friendships. For example, friends support academics directly by providing verbal encouragement and congratulations and indirectly by providing encouragement (or at least acceptance) for students to care about academic aspects of college.

Although peers can draw students away from academics, as existing research asserts, this research severely underestimates students' ability to develop coping strategies for this distraction. This is also true of educational research on younger students, such as James Coleman's (1961) now-classic statement that students strive to be a social success rather than an academic success. In line with Coleman, more contemporary research clearly demonstrates that students want to be seen as socially successful by their peers because that is what they believe their peers value, but this research focuses less on students' responses to these pressures. In contrast, I identify a range of strategies that students use to achieve their goal of balance and avoid the specter of "imbalance." Students' friends were important not only for the "good times" and "college memories" they provided but also for the ways they promoted academic success. Time with friends is not always a distraction from academics, because many friends do have academic benefits.

## Balancing Academic and Social Life

> I don't want to be so focused on school that I miss out on the social life, because after college you're not gonna be able to do this because you're gonna have a job. And I don't want to be so focused on the social that I don't make it out of college. [*laughs*] So I just want a balance.
>
> —Margaret

Margaret's comments reflect those of nearly every student I interviewed. College students reported two goals—to "do well" socially and academically—and most sought balance between their social lives and their academic lives. As detailed later in this chapter, most students actively worked toward balance. But what does balance mean?

### Cautionary Tale Testimonies of Imbalance

In describing their pursuit of balance, students frequently told me stories about students who were imbalanced. I refer to them as "stories" not because I assume they were false but because they followed a common structure and plotline (Maines 1993). They involved the participant or someone they knew, often a friend, who was "too social" or "too academic" and faced negative consequences as a result. Narrative analysis characterizes "testimony" as a type of story told through firsthand accounts (Bonilla-Silva 2014). Therefore, I use the term *"cautionary tale testimony"* to refer to the firsthand accounts that students told me of people who were imbalanced. Like other types of testimony, cautionary tales reveal ideology; the stories we construct expose our shared understandings of the world (Bonilla-Silva 2014).[2] Through reinforcing the risks of not achieving a balance between academic and social life, these cautionary tales reveal general understandings about college and what is important to students.

Cautionary tale testimonies frequently included stories of both peers who were "too social" and those who were "too academic," emphasizing the dangers of both extremes. Carlos described his friends Caitlyn, who was "too social," and Frank, who was "too academic." He started by describing Caitlyn: "She almost didn't come back last semester, and so this semester she's been trying hard, which, like, I've been trying to help her. . . . Because I understand that some people don't have that balance. They can't balance school and fun, I guess." By pointing to a commonly discussed cost of being too social—low GPA, perhaps low enough to lead to probation or expulsion from MU—Carlos's testimony of Caitlyn assumed and reaffirmed the importance and desirability of balance. Other cautionary tales highlighted this through pointing out friends who "still haven't grown up." Being too academic, however, also came with costs:

> All Frank does is study. He has no social life whatsoever. He just studies. And he's a social person; like, when I get him to come out, he's a lot of fun. But it's just, he refuses. . . . I could never do that. I need that social interaction or else I'll go crazy. . . . [Frank] is the type that's like, "I'll play later when I'm making millions of dollars," which [has] been an advantage to him because he's already [had] a paid internship. . . . But I value experiences too. You

know? I value being older and being like, "Oh, I remember when we did this, and that was crazy, du du du du da." So, it's kind of a trade-off. Yeah, he'll be making $200,000 a year, but when he looks back to college, it's more like, "Yeah, so I studied most of my college experience."

Carlos's cautionary tale positioned Frank's academic focus as admirable, yet a sacrifice Carlos would not personally make because "I value experiences too." Carlos does not want to reflect on college and feel that he missed out on the full experience, as he believes will happen to Frank. Students cited other costs of being too academic, such as "no extracurricular activities," "no friends," or being "way too stressed" (e.g., crying because of an A–). Time played an important role in cautionary tales. The dangers of being "too social" or "too academic" could appear in the near future, such as a grade on the next test or fun this weekend, and the more distant future, such as career achievement or college memories. In contrast to views of students as impulsive, this shows that students sometimes consider the future implications of current behaviors.

Although most cautionary tales focused on both extremes, the "too social" extremes were typically more vivid and concrete. Greg described imbalanced peers: "Most people here, it's like either one or the other. You're either just too involved in your books or too involved in being social, and you can't really find a healthy medium." Later in this chapter, I focus on the validity of his claim, but here, I want to note that despite Greg's acknowledgment of both extremes, his examples all focused on friends who were "too social":

> They devote their life to their friends or they'll devote their life to video games or they'll devote their life to pot or they'll devote their life to, like, one thing and it will impede how they do in school. . . . Friends will get in the way [of academics]. Like, I had a kid on my floor freshman year who played the video game Halo so much that he ended up failing out of school. And that was because everyone on the [dorm] floor was always like, "Come play Halo." And so he failed out of school.

Aligned with the concerns of parents and commentators, many cautionary tales focused on the negative academic consequences of being "too social."

When students gave cautionary tales involving their own past behavior, they emphasized personal transformation in which they learned balance by making mistakes. Fran explained, "Last year I had the going-out-partying experience and I saw that my grades suffered. And so this year I was just like, don't be that dumb." Margaret also described a personal transformation, but one in which she went from being "too social" to "not social enough": "My freshman year, I went out all the time and then I got bad grades." After she was put on probation and her parents found out, "I tried to change it around for my sophomore year and I hardly ever went out." Now, as the quotation at the start of this section suggests, Margaret described herself as "right in the middle. I don't think I go out too much, but I think now I go out enough to be social. I don't think that I overdo it."

Only one student told a cautionary tale where balance was an impossible goal. This exception came from Kirk, a premed student who framed choices as either purely social or purely academic. For him, each choice came with costs: "Most people come to college their freshman year and they get drunk, like, every weekend; they go out, and whatever your fancy, it can be drugs, drink, whatever." Kirk recounted what he told a first-year student on his dorm floor who asked for advice on the MCAT[3] in preparation for applying to medical schools:

> I keep telling her, "I see you going out every Friday. Every Friday I'll be coming in and you're going out." And I'm like, "You're not gonna make it. . . . I went out *two times* my freshman year.[4] *That's* what it takes. It's what you have to do. It's hard to balance things." . . . That one's a big one, though. It really is. I think it's very underrated for the academic people—the social aspect— because you really don't ever get to experience college. I mean, when you're a doctor and you're 30 and you make $200,000 a year, of course you can go to Acapulco every weekend, go ski in the Alps, do whatever. But you're old. [*chuckles*] I mean, yeah, you make enough money to go do all those fancy things, but you're getting old. . . . You've just got to decide what you want to do.

Kirk decided to focus on academics and to miss out on "the social aspect" in order to achieve career success. Like other cautionary tales, however, Kirk warned of the negative consequences that would face his floor mate, whose actions ("going out every Friday") failed to match her stated goal of attending medical school. Time appears again both in the near future (the MCAT) and the more distant future ("when you're a doctor").

Although cautionary tales appeared to be about other people's undesirable behavior, they revealed much about participants' own beliefs and actions. Cautionary tale testimony revealed students' belief that doing well in college involves both academic and social success, an often-elusive balance.[5] Students' cautionary tales and more general discussion of balance typically focused only on academic and social life, similar to the goals of Rutgers undergraduates during the late 1970s and 1980s, which were "to do well in classes" and "to make friends or have a good social life" (Moffatt 1989, 33). A few students, however, brought in additional areas such as sleep, paid work, religion, and extracurricular involvements. Through their common focus, cautionary tales thus highlight shared understandings among students about the potential dangers of being imbalanced and friends who may derail academic success. Social life is often overlooked in suggestions for improving higher education, but students' narratives clearly express that it is important to them. By highlighting the value of social life and paying more attention to students' friendships, we can better address criticisms that higher education is failing our youth and offer meaningful solutions.

### Degrees of Balance

One technique I used to look more deeply into students' understanding of "balance" involved asking them to rate themselves from academic to social. Using a paper-and-pencil scale, each student gave himself or herself a numeric score ranging from zero (academic) to 10 (social). I then asked why they rated themselves as they did, if they had changed over time, and ways they were similar to and different from their friends. This technique enabled me to get at the "narrative realities" and "self-dialogues" that were "[h]idden behind the scale items and their numbers" (Maines 1993, 25).

The cautionary tale testimonies of imbalance suggested that imbalance was common; for example, remember the claim from Greg that "[m]ost people here [at MU], it's like either one or the other." In contrast, almost everyone I interviewed placed himself or herself at or near the middle of the academic-social scale. Figure 2.1 illustrates this pattern. As shown by the tallest bar in this figure, half of participants chose the exact middle of the scale ("5"), including Margaret, the student quoted at the beginning of this chapter. Fully three-quarters of the students placed themselves within one point of the middle ("4" to "6"). And not a single student chose the extreme ends of the scale, either on the academic ("0") or social ("10") sides. Figure 2.2 shows the same pattern for each of the three network types—tight-knitters, compartmentalizers, and samplers. Although students frequently discussed others who were "too social" or "too academic" in cautionary tale testimonies, most students saw themselves as able to balance academic and social life.

Students rating themselves at or near the middle of the scale offered descriptions that valued academic and social life equally. For example, Madison described herself as "pretty balanced. I'm not, like, burning myself out

**Academic-Social Scale (0-10)**

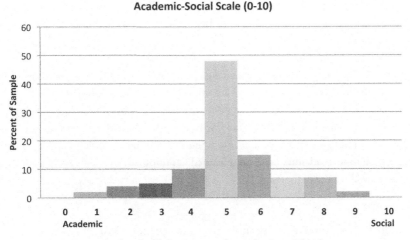

2.1. Students' self-placement on the academic-social scale

**Academic-Social Scale (0-10)**

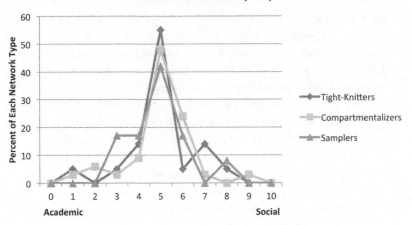

2.2. Students' self-placement on the academic-social scale by network type

on parties or books, so it's pretty balanced." Providing more detail about the process behind maintaining this balance, Krystal explained, "If it's, like, writing a term paper or going to the movies, I'm definitely going to go with the term paper that needs to be done. But sometimes I just feel like I have to blow off my homework and just relax and hang out and just have a good time." Krystal's comment also highlighted the possible competing concerns between academic and social life, which I focus on in more detail in the next section.

Students who sought a balance clearly differed in how easily achievable they perceived this balance to be. Some, such as Sean, identified it as a struggle:

SEAN: There's no road map to balancing it. . . . Grades slip because [some students] haven't had a support group, they don't have friends, no one's helping them, mentors, support, anything like that. I've learned now, after going through a lot, how to balance the involvement, learning where I need to pull back and like, "Okay, no, I'm not doing that. I don't care what happens, I need to do academics first." So, I learned to prioritize.

JM: How'd you learn that?

SEAN: Falling on my face flat on the floor.

Sean learned through trial and error, noting the lack of a "road map" to achieve balance. Whereas others, like Betsy, described achieving balance as effortless: "I feel like I'm an extreme on both [academic and social] because I will study and I will get good grades, but I will also go out almost every night. It's funny because my friends . . . , they're like, 'Blah blah blah. Are you going out tonight? Of course you are! I don't know how you do it.' But I think some people can be both. Easily." Although balance was nearly universally students' goal, it was not easily achievable for all.[6]

Some students who did not place themselves in the middle of the scale saw social life as worthy of more effort and time. Although they viewed their success as college students in part by how well they were able to balance social and academic life, their balance point was more on the social side. Maddie, who rated herself as an "8," explained, "I put most of my time and energy into my friends rather than school. And not like—I do get my work done, but I guess I don't feel like I need to put that much effort into it." Jocelyn, who also rated herself as an "8," offered a similar explanation: "I spend more time socially than I spend on my academics. . . . But I do focus on academics. I have to have good grades. If I don't get at least a B average, my mom won't pay for me to go to school. So I focus on it, but it's not something that I think about all the time and do on the weekends." Both Jocelyn and Maddie spent more time justifying their lack of academic focus than their emphasis on social life. Kim rated herself as a "9," and her explanation shows much less interest in academic life, making her one of the few students not pursuing balance:

I definitely would choose a social event [over an academic one]. I like interacting with people more than I like sitting in a lecture or sitting and listen[ing] to somebody talk. My attention span is very short. . . . [A]nd then I don't see myself as a very smart person anyway. I don't like school at all. I'm just here just because I know I have to be. For my benefit, I have to be here because you can't really do nothing with [a] high school diploma. I realize that. So I'm trying to do what it takes.

Interestingly, as shown in figure 2.3, students who rated themselves as more social did not necessarily have lower GPAs than other students. Students at the social end of the scale ("8" to "9") had GPAs that differed little from those in the middle ("3" to "6").[7]

The other students who placed little emphasis on balance were those at the other end of the academic-social scale. These students focused on school, like the "grinds" discussed by previous scholars (Horowitz 1987; Moffatt 1989). For example, Noleen, who had a 3.8 GPA and planned for a career as a journalist, placed herself as a "2," saying, "A lot of times I don't do things socially because of academic reasons. I don't go out because I do have things to do for school." The other students who placed themselves as a "1" or "2" on the academic-social scale were similar to Noleen in having a higher-than-average GPA (see fig. 2.3), with most planning for graduate or professional school. Kirk, who had a 3.7 GPA, rated himself as a "1," explaining, "I have a friend . . . [who] told me you can go out all your life, but in your four years [in college], if you want to go to medical school you just gotta hack at the books. So that's pretty much what I've done so far. . . . Being so academic really affects your social life." The only other student

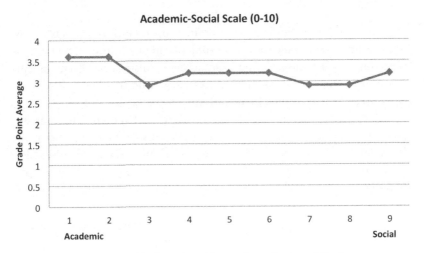

2.3. Average GPA for each position on the academic-social scale

who self-identified as a "1," Valerie, a nursing student with a 3.5 GPA, also focused on the future. She very bluntly said, "I consider myself more academic than social because academics will get me somewhere."

Cautionary tale testimonies suggest that students believed that many of their peers were imbalanced, a belief shared by research showing that college peer cultures often reward social success over academic success. Clearly, these descriptions do not agree with students' self-ratings, where most believed that they personally achieved balance. My interest in meanings led me to focus not on assessing how balanced students objectively appear, as other researchers have done, but on how friends play a role in students' efforts to achieve balance.[8] To most students, being balanced means having fun with friends and getting "good grades," without being overly focused on either. This again shows that advice or policy aimed solely at improving academics will miss the mark because it overlooks the importance of friendship to the college experience.

### Friends as a Distraction

If I didn't have friends here, I'd be a 4.0 student [who received all As]. . . . As a whole, academics impede my social life. But there's times where I have to make compromises. And I'm sure my parents wouldn't be too thrilled to hear that I'm going out on a Wednesday night when I have a Thursday test. . . . Peer pressure can definitely be an issue. There's always people banging on my door wanting to hang out.

—Greg

In nearly every interview, students brought up friends as a potential distraction from their academics. Most students, in fact, admitted that friends were not only a temptation but also an actual distraction. Even students who were doing well academically, like Greg (who had a 3.4 GPA), conceded that friends tempted them and sometimes they gave in.

I was not surprised that students' friends distracted them, but I was surprised by how frankly and directly many students described this persistent "peer pressure," as Greg termed it. The following focus group discussion with sorority members illustrates the seeming inescapability of the temptation of friends:

AUDREY: I feel like having a hundred girls around you, being like, "We're going out," makes it a lot harder to balance your academics.
JM: Just because there's always someone to go out with?

KELLY: Yeah, there's always somebody that wants to go out. You may have so much stuff to do, and *one person* wants to go out and they can somehow convince *everybody* [*group laughter*] to drop what they're doing.

Peer pressure need not come from all "hundred girls," as Audrey mentioned, but from just one who wants to go out, as Kelly remarked. Even *while* studying together or attending class together, students noticed that their friends distracted them. For example, John discussed how he decided to "never" study with friends because "we'll end up talking and it'll be unproductive." Students also referred to themselves as a source of peer pressure, as Bryce explained: "I probably do the same thing to them [my friends], so it doesn't annoy me. Actually, it does annoy me at the time, 'cause I'm like, 'No, dude, I'm not going out.' But I never get angry with them. I don't get, like, frustrated over it because I know I do the same thing."

Some students described the peer pressure as indirect. In other words, the pressure from friends was subtle, yet pervasive. Students developed rationales, sometimes quite elaborate, about when they would and would not give in. Noting that it was not "really peer pressure . . . because I know they want to go out," Ridge commented, "I can always tell if they *really* have to get it [schoolwork] done or if they can push it off a little bit." Juan described the indirect pressure as a series of daily decisions, like one he made earlier that day: "Do I study now or do I take my friend to the mall?" John presented more detail about this nuanced view of the study-versus-socialize dilemma:

> What we'll be trying to do, which is not good, probably, is rationalize it or try to reason why you *should* go out and not study. So not that you *don't* need to study, but you don't need to study *right now* or you don't need to study *for this long* or you don't need to study *today*. . . . We try to rationalize it knowing that school is the ultimate goal. . . . We'll say, "Let's all go to [dinner at] Applebee's." And you have something to do but you'll just be like, "Well, I haven't seen my friend in a long time" or "We never go out anymore" or "The paper will be here when I get back" or "I already wrote an outline" or something.

Like Juan's and Ridge's descriptions, John's account does not have friends actively telling each other, "Don't study, go out"; the pressure was more indirect.

Nearly every student in the sample described friends as a distraction from schoolwork. Some suffered negative consequences, while others changed their behavior in time. Some described friends as a current distraction, while others confined this experience to the past. Friends were a distraction electronically as well as in person, through contacting them on the phone and computer when students were trying to study. Students' descriptions of friends as an academic distraction correspond with prior research that paints a negative picture of college social life and more generally views peers as drawing students away from academics and hurting their academic performance (Armstrong and Hamilton 2013; Arum and Roksa 2011; Coleman 1961; Holland and Eisenhart 1990). Prior research, however, underestimates students' ability to develop coping strategies. Students described a range of strategies to achieve balance, which I group into two broad categories: (1) strategies that separate academic and social life and (2) strategies that integrate them. In the next sections, I describe these strategies. In chapters 3–5, I analyze how students use these strategies in different types of friendship groups.

While it is analytically useful to discuss the strategies one at a time, it is important to note that they often appeared together. The specific combinations in which students used these strategies are centrally important in distinguishing what happens in the network types discussed in chapters 3–5. Importantly, students can intervene in their own friendships by recognizing and appreciating friends who are academically involved in multiple ways. They can also take specific steps to cultivate these friends with academic benefits.

## Strategies of Separation

One way students dealt with the distraction of friends was to keep friends separate from academics. I categorized students' efforts to do so into three strategies: (1) dividing their lives into "academic time" and "social time," (2) using time with friends as a break from academics, and (3) using time with friends as a reward for academics. By keeping them separate, students believed they could "do well" academically and socially, thereby balancing these two goals.

### "Academic Time" and "Social Time"

BETSY: I know how to party. I'm not out of control, but I do know how to have fun. But then, when it comes to academics, I will study. . . . When it's study time, study; party time, party. That's my theory behind it.

JM: So you have certain times for certain things?

BETSY: Yeah. Like Friday afternoons, [I] cannot do homework. . . . I'm done [with classes] at 1:10 on Fridays. From Friday till Sunday afternoon, I don't do homework. We'll just have fun. We'll lay around [or] go to the mall.

The most general and most common strategy of separation was for students to divide their time at MU into "academic time" and "social time." While there were activities that blurred these boundaries (which are discussed later in this chapter), students tended to view time as rigidly divided into these two spheres. Betsy, for example, earmarked the weekdays for schoolwork and the weekends for fun with friends. Some students also talked about segmenting their time within the semester, with the beginning being more social and the end being more academic.[9] Others segmented their time within the day. For example, Kathryn discussed how her friends were a distraction from academics last year, so this year she separated friends and academics by dividing her days. Her social life happens "after 10:00 p.m., so I really have the whole day to focus on school." Segmenting time within the day was less frequent than segmenting the week. Some students added a third dimension, such as sleep, paid work, religion, or a student club, to their segmentation. Whether or not they were able to keep to these schedules, students believed that a more rigid temporal division between academic and social life allowed them to maintain balance and block their friends from being too distracting.

### Friends as a Break from Academic Pressure

[My friends and I,] we'll say, "Hey, let's study for a few hours and then we'll take a break; we'll go do something else." We do that a lot.

—Maddie

Even when students did not segment their weeks or days into "academic time" and "social time," they frequently separated the two by using time with friends as a break from academics. Not all students actually referred to it as a "break," as did Maddie; some called it an "escape" or "release" or "vacation from school." The last term comes from Emily, who saw her friends' primary academic impact as providing a "vacation" from the work: "We've studied all day. When we're together, it's time to be silly. It's time to do cartwheels and run all over the place and just sing superloud. Stuff like that. We're just kind of on vacation from school." Students remarked that this break with friends was important for their health and well-being. It was necessary, even when it might detrimentally affect their grades, as Matthew explained: "I decline socially or physically, I've noticed, if I'm overworked academically, [and] I *have* to take a break. I *have* to be social. Even if it's going to cause me to get a poor grade on something, that's more important to me because I will go crazy. I just have to keep myself healthy." Whitney noted how she developed this strategy when her past behaviors were counterproductive: "I was very much obsessed with my academics. . . . I had stressed myself out so much that I was sleeping probably about 20 minutes a night for two weeks. So, definitely, I've learned since then. . . . If you've been working on this paper for six hours and your friends want to go see a movie and you're really stressed out, just go see the movie!" Friends provided a break from, and a way to deal with, academic stress. Alberto elaborated on the necessity of having some time with friends separate from academics: "We deal enough with our grades in school that when we're with each other, we kind of want to get away from all that, so I think that's why we really don't talk about it [grades]."[10] Particularly in times of high stress or high workload, students described using time with friends as breaks that helped sustain them. Certainly, overusing breaks can be detrimental to students' grades. However, I agree with students that using breaks moderately and consciously can improve academic performance and commitment, allowing them to be balanced.

### Friends as a Reward for Academic Work

I feel like I can't have the social part until I finish the academic part.

—Nicole

Students also stated that engaging in the pleasures of friendship was a reward for studying, hard work, or good grades. Nicole's philosophy reflected this belief. Not only individuals but friendship groups enacted this. For example, Wendy described: "I've been in class all day, I'm tired of school, but then I have my roommates, my friends, like, 'Oh, Wendy, you gotta get this done. You have to get this done.' And I'm like, 'Ahh, I don't want to.' And they're just like, 'Just get, like, blank,' [and then] they try to give me some incentive or reward: 'Just get like half of this page written and then you can go watch TV for a half hour,' or something. Which works [*laughs*]!" Implicit in Wendy's friends' active role in setting social incentives for her is their shared belief in academic rewards. This shared belief—"norm," to use the term sociologists would use—also appears in a collaborative discussion among friends in a focus group I organized with sorority members:

DANA: It only makes you work harder because you want to get that paper done just so you can go out. [*group laughter*]

BRITTANY: Yeah. And I would rather stay up all night studying for a test the next day than spend, like, two or three nights wasted—well, not wasted—studying for it, but I just mean, studying till 10:00, going to sleep by 11:00. I'd rather just go out those nights or go hang out with friends and have fun, relax, [or] watch a movie. By the way, I can stay up all night and do fine on the test.

AUDREY: I get up and go all day. Like today, I had a ton of things due today, so I got up so early and I did that—went to this class, turned that in, finished that other thing. And then I can go out.

These friends built on and did not dispute each other's statements that friends were a reward (in Dana and Audrey's comments) and a break (in Brittany's comment), suggesting that these were common beliefs and behaviors among some friendship groups. Like breaks, moderately and consciously using friends as a reward can help students achieve success and balance.

As students worked toward achieving balance, they recognized time with friends as both important for social success and yet a potential barrier to academic success. Even students who rated themselves as more social or more academic often expressed these beliefs. One way to achieve balance was to separate time with friends from academics either generally, by marking time as academically or socially focused, or more specifically, by viewing time with friends as a break from or reward for academics. Prior research tends to focus on the distraction (Armstrong and Hamilton 2013; Arum and Roksa 2011; Moffatt 1989), whereas I identify ways that students' friends help them cope. Researchers, administrators, and policymakers should recognize friends as possible solutions, not only as problems. I demonstrate an unexpected path to friends' involvement in academics: students involve their friends in their quest to "do well" academically through actively separating their friendships from their academic life.

## Strategies of Integration

The second tension in this chapter is that nearly every student mentioned that they separated academic life and social life, at least at certain times, yet, when I asked about specific ways friends might be involved in academics, nearly everyone also described at least one way friends were involved in their academic lives. I refer to these ways that students involve their friends in academics as "strategies of integration." The breadth of the help students' friends provide has not been adequately captured in existing literature.[11] In fact, the study that most directly addresses this issue concluded that "when they talked to their friends about their academic work, it was almost always about generic issues such as workloads and deadlines, rather than the substantive content of their courses" (Brooks 2007, 699).[12] Although my findings confirm this difference in frequency, these are only two of the ways students' friends were involved in their academic lives. I identify four broad categories: (1) instrumental assistance, (2) emotional support, (3) intellectual discussions, and (4) competition. Previous research overlooks many ways in which students' friends help academically. Chapters 3–5 discuss how students in different types of friendship networks use these strategies differently, offering suggestions for improving their experiences given their friendship network type.

### Instrumental Help from Friends

[My friends give] study tips. My friends might be better at writing a paper, so I've learned how to write through them. I've helped with Spanish. . . . Sometimes, your friends are your best outlet for learning. I've learned a lot through them, as well as they learn through me.

—Julio

Like Julio, students typically brought up at least one way their friends have provided informational, tangible, and problem-focused assistance with academics. This instrumental help encompassed a range of activities, including tips for which classes or professors to take or avoid, editing papers, quizzing each other in preparation for exams, studying at the same time, and studying together in study groups.[13] It may not be surprising that students sometimes did these things with their friends. Indeed, instrumental help is described in some qualitative studies of college students' experiences (see Beasley 2011; Chambliss and Takacs 2014; Lareau 2015; Mullen 2010; Willie 2003). I add important details to better understand the mechanisms through which this help occurs and differences in who uses these strategies.[14] In addition, I identify a range of types of instrumental help, including some I found more surprising, such as students' friends driving them to class, walking with them to class, making sure they were awake in time to go to class, and reminding them about due dates for readings, assignments, and exams.

Student after student discussed academic tips their friends gave them.

Friends recommended certain classes, sometimes because they learned a lot in the class, other times because the class "wasn't too much work" or the professor was "nice" or an "easy grader." Friends helped each other solve academic problems, as Gina described: "My best friend that's here, I go to her a lot for stuff and I'll be like, 'Hey, can you help me with this?' Or like, 'How should I do this?' Or 'Have you had this situation before? What did you do?' And like, 'Can you do that with me?' My girls that are the freshmen, they'll do that to me and they'll be like, 'Okay, when you have three tests in one day, how did you do that?' . . . I'll give them suggestions." They gave each other tips on not only what to study and how to study but also "the good places to study," as Matthew learned from his friend Marilyn. Students also exposed each other to new classes and majors. For example, before Justin's friend introduced him to his major of information science, he "didn't know it existed": "He said, 'Well, why don't you try information science?' I was originally, like, [a] computer science [major] because I took a couple courses like that in high school. But then he kind of showed me about that, and I switched my major sophomore year once I realized I didn't want to do computer science." Although finding out about a major from a friend was not typical, Justin was not the only student in my sample who discussed this type of help from friends.

Students also frequently helped each other improve their performance in class by proofreading papers and studying together. Almost every student mentioned doing one of these activities with friends during their time at MU. More often than studying *with* friends, students discussed studying *alongside* friends, with each person reading, working on assignments, or studying for different classes; chapter 3 discusses the benefits of these specific types of instrumental help for lower-achieving versus higher-achieving tight-knitters. Friends also helped each other prepare for exams. Molly described doing this frequently with friends, such as: "I'll hand her flash cards and tell her to quiz me in Spanish." Although Arum and Roksa (2014, 34) say that time studying with peers is "not time well spent, at least not for developing general collegiate skills," I argue that it can be time well spent if the goal is balancing academic and social life.[15]

One other category of instrumental help that students' friends provided involved driving them to class, walking with them to class, making sure they were awake in time to go to class, and reminding them about due dates for readings, assignments, papers, and exams. While other categories of instrumental help were performed and accepted by most students, this one was not. There was a split between those who saw this type of behavior as a way friends could help and those who saw it as intruding on what they themselves should do. Abby put it succinctly: "I'll complain to my friends when I have a paper due and stuff, but for the most part my academics are just kind of for me." Chapters 3–5 explain how students' preferences for these academic "reminders" differ by network type. By expanding our understanding of the range of instrumental help students' friends provide, we can better acknowledge when friendships come with academic benefits and when interventions could help students be more successful.

### Emotional Support from Friends

[My friends,] they wish me luck. They're sympathetic about things. They encourage me. They ask after the fact how it went. All my good girlfriends are pretty good about that, asking, "So, how did it go?" "What do you think?" "Well, that's okay, you'll get it next time," if it didn't go well or whatever. Or they encourage me: "You'll do fine. Don't be nervous about it, you'll do okay." So, mostly just words of encouragement.

—Beth

The second strategy of integration involved friends providing emotional support or encouragement for academics. Like Beth, students discussed how their friends motivated them, provided an environment conducive to academics, and congratulated them when they did well. As discussed in later chapters, academic emotional support is a particularly important way that friends matter during and after college.

Friends provided direct emotional support through verbal encouragement and congratulations. Jim's description was similar to that provided by Beth:

Generally, my friends will know I have a big exam coming up and they're very quick to say, "How did it go?" Or I'll wake up in the morning and I'll have four or five messages: "Good luck on your exam. You're gonna do great." And I do the same thing. If I know that one of my friends has a big exam coming up, I'll send them a message right before I go to bed: "Good luck on your exam." Or if they do really well on their exam, if we go over to [the cafeteria] for dinner, I'll buy them ice cream for dessert. Something like that. We use each other for support a lot.

Students also used social media to post messages that said something like "studying for this damn psychology test" and commented that the next day people would "always ask, 'How'd it go?' It's nice that people look and listen for stuff like that." Wishing each other "good luck," asking how the test went, and congratulating and commiserating with each other afterward showed care about each other's academic success.

Along with this direct support, students also frequently discussed how friends implicitly supported academics by providing an environment where academics were encouraged, or at least tolerated. Friends provided support by listening to one another's complaints and understanding what they were going through. Indeed, previous research has noted that undergraduates frequently talk to friends about workloads and deadlines (Brooks 2007). As Ruth put it, "Sometimes, I complain to my friends: 'Oh, I have this and this and this due. Can you believe it? Oh, this crap is making me crazy!'" Friends also implicitly supported academics through expressing understanding. For example, Krystal trusted that her friends respected her academic focus: "If I say, 'No, I can't go out 'cause I have to do my homework,' they're very understanding. They're like, 'Oh, okay, that's blank.' They're supportive of that. They're not going to tell me to go quit school so I can party with them. I'm the same way. If someone wants to do their homework and I want to go out, I will leave them alone."

Students pointed to both direct and indirect emotional support for academics as important ways that friends facilitated their academic involvement and success. Both men and women described friends as emotionally supportive, although this was mentioned least often by white men.[16] The importance of caring and supportive relationships is confirmed by some research on elementary to high school students (Lewis et al. 2012; Ream 2005; Stanton-Salazar 2001; Valenzuela 1999), and Nancy Schlossberg (1989) has shown that such connections matter to college students. This research, however, tends to focus on relationships with institutional agents, such as teachers, whereas I focus on friendships with other students. My findings reveal the processes through which students' friends emotionally support their academic interests and activities. As social capital, friendships provide academic support and resources. As chapter 6 shows, not only are friends who provide emotional support regarding academics important during the college years, but these friendships were invoked frequently in students' reflections on college during the follow-up interviews and were more likely to have been maintained five years later. Emotional support is a particularly important way that friends matter during and after college.

## Intellectual Discussions with Friends

Somebody brings up something that maybe they talked about in their class or whatever, and we'll just sit and talk about it for a while. Maybe how we feel about it, what we would do in the situation. . . . I took a philosophy class my first semester here and that brought up a lot of theories and ideas that I'd never really thought about before. So sometimes, when we would hang out or do whatever, I'd be like, "Oh, this is what we're talking about in philosophy." And it became a trend throughout the semester; every time we would see each other, they would be like, "So what are you talking about in philosophy?" It would always start with a big conversation about God and all this theoretical stuff: and what if this, and what if that?

—Noleen

A third type of integration involved intellectual discussions with friends. Previous research documents important "social" learning from friends, particularly from interactions across diversity (antonio 2001; Aries 2008; Brooks 2007; McCabe 2011; Mullen 2010). My findings build on these insights by investigating how these interactions integrate social and academic life, and differences in who uses these strategies by network type.

Sometimes these discussions stemmed from ideas discussed in class, as mentioned by Noleen, a journalism major; other times, discussions were unrelated to classes, covering a range of intellectual ideas, including politics, art, the news, race, or religion.[17] Not all students talked about controversial ideas, profound knowledge, or such clearly intellectual issues as God and philosophy with their friends. Intellectual discussions with friends could also revolve around "small facts," as Akira, a health administration major, described it:

I get to learn new things I didn't know, like a fish has only a five-second memory. [*laughs*] You learn all this—it's not, like, *wow,* deep knowledge, but it's that general knowledge that you wouldn't ever think about. Like, who thinks about, do they get tired swimming in the same tank? They don't remember it. . . . It's just knowledge that you increase when you're with your friends. . . . We just don't talk about, like, "Oh, how's your day?" [But] like, "So, did you hear about the news? Did you hear about this?" Or "Did you know an eye can see over 12 million shades of gray?"

A final way that intellectual discussions with friends came up was in some students' desire for more. Brandi, for example, mentioned how she and her best friend "think beyond the norm," something that she does not experience with other friends:

BRANDI: [My best friend and I] are so intellectual. . . . We both feel like we're on such a different level than other people. . . . Way beyond the flat line that most people think on.

JM: So, do you have that with your other friends too?

BRANDI: No, I don't really talk intellectually like that with other ones. . . . A subject like gay marriage—people will usually be, like, "Yes" or "No, I don't agree with it." We will talk about it in such a higher level.

Brandi's intellectual discussions with her best friend were an important and distinctive part of their relationship. She also mentioned wanting more, a sentiment shared by others. Greg, for example, expressed disappointment with peers and friends at MU who "don't tend to challenge me intellectually." The frequency and depth of intellectual discussions with friends varied.[18] Intellectual engagement with friends was not present in all students' experiences, and the desire for more or deeper relationships was even less common. Chapters 3–5 discuss these differences as they relate to types of friendship networks. However, these behaviors and desires were present among many students, in a range of majors. Intellectual discussions with friends thus are a meaningful way that students integrate and balance their academic and social lives.

### Competition with Friends

Having my friends around . . . I feel almost competitive sometimes. Like, oh, so-and-so is getting a 3.5 [GPA], I've got to get a 3.6. Something to that effect. So I think it encourages a little competition from time to time.

—Krystal

The fourth, and least common, way that students' friends were involved in their academic lives was through fostering friendly competition over schoolwork and grades. Students aimed to improve by comparing their performance with that of their friends, as Krystal explained. For most students, such competition was not a central part of the relationship. However, even when it happened only "from time to time," as Krystal put it, students said that friendly competition could motivate them to equal, if not surpass, their friend. Ruth offered a similar description: "[My friends and I are] competitive academically. Who's going to get a better GPA this

semester? We seriously do that. And it's not that it's malicious academically, but it pushes you. . . . That really pushes you when your friends are
like, 'You didn't do the homework? Are you crazy? You know she's collecting [homework] today.'" Friendly competition motivated students to study
and earn grades they were proud to share.

Competition with friends was mentioned much less frequently than the
first three ways of integrating social and academic life: instrumental help,
emotional support, and intellectual discussions. Some students said they
did not discuss their grades with anyone or they discussed them only with
close friends or family, especially parents. My findings stand in contrast to
those in a small study of UK college students' friendships, which concludes
that "[n]early all students thought that it was important to compare the
grades they received with those of their friends and peers" (Brooks 2007,
701). This sentiment, however, was more common among samplers than
the other network types; chapters 3–5 discuss this difference by friendship
network type. Friendship structure, a factor unexamined in prior research,
appears to mediate how frequently students draw on particular strategies.

## Cultivating Academically Supportive Friendships

I always encourage them and they always encourage me—the friends that I have
now. The friends that I had before, they didn't even care what you were doing. . . .
But now, I don't want to be around people who are not ultimately looking out
for my good, and part of my good is getting a degree. Right now I'm in college, so
I should be getting a degree, which means I need to be going to class and I need
to be doing my homework, which means I need people around me who support
that. I don't have any friend who . . . would tell me not to go to class, because
they know that I'll be like, "What do you mean not go to class? You're supposed
to be my friend!" I like people who push me toward that. And I've learned to
push other people toward that because I know it helps me. . . . I try to be [for
them] what I want them to be for me.

—John

While students did not always use these strategies intentionally, they sometimes were quite deliberate in cultivating academically supportive friendships. A gardening metaphor is apt here because the strategy involved sow-
ing the seeds of these relationships by seeking out academically serious
and successful students, nurturing the plant by maintaining positive relationships, and keeping the weeds away by avoiding friendships that seem
academically destructive or distracting. John discussed each part: choosing

friends who supported his academic goals, providing this same support for his friends, and avoiding friends who did not "push me toward that."

The first part of the strategy involved surrounding oneself with successful, smart, and serious friends. Adriana described it as "try[ing] to put people around me who have some kind of potential to do well, who are pretty intelligent, . . . [and] they have a good goal already." She elaborated: "They are good examples, and I want to do things to try to be [that way]. . . . I see the success that they have in their things they're doing, so I want to try to be able to do that too. And they show you the importance of being a good student. Being a role model, they show you." In line with prior research showing that junior high and high school students were more likely to become friends with peers who attended classes with them (Frank, Muller, and Mueller 2013), students often mentioned friendships formed in class. Mya explained: "I just sit down [in class and say], 'Hey, how are you doing today?' [*chuckles*] And you see that person every day. You go sit by them or they come sit by you and you guys just start talking and be like, 'Oh, you want to study together?' Go study, go out to dinner, or something like that. That's how I developed most of my friendships." Although meeting most of one's friends in class was not common, the progression Mya described of talking in class leading to study groups and friendships was typical. Greg's description shows that this strategy is quite conscious and deliberate for some students: "I will try to make a friend or two in my class and look for people I already know the first day or second day. And I've been very, very lucky with that. I've never just gone to a class and not made a friend. With group projects and stuff, I've always known who my groups were going to be right away because I would make friends with people in class." While sharing a class signaled some common interest, this signal came through stronger when students shared a major, multiple classes, or activities, such as internships. Daniel, for example, discussed a "kind of cheesy" off-campus "team-building experience" for honors students in his major that fostered friendships because "[i]t made it easy to meet people and formed some sense of camaraderie together as we embark on our business pursuits. . . . When we came to class the first couple days, it was easy to be, 'Oh, I saw you at the [team-building] thing.'" This common experience and interest seemed to increase students' willingness to talk to peers by making them feel more comfortable doing so. Such interactions could be the first step to an academically supportive friendship.

The second part of the strategy involved making the effort to maintain academically supportive friendships. Nicole described how taking additional classes together nurtured a friendship she made in a class: "We became friends by studying for tests together. So the more we studied, the more we got to know each other. We're in a class together now, actually, that we chose to take together. I just really enjoy that friendship because I feel like that's one of the most intellectual people I know." Students often maintained these relationships by engaging in other strategies of integration, including studying with friends, having intellectual conversations with them, and offering explicit and implicit emotional support. Maintaining these relationships could involve redirecting friends' behavior when their academic focus strayed—for example, by encouraging them to attend class or taking them to the library—actions most common among high-achieving tight-knitters (see chapter 3).

The third part of cultivating academically supportive friendships involved avoiding friends who were not supportive. Jenny succinctly remarked, "I really don't surround myself with people that just don't care about school." Some students mentioned that they avoided specific types of friends, such as "excessive partyers" or "toxic friends." Amanda asserted, "I tend to avoid all partyers. Someone who identifies themselves as a partyer is not usually my friend, or at least not a close [friend]. . . . If I get into that kind of a lifestyle, that affects, like, how much time I spend on homework. . . . If I'm at the bars, I'm probably not going to be doing homework." Similarly, Carlos avoided a specific personality type, which he termed "intoxicating": "There's definitely those people that are intoxicating. You're just like [*exhales loudly*]—you completely forget about things. I have some of those friends that I cannot say no to. If they're like, 'Hey, let's go out,' and it's a Monday, I'm like, 'Okay, let's go!' And *those* are the people you want to stay away from [*laughs*], at least for the first half of the week." Implicit in Carlos's explanation was that even academically focused students like him can get distracted by certain friends. He worked to avoid academically destructive friendships. The last part of his comment alludes to his temporal separation between "academic time" and "social time." Analyzing how students coped with the potential distraction of friends by integrating their friends into academics provides important insight into how friends may positively affect academic outcomes, such as grades. The three ways students cultivated academically supportive friendships also provides a model for students wishing to gain more friendships that yield academic benefits. By choosing friends who support one's goals, maintaining these friendships through providing similar support, and avoiding friends who are not supportive, students can maximize the academic benefits of their friendships.

## Conclusion

In sum, prior research often asserts an either/or perspective on friends and academics: friends *either* distract *or* help. For example, other studies of students' everyday experiences on college campuses highlight how even students with high academic aspirations can be drawn away from academics by college social life. Scholars have documented how the university itself rewards this "party pathway" (Armstrong and Hamilton 2013), how "romance culture" draws women away from academic achievement (Holland and Eisenhart 1990), and how "talk about academics . . . accounted for less than 5 percent of the total subjects . . . discussed" (Nathan 2005, 99). While I find that distraction is present, I also find that many students forge relationships that help them academically. Students integrate their friendships into their academic lives in a variety of ways. This occurs even for students who employ strategies to separate their friends from academics and for students who see themselves as "equally balanced" on the academic-social scale, as well as those who are more social or more academic. Put simply, students are savvier than we give them credit for.

Another strand of research recognizes that peers help students but provides little detail about how this occurs and typically does not distinguish between friends and other types of peers. For example, a recent book notes "the centrality of the social sphere to what happens in college" (Arum and Roksa 2014, 27), and a classic text in student development asserts, "A student's most important teacher is often another student" (Chickering and Reisser 1993, 392). In general, researchers in these traditions focus on specifying how much peers matter for particular outcomes and in what contexts.[19] I draw on this research but differ in focusing specifically on friendships and in analyzing rich accounts of students' experiences to explore the processes through which friends help and hinder each other academically. My findings add concrete details to support researchers' claims about the importance of social integration and the potential of academically oriented friendships to be academically beneficial. They fit with the growing body of evidence on peer effects, which argues that students influence one another's behavior, providing much-needed detail about *how* peer effects occur.[20] I identify a range of ways that students actively (even if not always intentionally) involve friends in their academic lives.

For nearly every student I interviewed, friends were *both* a distraction *and* a help. These elements exist alongside each other. Students described friends as at least a potential distraction from academics. And they described a range of ways their friends were involved in their academic lives. Students often recognized which friends pulled them toward academics and which pulled them away. To achieve balance, they cultivated relationships with those who tolerated or encouraged academic involvement and used strategies of separation to protect their academic lives from friends who were academic distractions. Not all students made these distinctions, but looking at their friendships through this lens would allow students to maximize the academic benefits of their friends. The strategies of integration show a range of ways friends support students' academic involvement. The potential of friends to distract students, however, was present as well. In line with nuanced conceptions of social capital as both positive and negative (e.g., Portes 1998), I show social capital as facilitating as well as constraining students academically and their ability to balance academic life and social life. By failing to recognize the value of both integrating and separating friends from academic life, students, parents, administrators, and policymakers overlook one of the most crucial aspects of college—friendship.

Another false dichotomy is thinking about academic life and social life as either separated or integrated. I find that students often asserted that they tried to separate their friends from their schoolwork, but they found them involved in a range of ways. Nearly every student I interviewed used both strategies of separation and strategies of integration. These strategies are not mutually exclusive.

Students' friends were most often involved academically through face-to-face contact, although there certainly were times that they used electronic messaging to connect with friends. Academic involvement with acquaintances was more likely to be electronic, perhaps because acquaintances were more likely to be involved in students' academic life in just one way than through multiple strategies of integration. Future research should explore how much the rise of social media has changed the ways friends are integrated and separated from academics and how university context changes this role (e.g., students at nonresidential and commuter campuses may involve friends in academics more often via electronic messaging).

These findings imply that parents, administrators, and researchers can improve students' college experiences through some simple yet powerful approaches. First, acknowledge that students value both academic and social life. The "testimonies of balance" and the "cautionary tale testimonies of imbalance" reveal that students cherish both aspects. Efforts to get students to focus on academics are certainly worthwhile but should recognize that social life can also be meaningful for students. Second, recognize that students' friends are both involved in and separated from academics, and that both expedients can be helpful sometimes. Even the most successful and balanced students engaged in strategies of separation at times. The strong claims from students that they separated their friends from academics seemed to be reactions to their awareness that friends can be academic distractions. This relates to the last suggestion, which is that friends who either share their friends' goals, motivations, and behaviors or serve as a model for these characteristics are incredibly helpful in supporting students' efforts for balance. Students should know that their friends appreciate these efforts. As I showed earlier in this chapter, students can cultivate these types of friendships.

This chapter paints these strategies in broad strokes, focusing on identifying the specific methods students use to keep friends separate from and involved in academic life. In later chapters, I address the combination of strategies students used, which strategies were academically and socially successful (and which were less so), and how they influenced students' lives after college. I begin, in chapter 3, by focusing on students with very dense networks, in which almost all their friends knew each other.

# THREE

# Tight-Knitters

Although nearly all students both separated their friendships from their academics and integrated the two, they did not do so in the same ways. The next three chapters highlight how students' strategies to separate and integrate their friends differed by type of friendship network: "tight-knitters," students with one densely woven friendship group; "compartmentalizers," those with multiple friendship groups; and "samplers," those with friends with few connections to each other. In this way, these chapters bring together the key insights of chapters 1 and 2 to analyze network structure (measured primarily by density) and content (what happens inside these networks), revealing that both matter for students' academic and social experiences.

In this chapter, I focus on "tight-knitters," students with one densely woven friendship group in which almost all their friends know each other. I show that tight-knit networks provide social support, circulate information well, and exert social control; however, these effects are not always academically positive. Although tight-knitters graduated from college at lower rates than compartmentalizers and samplers, density itself is not the problem. Network content matters. Tight-knitters who did well academically had friends who provided instrumental help, emotional support, and intellectual engagement, and those who did poorly had friendship networks lacking this academic involvement. Put differently, higher-achieving tight-knitters experienced positive peer pressure, whereas lower-achieving tight-knitters experienced negative peer pressure for academic achievement. Tight-knit networks intensify friends' (positive or negative) impact. As chapters 4 and 5 show, less dense networks leave open more opportunities to engage in different types of academic involvement with different friends. Specific types of networks encourage, but do not determine, particular types of academic assistance from friends.

Almost all tight-knitters in my sample are black or Latino, and the racial isolation many of these students experienced drove them to actively seek networks that provided a sense of "home" and comfort on campus. Dense networks provided this social support and comfort. By linking network structure to what happens in these networks, this research contributes to understanding educational inequality in terms of recruitment, retention, and graduation rates at predominantly white campuses. Black and Latino tight-knitters achieved a sense of belonging through their friendship networks, but their own academic outcomes varied according to the academic involvement of their friends. Among tight-knitters, academic outcomes and social experiences did not always match.[1] As the experiences of Alberto and Keisha show, tight-knit networks typically socially support students but can be positive or negative academically depending on friends' academic orientations.

## Alberto's Story of Tight Friendships

When I first interviewed him, Alberto was in his fifth year in college.[2] He attended a college in a nearby state for one year and then transferred to MU. Alberto was a Latino man who self-identified as upper class and gay. Throughout his four years at MU, Alberto had been very involved in campus clubs and activities; for example, he founded the chapter of his Latino fraternity at MU and was president of MU's Latino Student Alliance. Alberto's active social life also involved hanging out with his friends and his fraternity brothers. He balanced his social life with an academic focus, describing himself as academically "serious" and "engaged." He excitedly and repeatedly told me, "I want to learn everything I can."

As Alberto described his friendships, the tone in his voice became sentimental. He began by talking about his friends from his hometown, describing his friend Natasha as "almost like a sister." When I asked if there was anyone at MU he considered a friend, he responded, "Definitely. I consider my fraternity brothers my best friends here—like my family away from home." Alberto explained:

I've lived with them for the last two years. It's kinda like a family. If there's a birthday, we'll get a cake or we'll go out to dinner. [At] Christmas, we'll all buy each other presents. We all know everything about each other; we don't really hold back with anything. If there's anything that's going on or anything that's an issue or anything that we're going through, we talk about it with one another. If someone's going through something serious—like, crying in front of each other, it's no big deal. They're definitely someone I can tell everything to.

Alberto's network reflected the sense of "home" he felt among his friends. His MU "family" included some of his fraternity brothers and two other friends—Sasha, a former MU student, and Teresa, whom he met at a Latino festival on campus. In describing his friends from MU and those from home, he constantly noted the support and acceptance he felt from each friend, including for his marginalized ethnic and sexual identities.

Alberto's "tight-knit" friendship bonds are shown in figure 3.1.[3] Alberto's network seamlessly integrated his 14 friends into one highly connected group, weaving together friends from multiple spheres, including friends from various aspects of MU, such as campus clubs or residence halls, and friends from home.[4] Accordingly, figure 3.1 does not divide his MU friends from his hometown friends.[5] Almost all his friends knew each other, with Pedro being the least well connected.

Not only did Alberto's friendship network provide him with social support, but it also supplied a supportive academic environment.[6] Alberto described instrumental and emotional ways that his friends helped him academically: "We kind of push each other and make sure we're getting good

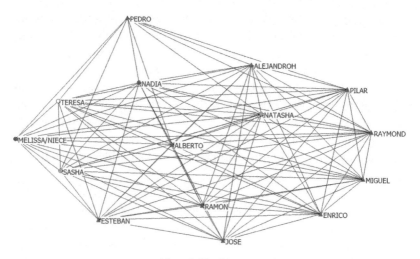

3.1. Alberto's friendship network

grades. At midterm, we'll just be like, 'Well, where's everyone at? Is everyone okay? Are you guys going to class?' Or 'Why aren't you going to class?' Or 'Are you doing this?' and 'Why aren't you doing this?' We definitely help each other." Their support included being accountable to each other. He also discussed a more formal social control agent, his fraternity's elected "academic chair, who is always making sure that the members are keeping their grades up and focused." Alberto told me he did not purposely take classes with friends—"I wouldn't go out of my way to do it"—but it had been a good experience when it worked out that way: "It made us stay on top of each other to 'keep on studying.' And, like, 'Don't forget your readings' or 'We have this assignment due; don't forget!' Or if there's a paper due, we'll proofread it for each other because we're both in the same class working on it together. So I think it makes getting through the class easier when a friend is in it." The help, accountability, and support Alberto's friends provided one another were similar to what a supportive family offers. In his words, Alberto's friendship network feels like "home."

Alberto's friends engaged in intellectual discussions to a greater extent than most students, including most tight-knitters. Alberto described a deep intellectual community where insights were shared with friends, including his friend since second grade, Natasha: "She's done all kinds of classes. . . . Every time I talk to her, she's doing something new, like a self-defense class now." He described a tight connection between academics and social life: "People I meet in classes . . . [and] programs I've been involved in tend to flow into my circle of friends . . . [because] we have more of a common interest, rather than just someone I met at a party." Alberto easily rattled off several examples of times he introduced ideas from class to his friends. One example was from a fraternity meeting the week prior to our interview:

> In a class that I took, we did an exercise on evaluating: . . . Do you have a short fuse [or] are you patient? Do you like to collaborate with people when you're in a conflict or do you want to get your own way? We did this exercise in class, and then I went back to the fraternity. While we were sitting at our chapter meeting, there was an issue that came up and I was like, "Okay, we're gonna do this exercise 'cause I think it's great." And they're just like [*exhales*], "Okay, there's Alberto." But, like, it intrigues them.

Ideas, books, and documentaries from class were common topics of conversation among his friends. Alberto commented, "[Friends have] read a book and said, 'Oh, this is a really interesting book; you should read it,' so I'll read it. We'll pass on things like that. Or maybe documentaries that someone's seen and they say is really interesting. So I might go online and do some research about it or just look articles up. If someone's taken a class here that they found really interesting, they might share that. And then I might talk about that or look stuff up or even take the class." His friends also discussed broader intellectual ideas, including politics, news, race, and ethnicity. Alberto noted that his home page was the *Washington Post* and "I talk to everyone about it." His friendship network also expanded the types of intellectual issues he was exposed to:

> One of my friends feels really, really strongly against [Che Guevara], and he saw a guy walking down the street with a Che Guevara shirt. He sat there and talked to him for like 15 [or] 20 minutes. He told him how bad Che was and how he killed all these people and how he's horrible, and he doesn't know why people glorify him—to the point where this guy, like, flipped his shirt inside out, like, right then and there. And I was like, wow! I don't really know that much about Che Guevara, so I read up on him. Stuff like that just happens.

Rather than just taking on his friend's views as his own, Alberto became curious about the topic and "read up" on it. Having intellectual discussions with friends does not mean that everyone must hold the same beliefs, even in tight-knit networks.

Throughout my interview with Alberto, he mentioned a variety of ways that his academic and social lives were integrated. For example, he and his friends studied together for class, they proofread each other's papers, they debated intellectual issues, and they discussed ideas from class. Most important to Alberto was the emotional support surrounding academics that his friends provided each other. He received academic emotional support not just from one friend or even a couple of friends but from his entire friendship network.

Although Alberto typically integrated his friends and academic life, there were times when he sought to separate them. He referred to his friends as a needed break from stress associated with school: "I go out, just party with friends, just hang out, just get my mind off of it, . . . the pressure of academics." He also described his friends as a possible distraction and admitted there had been times he had encouraged friends to "just go out; you can go to sleep right after class—no big deal." Alberto was typical in viewing friends as a possible distraction from academics and as a break from academic pressure. His academically supportive network, however, provided "checks" to ensure that breaks and hanging out were kept to a reasonable amount.

Tight-knit networks can provide emotional support, instrumental help, and intellectual engagement to students, as they did for Alberto. However, tight-knitters do not always find these types of support in their friendship networks. In some cases, the networks provided some general social support but not the same high degree of academic emotional support, instrumental help, and intellectual engagement.

## Keisha's Story of Tight Friendships

In many ways, Keisha resembles Alberto. They both had dense networks in which their friends knew each other (see Keisha's friendship network in fig. 3.2). Their tight-knit networks similarly provided both of them with important social support. When I asked Keisha about her friends, her cheeks lifted in a big smile. She then explained, "If any of them are having anything, we're always at each other's birthday parties and graduation parties. Anything like that, we're always there. We go out to eat, go to movies, and we hang out at each other's houses. . . . [We talk about] relationships mostly. That's what girls talk about [*laughs*] most of the time. . . . If we have any problems or anything, we'll always like run right to each other." Keisha and Alberto were both fifth-year seniors at MU when I first interviewed them. They both described themselves as academically serious yet balanced

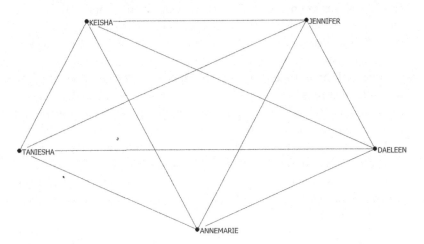

3.2. Keisha's friendship network

between academic and social life.[7] Both are students of color who joined minority Greek organizations. For both of them, their tight-knit groups seemed intentionally crafted to overcome the social isolation resulting from being a minority on a predominantly white campus. They differed greatly, however, in the ways their friends were involved in their academic lives and in whether they graduated from MU.

Keisha mentioned emotional support regarding academics that her sorority sisters and other friends provided. Compared with Alberto, however, this support appeared limited:

> Your friends affect your academic life if you let them. Good or bad, because you do have those [friends] that may not study as much as others. Everybody has their different ways. You know individually how much time you need to study, and you know just how you are and what's good for you. But you do have those [friends] that try to kind of influence that: "Hurry up and do your homework and just come [out]." It's just that easy to do. But for the most part, everybody's supportive of each other—very supportive of academics. . . . One of our principles [as a sorority] is scholarship and academics and stuff, besides just being there socially or just personally [or] relationship-wise as sisterhood and stuff like that. That's just one of the things we really hold important.

When I asked Keisha for specific ways that her friends support her academically, she stumbled to provide examples of any type. Whereas Alberto gave numerous examples of intellectual engagement, emotional support, and instrumental help, Keisha noted that her sorority sisters worked to keep their grades up to the 2.5 GPA (between B− and C+) required by the chapter, she sometimes studied alongside friends, and her friends reminded each other to attend class. In response to my question, "Do you tell each other to go to class when you don't want to go?" Keisha laughed, then responded: "Yes. All the time. . . . We [have] talked about it: 'Man, I do not want to go to this class. I just want to go home.' And, like [we tell each other], 'No. Go to class. Then don't do nothing after that. Go home and go to sleep.' We encourage each other and keep each other up on our toes." Encouragement to attend class is certainly a good thing and signifies some support from friends, but Keisha's friends' academic involvement was clearly limited.

Keisha did not stumble in providing examples of the "bad" academic effects of her friends. She mentioned that it was "easy" for friends to distract her from studying and encourage her to go out instead. When I asked her how her academic life influences her social life, Keisha responded quickly:

> I try to keep them very, very separate. . . . I don't think they influence each other at all unless I'm doing too much of one. Like, if I'm being too socially active, yes, my academics does, it starts to suffer, just a little bit. And if I'm doing too much academically, I don't think it influences social at all because you could always do social things; you could always make time for that. But if you don't make time for academics, you're more at a loss because you're losing out in GPA and in time and in everything.

Keisha recognized her friends as a possible distraction from academics, particularly her friends who did not "study as much as others" and would try to "influence" her to go out. To make time for school, Keisha's strategy was to keep her friends "very, very separate" from academics.

As a result, only a few of Keisha's friends were involved in her academic life, and their involvement was limited. Keisha's conversations about academics did not permeate her entire network as they did with Alberto. This was particularly striking because her network was smaller than Alberto's, with only four friends.[8] In fact, most of her discussion about academics involved recounting the advice she gave her younger sister and how she studied with her boyfriend. Interestingly, Keisha did not consider either her sister or her boyfriend to be a "friend," so neither appears in her friendship network.[9] In contrast to Alberto, who gave several concrete reasons why it helped to have friends in classes, Keisha responded to my question about whether she ever takes classes with friends by noting, "No. All of us have such different majors." The limited academic involvement of Keisha's friends stood in sharp contrast to the broad range of emotional support, instrumental help, and intellectual engagement in Alberto's friendship network.

## Who Are Tight-Knitters?

Most tight-knitters were black and Latino students who were the first in their families to attend college, like Keisha and Alberto. Specifically, 63 percent of black and Latino students were tight-knitters, compared to 6 percent of white students (only two tight-knitters—Justin and Ridge— were white; see table 3.1).[10] Over two-thirds of tight-knitters were first-generation college students, all of these were black or Latino, and almost

Table 3.1 Selected characteristics of higher-achieving and lower-achieving tight-knitters

| Name | Graduated from MU | GPA | Race/ Ethnicity | Gender | Class | First-Gen. | ACT | Instrumental Help from Friends* | Intellectual Discussions with Friends | Emotional Support from Friends | Academic Multiplex Ties |
|---|---|---|---|---|---|---|---|---|---|---|---|
| **Higher-achieving tight-knitters:** | | | | | | | | | | | |
| Justin | Yes | 3.6 | White | Man | Lower | No | 22 | Study group, proofread, homework, advice | Yes | Limited | Multiple |
| Valerie | Yes | 3.5 | Black | Woman | Upper | No | 23 | Study group, quiz, proofread | Limited | Yes | Multiple |
| Angela | Yes | 3.4 | Black | Woman | Middle | Yes | 21 | Study group, study alongside, proofread, homework, quiz | Yes | Yes | Multiple |
| Carlos | Yes | 3.3 | Latino | Man | Upper | Yes | 24 | Study group, advice | Yes | Yes | Multiple |
| Ridge | Yes | 3.3 | White | Man | Upper | No | 29 | Homework, proofread, advice | Limited | Limited | No |
| Ana | Yes | 3.2 | Latina | Woman | Middle | Yes | 20 | Study group, remind, wake | Yes | Yes | Multiple |
| Teresa | Yes | 3.2 | Latina | Woman | Middle | Yes | 22 | Study alongside, homework | Yes | Yes | Multiple |
| Bryce | Yes | 3.1 | Asian | Man | Middle | No | 27 | Study alongside, proofread, remind, drive | Limited | Limited | One |
| Alberto | Yes | 3.0 | Latino | Man | Upper | Yes | 27 | Study group, study alongside, advice, remind, proofread | Yes | Yes | Multiple |
| Julio | Yes | 2.9 | Latino | Man | Lower | Yes | 15 | Proofread, advice, homework | Yes | Yes | Multiple |
| Octavia | Yes | 2.9 | Black | Woman | Middle | Yes | 18 | Study group, study alongside, proofread, advice, wake | No | Yes | Multiple |

Lower-achieving
tight-knitters:

| Name | | GPA | Race | Gender | Class | | SAT/ACT | | | | |
|---|---|---|---|---|---|---|---|---|---|---|---|
| Madison | Yes | 2.8 | Black | Woman | Lower | Yes | 23 | Proofread, wake | No | Limited | No |
| Latasha | Yes | 2.7 | Black | Woman | Lower | No | 25 | Study alongside | Limited | Limited | No |
| Claudia | Yes | 2.6 | Latina | Woman | Lower | Yes | 20 | Study alongside, wake | Limited | Limited | One |
| Adrianna | Yes | 2.6 | Latina | Woman | Lower | Yes | 20 | Study group, study alongside | No | Limited | One |
| Sean | Yes | 2.3 | Black | Man | Lower | Yes | 20 | Remind | No | Limited | No |
| Keisha | No | 3.0 | Black | Woman | Middle | Yes | —† | Study alongside, remind | Limited | Limited | No |
| Mya | No | 2.7 | Black | Woman | Lower | Yes | 20 | Remind | Limited | Limited | One |
| Erica | No | 2.5 | Black | Woman | Upper | No | 22 | Study group, study alongside, quiz, wake | No | Limited | No |
| Rachel | No | 2.5 | Black | Woman | Middle | Yes | 18 | Study group, proofread, homework | Limited | No | No |
| Kim | No | 2.2 | Black | Woman | Middle | Yes | 19 | Study alongside, proofread | No | Limited | One |
| Chris | No | 1.9 | Black | Man | Lower | Yes | 24 | Study group, borrow books | Limited | Limited | No |

*Note:* See table 0.2 notes for discussion of socioeconomic class, first-generation college students, and ACT scores.

* Possible responses in this category are **study group** covering the same material; **study alongside** friend, each focusing on own work; **quiz** each other in preparation for exams; give each other **advice** about classes, majors, or professors; help each other with **home-work**; **proofread** papers; help each other on own work; **remind** each other about assignments or to attend class; **drive** each other to class; **wake** each other up for class; and **borrow books** for class.

† Keisha reported that she did not take either the SAT or the ACT. I was not permitted access to MtI records to be able to confirm this.

half self-identified as lower class and almost half as middle class (only two first-generation tight-knitters were upper class). Most (86%) were also from the state in which MU is located. Seven tight-knitters were in sororities or fraternities, although only one of these was a "mainstream" fraternity, the phrasing most students of color used to refer to historically white houses. Although more tight-knitters were employed than other network types, they worked fewer hours: two-thirds were employed, working 18 hours per week, on average. Similar to compartmentalizers, slightly over half lived on campus and half were in a romantic relationship. In other words, the main ways that tight-knitters differed were their racial and class backgrounds.

Race is the most distinguishing feature of tight-knitters. Indeed, past research finds that students of color tend to bond in tight-knit groups (Martinez Alemán 2000; Solórzano, Ceja, and Yosso 2000; Stearns, Buchmann, and Bonneau 2009; Tatum 1997; Willie 2003). Solórzano and colleagues (2000) refer to this bonding among blacks as creating "counter-spaces," and Lasley Barajas and Pierce (2001) refer to these relationships among Latinas as "safe spaces." These studies focus primarily on the homophily of these networks.[11] Research has also pointed to the importance of friendships and other peer relationships in facilitating the on-campus integration and comfort of students of color (Beasley 2011; Lasley Barajas and Pierce 2001; Martinez Alemán 2000; McCabe 2009, 2015; Solórzano, Ceja, and Yosso 2000; Willie 2003). My findings build on previous research by more precisely documenting the ways in which friendships provide help and support for students of color and noting how support differs by network type.[12] My findings also illustrate how students of color can be harmed by the very structures to which they turn for support. In other words, the lower graduation rates of students of color may be mediated by antiacademic norms in the dense friendship networks of lower-achieving tight-knitters. This provides a clear example of how friendships can have clashing effects on the inequalities plaguing higher education, such as racial differences in graduation rates: friendships reduce existing inequalities when networks provide social and academic support in response to racial isolation, yet they intensify existing inequalities when networks fail to provide social or academic support.

Race matters also in terms of whether students happened upon their friendship networks "accidently" or consciously sought out particular types of friends. Black and Latino tight-knitters were more likely than white students and black and Latino compartmentalizers and samplers to strategically build their own network structures, whether by creating an informal friendship group or by joining a formal organization. The racial isolation many black and Latino students experienced drove them to actively seek networks that provided a sense of "home" and comfort on campus. Dense networks supplied this social support and comfort.

## Network Structure and Academic Outcomes

When I looked at the academic success of all participants in my study, tight-knitters were the least likely to graduate. Only 77 percent of tight-knitters graduated from MU, compared with 91 percent of compartmental-izers and 92 percent of samplers (see table 3.2).[13] GPAs were more similar across network types, but tight-knitters again showed the lowest academic achievement, with an average GPA of 2.9, compared with 3.3 among com-partmentalizers and 3.2 among samplers (roughly a B vs. a B+). While these differences reflect racial disparities in academic outcomes found among college students generally, black tight-knitters had lower academic outcomes than black samplers and compartmentalizers.[14] I was initially puzzled about why some of the students with vibrant and supportive tight-knit networks would have the lowest academic outcomes. Upon closer analysis, it became clear that not all tight-knit networks worked the same.

Tight-knit networks provided social support, but the academic benefits varied greatly. I found that some tight-knit networks were like Alberto's in providing emotional support, intellectual engagement, and instrumental help. Students in these networks tended to be those who graduated from MU and had high GPAs. In contrast, other tight-knit networks provided limited academic involvement, including emotional support regarding academics. Students in these networks tended to be those who did not graduate from MU or had lower GPAs. Keisha, for example, did not gradu-ate. She attended MU for five years and a nearby community college for a couple of semesters, but she was short a few credits needed for her major. Both she and Alberto ended up with 3.0 GPAs (see table 3.1), so it was not GPA that separated them but whether they ultimately earned a degree. Keisha's friendship network gave her social support but not the supportive

Table 3.2   Academic outcome by network type

|  | Graduated from MU (%) | Mean GPA |
|---|---|---|
| Tight-knitters (N = 22) | 77 | 2.9 |
| Compartmentalizers (N = 33) | 91 | 3.3 |
| Samplers (N = 12) | 92 | 3.2 |

resources—the multiple types of academic involvement found in Alberto's network—to help her achieve a college degree.

These same patterns appear when comparing other higher-achieving and lower-achieving tight-knitters. Table 3.1 shows the types of friends' academic involvement for these two groups. Higher-achieving students are those who graduated from MU with a GPA of 2.9 or above. Lower-achieving students are those who did not graduate or had a GPA below 2.9, which means their GPAs were in the bottom 30 percent of my sample. These differences between higher- and lower-achieving students cannot be completely explained by prior academic achievement (measured by the ACT and SAT scores students received in high school). They do, however, seem related to their parents' college attendance.[15] My findings are in line with other research arguing that higher education reproduces class inequalities (e.g., Armstrong and Hamilton 2013; Mullen 2010; Stuber 2011): students who entered college with a class-based disadvantage as first-generation college students were more likely to end up as lower-achieving tight-knitters.

Networks may also be a critical mediating variable that mutes or amplifies the effects of family background on academic performance. Lower-achieving tight-knitters seemed to have friends from more disadvantaged backgrounds than higher-achieving tight-knitters did. This finding is more speculative than others I report because I did not systematically collect data on friends' class backgrounds.[16] Nonetheless, it points to the need for future research to explore networks not only in terms of their direct effects but also in terms of their mediating effects.[17]

As shown in the last four columns in table 3.1, higher-achieving tight-knitters received more types of instrumental help from friends[18] and were more likely to discuss intellectual issues with and receive emotional support from them. Drawing on the network concept of multiplexity, which refers to connections through multiple types of ties,[19] I use the term *"academic multiplex ties"* to describe relationships providing at least two of the three types of academic assistance: emotional support, instrumental help, and intellectual engagement. Higher-achieving tight-knitters, including Alberto, were more likely to have academic multiplex ties.

Previous research on network density may shed some light on these findings. Researchers interested in network density typically have looked at its relation to social support, information flow, and enforcement of social norms. Generally, they view dense networks as supportive.[20] Researchers also find that density affects social control, with greater norm enforcement in dense networks. Theory suggests that individuals are less subject to social control when their networks are made up of overlapping circles rather than concentric ones (Simmel 1955, 146–47), and some empirical evidence backs this up. For example, social closure (networks in which individuals know each other) facilitates information exchange between network members, as in the case of parents who monitor and discuss their children's activities and behaviors (Coleman 1990). Dense networks also influence information flow. Although information freely flows among members of a dense network, some researchers have asserted that such networks can lead to "inbreeding" (Wellman and Gulia 1999, 104), where new information is difficult to acquire within the network (Burt 2004; Schweizer, Schnegg, and Berzborn 1998). In other words, redundant information flows within ,the network, but new information cannot enter. My findings are similar to those on peer delinquency, where junior high and high school students are more likely to be delinquent if they are in a dense network with others who are also delinquent but are less likely to be delinquent if they are in a dense network with others who are not delinquent (Haynie 2001). Building on research that social capital can be both positive and negative, I find that tight-knit networks provide social support, circulate information well, and serve as social control, as prior research asserts; however, these effects are not always academically positive.

As we would expect from high-density networks, I find that tight-knitters get support from their friends. Race influences this experience and its benefits. As described later in the chapter, tight-knit networks provided an important sense of "home" for black and Latino students who felt marginalized at MU. However, these supportive networks did not provide academic benefits for all tight-knitters.

Information flow and social control's effects varied according to the content of the network. Higher-achieving tight-knitters' friends frequently talked about academics, circulating academic information throughout the network. Friends generally were involved in each other's academic lives instrumentally, emotionally, and intellectually. All but two higher-achieving tight-knitters had multiple academic multiplex ties in their network. Their friends expected and encouraged them to do well academically. Although friends still provided academic distractions, it was more often redirected than tolerated.

Lower-achieving tight-knitters also experienced increased social control and information flow in their networks, but these effects were not academically positive. These students' friends provided limited or no instrumental help, emotional support, or intellectual engagement, and some friends had low levels of academic skills and information. Friends frequently talked about other topics, such as relationships and social life. In their dense networks, information about these other topics flowed well; thus, social information rather than academic information circulated well throughout the networks. Social control operated so that it was acceptable for lower-achievers' friends to be minimally involved academically and for their friends to distract them academically.[21] In these examples, social capital can be negative.

In addition to tight-knitters being characterized uniquely by their high levels of network density, they also stand out in terms of modularity and betweenness centrality. All three measures (density, modularity, and betweenness centrality) are mathematical properties of networks. Because most of their friends are connected to each other, tight-knitters have high density scores (0.67–1 from a possible range of 0–1), low modularity scores (0–0.08 from a possible range of –0.5 to one), and low betweenness centrality scores (0–0.28 from a possible range of 0–1). As explained in chapter 1, density is the proportion of ties present out of possible ties. Betweenness centrality is a measure of how central a person is in a network in terms of how many others in the network are connected only through that person. Modularity measures the number of communities in a network, calculated by comparing the number of ties present with the number expected by chance (Newman 2006). The low betweenness centrality scores suggest that few people in tight-knitters' networks are connected principally through the tight-knitter (the ego, to use network language).[22] The low modularity score suggests that tight-knitters' networks do not fall into groups or communities.[23] Tight-knitters instead have one group of friends.

## The Negative Side of Tight-Knit Networks

While they are not the only factor that matters for college success, I argue that friendship networks are an important overlooked factor. A tight-knit network can amplify academic success (as it did for Alberto) or constrain it (as it did for Keisha, who failed to graduate). The differences described earlier between Alberto and Keisha highlight several of the academic problems for students with tight-knit networks. Here, I analyze the negative side of tight-knit networks in more detail.

### Friends' Limited Instrumental Involvement

Chapter 2 discussed a range of ways that students provided instrumental help to each other, including participating in study groups, asking for help with course material, editing each other's papers, quizzing each other in preparation for tests, sharing notes, and waking each other up for class. As shown in table 3.1, lower-achieving tight-knitters were involved in fewer types of instrumental help than were higher-achieving tight-knitters (two vs. 3.5 types of instrumental help, on average). The most frequent type of instrumental help from tight-knitters with lower academic achievement was studying with friends. For example, Mya discussed how she occasionally studied in the same room as her roommate in order to keep from falling asleep: "We just go in the living room, set out our books, turn on the TV, and we read and study. I have to have things going on around me; otherwise, I fall asleep. [*laughs*] Like, reading something—next thing I know I'm waking up. I'm like, 'What?' So that's what we do." Mya's statement illustrates a further distinction between these two groups: lower-achieving tight-knitters were more often studying *alongside* friends rather than *with* friends. Table 3.1 shows these differences: whereas higher-achieving tight-knitters often mentioned participating in study groups with friends, lower-achieving tight-knitters were more likely to discuss studying different material with their friends nearby, like Mya and her roommate studying in front of the TV.

While studying at the same time as friends was most common, lower-achieving tight-knitters also mentioned reminding each other about due dates or attending class, quizzing each other with flash cards, waking each other up for class, and sharing books. For example, Erica noted, "We'll quiz each other. I had flash cards for my German class and [my friends would] go through the flash cards so I could memorize them." Erica also remarked: "We'll write reminders on our door, like, 'Wake me up at 11:00 so I can go to class' or 'Call me so I'll get up. Get me outta bed.' But, yeah, sometimes we didn't make it [*laughs*]." While flash cards and waking each other for class may help, these actions involve little academic engagement. Similarly, Chris mentioned how his friends borrowed books from each other to save money. Latasha made clear the limited extent of her friends' academic involvement: "Studying. That's really it. If we're not studying together, there's, like, no other discussion that we have. It's not like we have talks about the class—like, what happened in class. We don't do anything like that, no." All these examples, even the most frequently mentioned one of studying alongside friends, were more limited ways friends were involved instrumentally. Rather than answering questions about course material, proofreading papers, or participating in study groups, the types of instrumental help that lower-achieving tight-knitters engaged in typically provided little academic engagement.

### Friends' Limited Intellectual Discussions

Most of the higher-achieving tight-knitters engaged in intellectual conversations with friends, many on a regular basis. In contrast, most lower-achieving tight-knitters mentioned few, if any, intellectual discussions. Table 3.1 shows these differences.[24] For example, Erica was typical in seeing little incentive to engage: "I don't think we've ever really talked about anything that we went over in class here, like how we felt about it. . . . I don't really express myself like [that]. I don't do it." Kim also tended to view intellectual issues as unusual or undesirable topics among friends, noting that she does not talk about issues such as religion or politics with her friends: "Definitely not. . . . Nothing really intellectual. No intellectual conversation."

Even if they were not so direct in stating that they did not engage in intellectual discussions with friends, lower-achieving tight-knitters often failed to give examples or to be concrete in the types of issues they discussed. For example, Mya enthusiastically explained, "Everything. We talk about everything. Some of them I talk about everything with, and some I don't. It depends on the person. Like Tina—I talk to her about everything. That's my best friend; I talk to her about everything. But other people, [only] certain things." Rachel's description also lacks concrete examples: "I notice that sometimes if I'm out, I'll pick up on something that was said in class or that we did in class, just from being out in the community. Or friends just spark up random conversations and I'll be like, 'Oh, yeah, we just talked about that in class today!' So, I'll get talking about what we talked about in class." Without specific examples of the discussions, it was hard to get a sense of how they affected Rachel academically. Lower-achieving tight-knitters' rather-vague descriptions of intellectual discussions with friends differed greatly from the multiple concrete examples Alberto and the other higher-achieving tight-knitters provided.

### Friends' Limited Emotional Support

Whereas the higher-achieving tight-knitters described friends as providing intense emotional support surrounding academics, checking in with each other and providing an environment where doing well academically was encouraged (or even expected), lower-achievers described more limited emotional support from friends. The second-to-last column of table 3.1 clearly shows this difference.[25] Lower-achieving tight-knitters' discussions of grades illustrated how they kept schoolwork to themselves rather than relying on friends. Here's an excerpt from my interview with Kim, who quite candidly explained her reasoning:

JM: Do you tell [your friends] specifically what grades you got or just that you did well?

KIM: I'm not ashamed of my grades, because it's what I earned. Either I worked hard for it or I didn't. If I know I didn't try my hardest in that class, I really wouldn't be ashamed, because I know I didn't deserve a better grade. Now, if I work[ed] my butt off and still got a bad grade, then I probably would be like, "Uh, I don't want to tell you." Sometimes I feel kinda stupid or whatever when I do get bad grades compared to everybody else's 'cause it just comes so easy to other people than it does to me. I struggle.

Missing from Kim's description was mention of support from her friends. She discussed neither friends congratulating her when she does well nor friends encouraging her or offering advice when she does poorly, which were common behaviors among Alberto's friends and those of most other higher-achieving tight-knitters. Not only was explicit support missing but so was the implicit support of friends passively encouraging each other by acting academically interested or focused.

Some lower-achievers discussed providing emotional support to others without receiving it in return. Latasha, for example, described this among her friends regarding grades:

LATASHA: If somebody tells me, like, "Yeah, I aced that test," . . . if they tell me they did good, I'm like, "Yeah, that's great!" I'm saying, "Keep it up." So yeah, that's, like, pretty much a lot of encouragement going on.

JM: Do they encourage you too? [Latasha laughs] Or is it you encouraging them?

LATASHA: I tend not to say much about myself unless I do bad. [laughs] Pretty much, they'll [say], "What's the problem?" and "Why do you feel like that?" But that's basically it.

Latasha noted that her friends failed to reciprocate the support and encouragement she gave. This one-way support was more characteristic of the friendships of lower-achieving tight-knitters.

### Friends as a Distraction

Descriptions of friends from tight-knitters with lower academic outcomes were littered with examples of times when friends distracted them from academics. While all students mentioned this to some extent (see chapter 2), lower-achieving tight-knitters frequently discussed this throughout their interviews. Furthermore, their friends were not just a *possible* distraction but an *actual* and *constant* distraction. And their distractions were not counterbalanced by other academic involvement. In response to my asking her whether she and her friends tell each other not to go to class when they don't want to, Latasha laughed:

> We'll call and be like, "Hey, are you in class?" They're like, "No, I'm not in class." Like, "You going to class?" They're like, "No, I think I'm not going." "Oh, you're not going. I'm not going either." Or they'll come in, I'll be studying or reading or something, and they're, like, laying down in the bed and then I'm like, "Man, they look pretty comfortable laying down in that bed!" I'll still try to stay up studying, and then the next thing you know I'm laying down. And then somebody else will come in: "Hey, it's time for class!" and [I say,] "Man, I'm sleepy. I don't want to go." And then the person next to me is sleepy: "Man, I'm sleepy. I'm not going to go either." Then the person that came in to tell me it was time for class is like, "Well, I'm not going to go either!" So, it works for a negative effect more so than a positive.

Lower-achieving tight-knitters and their friends distracted each other from attending class and from studying. Chris discussed how friends distract each other while studying: "It's not *hard*, but it's *challenging* to study with your friends. Because it's your friends. You might start talking about something else or what went on during the day, get sidetracked—get sidetracked two or three times while you're trying to study." Their distraction often overshadowed the instrumental help friends can provide by studying together. This high level of distraction can be seen in Madison's response to my question "What would you say has been the biggest obstacle for you academically in achieving what you'd like?": "Biggest obstacle? I would have to say—I hate to say that I can't help but think about my friends. . . . I just think if we were apart for a little bit, then I would just be more focused. I wouldn't constantly have somebody knocking on my door [asking], 'Can you help me with this?' or 'Can you go here with me?' [or] 'Hi' [or] whatever. I don't know. They're nice people, they're my friends, but you just got to draw the line somewhere." Rather than seeing friends as helping her academically or as separate and benign, Madison clearly identified friends as an obstacle. In fact, friends were her "biggest obstacle." Although Madison's phrasing was harsher than that of others, the general sentiment was common. She recognized that she needed "to draw the line," but her actions do not clearly show that she took her own advice.

In networks of lower-achieving tight-knitters, students tolerated—and even seemed to expect—friends to distract one another academically.

### Friends' Lack of Academic Skills

Some tight-knitters found themselves in networks where they lacked the skills and knowledge to help their friends, and their friends lacked the skills and knowledge to help them. Often, students described this as being "on the same level" academically. Kim gave an example: "[My friend and I] had a class together. But we would both be on the same level. It was, like, we weren't able to build each other up. Because half the time if I wouldn't go [to class], she wouldn't go, and vice versa. I don't know. We was basically on the same level, so we couldn't push each other up. It's like she wasn't willing to work harder and then I wasn't willing to work harder." Kim discussed how her friend not only shared her academic skills and knowledge level but also her (low) level of academic motivation. Not only the description but also the indifferent tone she used was typical of lower-achieving tight-knitters' discussions about being "on the same level."

A few students even described their friends as a level below them academically. These students were even less able to offer help. As Madison admitted this about her friends, her demeanor shifted noticeably, her voice becoming softer and almost aloof: "I just feel like they're not on my level. You know what I'm saying? As far as conversation, they are just really not on my level. I mean, they're cool, but they don't stimulate me intellectually." While compartmentalizers and samplers sometimes expressed dissatisfaction with friends, Madison was more indifferent. Like other lower-achieving tight-knitters, she did not look for intellectual conversations with or support from friends or peers outside her network. Friends' lower levels of skills, knowledge, and encouragement had a particularly large impact in tight-knit networks because students' friendships were so interconnected.

Prior research on peer effects provides some insights here. Using data collected throughout a yearlong master's program in Italy, Alessandro Lomi and colleagues (2011) found that students with lower grades were more likely to choose other students with lower grades as friends than they were to choose higher-performing students as friends. Examining US high schools, Jennifer Flashman (2012, 2014) came to a similar conclusion: students often formed friendships with those of a similar level of academic achievement. By focusing attention to what happens in these networks, I add nuance to these findings. While lower-achieving tight-knitters' networks provided social support, circulated information well, and served as social control, they typically were not circulating academically helpful information or stopping friends who distracted each other from schoolwork.

### Friends' Failed Attempts to Help

Some students described times friends tried to help. These attempts, however, were not enough to combat the limited help and support their networks provided and the constant distraction of friends. Kim, for example, contrasted the actions of most of her friends with those of Tyrone, a friend she made recently. When Kim was with her friend Corentine, she found: "We procrastinate. We know that. And he [Tyrone] is just calling us out on it. And he'll help us write. He'll stay up late with us to help us write papers; . . . he would stay up and help us [study for a test]." Earlier that week, Tyrone helped a friend with her paper: "He went over her topic with her. And sometimes he'll, like, write out her first paragraph just to get her started. And then we'll just all put in our ideas. Like, he was asking me what I thought about her topic 'cause I'm not in their English class. So I would just throw in my ideas. And he'll just help us, like, put it out on paper and stuff." Although her friend Tyrone tried to counter the generally negative effect of her broader friendship network, one person's influence was not enough in a tight-knit network. Tyrone's positive influence was not contagious; it failed to spread throughout the network. Most tight-knitters with lower achievement gave examples of a specific friend who tried to help them or a friend whom they tried to help. These examples show that these students did not disregard academics. They also show, however, that limited academic involvement was not enough.

### Social Costs of Tight-Knit Networks

Some tight-knit networks also exerted pressure on participants' social lives. Students in tight-knit networks were more likely than others to tell me that although they felt differently than their friends, they kept these feelings from their friends. An assumed uniformity in norms seemed to exist.[26] Social control, which works to keep everyone in the network similar to each other, not only was academically problematic, as discussed earlier, *but* also could pose social problems. The main issue was difficulty associated with exiting one's friendship network. This is in line with the "blockage of exit options" as a form of negative social capital discussed by Alejandro Portes and Julia Sensenbrenner (1993, 1345). I find that this form of negative social capital is a particular problem for tight-knitters. If one leaves a tight-knit network, network members choose whether to stay with that one individual or the group. Among the students I interviewed, network members chose to stay with the group. This works out for students when they find a new group, as Octavia did. However, it does not work well for all students.

Erica's experience represents the most extreme example of the costs associated with exiting a network among my participants. When Erica was near the end of her first year at MU, she had a falling out with one friend, Tara. This began with an argument over a small amount of money that Erica had loaned Tara, but it escalated into Tara's physical assault of Erica in front of their mutual friends, who stood by and watched. Erica reported the incident to the campus police and the resident assistant, who did nothing, according to her. She ended up losing all her friends over this. Not only did she feel betrayed that her friends did not intervene during the assault, but they took Tara's side after the assault. Erica was baffled about how they could blame her for Tara's keeping her money and assaulting her. Erica felt isolated and alone. Tara continued to intimidate and physically assault Erica, and Erica continued to report these incidents to campus authorities. She was unable to focus on studying for final exams and ended up failing classes, which she attributed to the stress. Consequently, Erica lost her scholarship (which was based on GPA) and decided to transfer to a branch campus. Her parents, who had paid the rest of her tuition at MU, "kind of blame me for everything that happened" and withdrew their financial support. After transferring, Erica ended up taking out loans and working one or two jobs while taking classes. She was still hoping to finish her degree, but the prospects looked slim. Erica's friendship network, which had once provided her with important social support, basically removed her from their interconnected web, leaving her devoid of any support. Erica's situation shows how social life and academic life are closely intertwined; problems in one area can lead to problems in the other.

In sum, while tight-knit networks may look the same, what happens in these networks differ. With one exception (Madison and Latasha), the lower-achieving tight-knitters were not friends with each other, so it is not one friendship group or organization driving these findings.[27] Lower-achieving tight-knitters tended to experience friends as more of a distraction than a helping hand. Rather than integrating their friends into their academic lives, lower-achieving tight-knitters tended to separate friends from academics, viewing academics as "all on me."[28] Often, friends' negative influence was not active or intentional but passive and unintentional, occurring by simply not being focused on academics and not offering emotional support or encouragement to be academically successful. Even if they wanted to, friends often lacked the resources to be able to provide academic emotional support and help to each other.

## The Power of Tight-Knit Networks

Unlike the examples in the past section, Alberto and most of the other higher-achieving tight-knitters described friends who were involved in their academic lives in multiple ways. As mentioned earlier, I use the term *"academic multiplex tie"* to refer to a relationship providing at least two of the three types of academic involvement: emotional support, instrumental help, or intellectual engagement. While only four lower-achieving tight-knitters described any friend as an academic multiplex tie, all but one higher-achiever reported at least one and all but two reported multiple academic multiplex ties. Carlos, for example, excitedly described many ways his friend Sacora helped him academically:

> She'll be like, "Oh, did you do this?" and "Remember to do this." And I'll be like, "Hey, did you do that homework?" or "Do you wanna review this real fast?" And that helps out a lot, just for small stuff. Like, the power was out at my apartment one day that I had to wake up at 8:00—and if I don't have an alarm clock, forget it, I won't wake up—and so I called her. I was like, "Oh my God, Sacora, I don't know what to do; my power is out." And so she's like, "So, sleep over," and so I did, and we both went to class that next day and it was fine. So stuff like that helps out. And we can sit there and talk about, like, "Okay, so marketing—what did you think about it?" or "Just don't forget to read this" or "Was this reading hard?" [or] "Can you help me out with this?" Or when I have questions or she has questions, we'll go see a teacher together. So stuff like that helps out a lot. Just because having a friend there, you don't feel like you're alone. . . . She's there along with you, trying to learn and trying to succeed.

Sacora and Carlos provided each other with emotional support, such as going together to see a teacher; instrumental help, such as reviewing class material together; and intellectual engagement, such as discussing "what did you think about it?" The academically successful tight-knitters surrounded themselves with friends who provided these multiple types of academic support and help. Although academic multiplex relationships were important in each of the types of friendship networks, they made the biggest difference for tight-knitters. This was because tight-knitters were surrounded by one cohesive group.

Tight-knit networks were also academically powerful when students actively cultivated academically supportive friendships. Higher-achievers not only recognized the benefits of having friends who strove for academic success but also worked to surround themselves with these friends. Octavia, for example, ardently believed that having friends who were successful and supportive would motivate her to be successful: "The people I socialize around, they're really on that same focus; you know, they're trying to get their homework done. That's why I know I picked the right people to hang around, because their focus is trying to get out of school too. . . . They push me on: 'Well, you need to study.' They're good about that." Academically supportive friendships may provide explicit support, such as encouraging friends to study, as well as implicit support, such as simply being interested in academics. Valerie was quite direct in explaining why she wanted successful friends:

> If they're succeeding and whatever, then it's like, okay, my friend's succeeding [so] I should be succeeding. If my friend has an A in the class, then I want to be like [her]. Sometimes it's a good thing to be like your friends, and sometimes it *isn't* a good thing to be like your friends. But, yeah, sometimes you want to be like your friends or whatever because if they're getting all As, of course I want to be like you, I want to get all As too or whatever. So I think they have an influence on how you want to actually stand in gradewise.

Julio, Justin, and Angela also stated that they sought to surround themselves with academically focused friends. Higher-achieving tight-knitters tended to not tolerate friends distracting them academically, instead redirecting this behavior. Ana explained, "[When my friend] doesn't answer my phone calls and doesn't call me until hours later, I'm like, 'Did you go to class?' She's like, 'Yeah, I did.' I'm like, 'Are you lying?' She's like, 'No, I went to class.' I was like, 'Don't lie.' I was like, 'Did you really go?' And she goes, 'No.' [*laughs*] I'm like, 'What are you doing? Why didn't you go to class?' So I try to call her, make sure she's awake, stuff like that." Another higher-achieving tight-knitter, Carlos, noted that his friend Caitlyn's grades were "very low," so she was on academic probation and in danger of being suspended or expelled from MU. Consequently, Carlos provided Caitlyn with academic opportunities to "hang out": "My friend Caitlyn, I try really hard to, like, help her out because she's the type that isn't very motivated.

So I'll be like, 'Oh, did you do the work? Do you want to come study with me?' . . . I'll just try to bring her along to help her out." Ana and Carlos strategically intervened to help their friends and to keep themselves surrounded by academically focused friends.

## Race, Social Isolation, and Friends

A significant part of the social support that black and Latino tight-knitters received from their friends related to race-based experiences on campus. All tight-knitters discussed feeling alone during some of their time at MU. However, all black and Latino tight-knitters discussed how race or ethnicity played a part in their feelings of marginality and hypervisibility, experiences well documented in past research (see W. Allen, Epps, and Haniff 1991; Beasley 2011; Feagin, Vera, and Imani 1996; McCabe 2009; Myers 2005; Solórzano 1998; Willie 2003; Winkle-Wagner 2009). Even Alberto, who was involved on campus and had an academically and socially supportive community of friends, had some lonely times when he first transferred to MU. He felt "shocked" by the smaller number of Latinos on campus than in the diverse city where he grew up. He accurately noted that Latinos made up only 2 percent of the undergraduate population, and "then, half of that 2 percent actually does anything active in the community." Alberto believed that the Latinos on campus had unmet needs. He saw existing ethnic organizations playing an important role but felt there was only so much they could do. From his involvement at the Latino Student Center, he realized there were two Latina sororities on campus but no Latino fraternities. For these reasons, he decided to start a chapter of a Latino fraternity on campus: "I just started looking into the idea and I felt it was kinda necessary. It's good that the women had an active role in the community with the Greek life and everything, but I didn't feel like the men were as well represented. And there was definitely an opportunity for Latino men to do their role on campus, you know, being involved. So that's why I actually started the movements to start the chapter." Alberto spent several months looking for other Latinos who shared his interest in better representing Latino voices on campus.

Alberto worked with five other Latinos for two years to found the chapter and get the national organization of their fraternity and MU to recognize it. As do most Greek organizations, they held weekly chapter meetings and organized social activities. They also attended campus events—"basically, making sure everyone knew who we were"—and organized educational, cultural, and community-service events, both alone and in partnership with other Greek organizations. For example, on the Monday before our interview, Martin Luther King Jr. Day, the group did a community service project at a local school. They had Martin Luther King crossword puzzles, friendship bracelets, and coloring-book activities for the children. After the event, the fraternity members and some of their friends ate dinner together.

Alberto recognized his social isolation on campus, and rather than remaining alone, he discussed his experiences to find other students who shared them. He earnestly described his friends as united in "fighting for our equal rights as a minority on this campus." He explained, "There's been a couple times that I think professors have made comments that *they* don't think are derogatory but *are* really offensive. So we'll talk about that and kind of share those experiences. So, definitely, I talk to them about stuff that goes on and stuff I learn." Finding friends who can relate to these isolating experiences was important to many students, including Sean, who told me, "Being a black male—even a black student—on this campus, you just get here and you look for people that look like you and when you don't see that, then you can feel lost. You try to become socially involved to make up for feeling distant and no attachment to the university." Another black student, Valerie, succinctly summed up the race-based isolation and the support of friends that characterized black and Latino tight-knitters' experiences: "Being a minority, it's kind of hard coming here and finding people who [have] the same interests as you. . . . This [friendship group] is like being at home again. It's like when you come to college, you don't need the whole home but you want to feel somewhat of being at home." Like Alberto and Valerie, tight-knitters often described consciously bringing people together to form a friendship network. Other tight-knitters found a supportive "family" somewhat accidently, through a preexisting organization. For example, Julio, a Latino student, explained how a campus organization brought together peers who could relate to his experiences: "I'm used to being around a lot of minority people [in my hometown]. So when I came here, it was a culture shock. But the Team Up program[29] helped me. It was like a family, . . . that's where I met my friends, and I keep in contact with those friends today. It's just a tie that doesn't go away. . . . It's like a fraternity, but it's not a fraternity. [*laughs*] . . . It's a bond that won't be ever faded." The sense of alienation or "culture shock," as Julio termed it, attributable to their racial or ethnic identity in the predominantly white campus environment led some students of color to seek out friendships through organizations on campus and to weave these friends into a coherent network with friends from other sites on and off campus. These family-like networks were not always racially homogeneous; for example, Julio's network had 17 percent Latino students, and Angela and Carlos each had about 30 percent same-race friends.

Many other tight-knitters described their friendships and the support these friendships provided as "like home" or "like a family." Alberto described his supportive friendship network as "family away from home." Teresa, a Latina, similarly described her group of friends: "I have my own little family here. . . . We're really like brothers and sisters. It's really awesome, I think. It's great. I'm really happy that we built our own little family." Students perceived support from a group of people who cared—like a family—as crucial in helping them deal with challenging racial experiences on campus. Another Latina, Ana, described the small number of Latino students at MU as shaping both the content and the structure of her network.[30] "All my friends are kind of connected. I don't want to sound stupid, but the Latin [sic] community at MU kind of 'sticks together,' we say, because everybody knows everybody. . . . We've seen you at a party or we've seen you at the Latino Student Center or we've seen you at a gathering." The experience of being a "minority" on campus, such as the isolation Ana felt after finding racist slurs written on her dorm-room door, was a topic of group discussion in these tight-knit networks. In other work, I discuss students' responses to racist experiences on campus (McCabe 2009). When I subsequently examined these responses by network type, I found tight-knitters most likely to cope through bonding with other students on the basis of a shared racial identity. A sense of "home" was created in cohesive friendship networks that brought together students from campus organizations, other friends at MU, and friends from outside MU.

## Conclusion

The dense networks of academically successful black and Latino students provided social support and academic emotional support.[31] Dense networks were academically powerful when they contained academic multiplex ties—for example, the same friend provided emotional support and instrumental help, or emotional support and intellectual engagement. Dense networks could be problematic academically, however, depending on the level of intellectual engagement, emotional support, and academic skills of friends in the network. The social control and information flow facilitated by dense networks could be academically positive or negative depending on what happened in and who was included in these networks.

This chapter shows that not only the structure of the network matters but also the content. Higher-achieving tight-knitters drew on the strengths of both the structure and the content of their networks when they sought to surround themselves with academically focused friends. This idea has spread into the popular culture and is summed up quite well in some advice billionaire businessman Warren Buffett gave on how to be successful: "It's better to hang out with people better than you. Pick out associates whose behavior is better than yours and you'll drift in that direction."[32] Although this strategy could work in each network type, it is most powerful among tight-knitters, who are surrounded by one friendship group. Buffett's advice, however, does not fully capture how higher-achieving tight-knitters cultivated academically supportive friendships. They did not just "drift" toward their friends' success but actively intervened to help their friends and to keep themselves surrounded by success. Because tight-knit networks provide social support for friends, interventions can focus on sustaining positive academic involvement among friends along with tweaking network structure and content for students whose networks are pulling them down or away from academics. Students would do well to avoid the model of lower-achieving networks, who tolerated friends distracting them academically, and imitate higher-achieving students, who tended to redirect this behavior. In doing so, students might be able to shape the norms and actions of their friends.

It is important for students, as well as their parents, college administrators, policymakers, and researchers, to understand that each type of network has specific benefits and potential drawbacks. Tight-knitters should recognize that their friendship network has the potential to have a more powerful impact on academic and social outcomes than if it was less dense. With friends surrounding them, it is particularly important for tight-knitters to choose their friends wisely; friends who climb will bring you higher, while those who lag behind will drag you down. Because both network structure and content importantly shape students' success, interventions to avoid the drawbacks of tight-knit networks could target both of these elements.

In terms of intervening into network structure, if students find themselves in a friendship network that is pulling them away from academics, one relatively easy solution would be to reach out to other peers.[33] Specifically, attending a meeting or event related to their interests—whether a yoga class, African American student association, political science club, or intramural basketball team—could add a new, unconnected person to their network. Of course, this approach will be most impactful if the student attends unaccompanied by friends from his or her tight-knit network. It does not take much to change someone from a tight-knitter to a compartmentalizer. Meeting one new person who introduces the student to his or her friends could add a second dense cluster, which might have a more academic focus. Less dense networks leave open more opportunities for different friends to engage in different types of academic involvement. College administrators can support these actions by maintaining or increasing support for campus clubs and social activities. Parents can support these actions by encouraging their children who are in tight-knit networks to interact outside their friendship network.

Another solution to the problem posed by lower-achieving dense networks is to target network content. Relationships that provided multiple forms of academic support—instrumental, emotional, or intellectual—were particularly helpful in promoting academic success, so this is where students should focus their effort. Group norms may not be easy to change, but they can change. A student could start by providing emotional support regarding academics to his or her friends along with instrumental or intellectual engagement. Hopefully, these actions would be reciprocated, and others in the network would act similarly. Because the network is dense, ideas typically spread quickly within the network. As this chapter shows, the content of the network can reinforce academic success or pull students away from academics. Interventions should reinforce the former and ward against the latter. College administrators can foster these actions by supporting group study spaces on campus and clubs related to a diverse range of academic and intellectual interests. Faculty can help students to get to know each other in classes through meaningful group work. Parents, along with administrators and faculty, can support these actions by not always encouraging students to stay away from friends during times of academic pressure; leaning on friends for multiple types of academic support can be particularly powerful within tight-knit networks.

As the next chapters show, less dense networks offered more opportunities for different friends to engage in different types of academic involvement. In the compartmentalized networks that are the focus of chapter 4, a student may have, for example, one group of friends providing academic emotional support and another providing instrumental help. In each type of network, the friendships that students form in college have important implications for their success.

# FOUR

# Compartmentalizers

Compartmentalizers are students with middle-density networks—where roughly half their friends know each other—containing distinct clusters of friends. Their networks usually have two or three clusters; a few have four clusters. These clusters might be composed of friends from a first-year dorm who proofread each other's papers, friends from an academic club who provide emotional support regarding academics, and friends from home who party together. Within each cluster, compartmentalizers' friends are tightly connected, but friends rarely know each other across clusters. Nearly all compartmentalizers discussed friends as helping them balance their academic and social lives. Friends helped in two ways: (1) through different clusters of friends being involved in students' academic and social lives in different ways, which I refer to as "segmented academic involvement," and (2) through friends who provide multiple forms of academic assistance, what I referred to earlier as "academic multiplex ties."[1] According-ing to whether each of these two features was present or absent, compart-mentalization exhibited four patterns, as shown in table 4.1.

Students' backgrounds are not monolithic across these four patterns in how friends helped. Most compartmentalizers are white and middle- or upper-class, and this is especially true for compartmentalizers whose net-works had *either* segmented academic involvement *or* academic multiplex ties. Students from these more privileged backgrounds seemed able to bal-ance their academic and social lives with only one of these features. Most said that making friends was easy because they perceived most people around them as "like me." Even when they discussed problems making friends when they first arrived at MU, they were able to solve this pretty easily, often by joining a particular organization, as shown in Mary's story (see below). In contrast, black and Latino compartmentalizers and those

Table 4.1 Selected characteristics of compartmentalizers

| Name | Graduated from MU | GPA | Race/Ethnicity | Gender | Class | First-Gen. | ACT | No. of Friends | Groups in Network | From Different Groups: Segmented Academic Involvement | From the Same Group: Academic Multiplex Ties |
|------|------|-----|------|------|------|------|-----|------|------|------|------|
| Segmented academic involvement: | | | | | | | | | | | |
| Lacking academic multiplex ties: | | | | | | | | | | | |
| Beth | Yes | 3.7 | White | Woman | Middle | No | 24 | 23 | 3 | Yes | No |
| Vanessa | Yes | 3.7 | White | Woman | Upper | No | 25 | 19 | 2 | Yes | No |
| Mary | Yes | 3.5 | White | Woman | Middle | No | 28 | 17 | 2 | Yes | No |
| Logan | Yes | 3.5 | White | Man | Middle | No | 23 | 35 | 3 | Yes | No |
| Greg | Yes | 3.4 | White | Man | Middle | No | 26 | 15 | 2 | Yes | No |
| Krystal | Yes | 3.4 | White | Woman | Middle | No | 29 | 16 | 2 | Yes | No |
| Heather | Yes | 3.3 | White | Woman | Middle | No | 29 | 31 | 3 | Yes | No |
| Maddie | Yes | 3.2 | White | Woman | Upper | No | 26 | 24 | 2 | Yes | No |
| Jenny | Yes | 2.9 | White | Woman | Middle | No | 26 | 15 | 3 | Yes | No |
| Betsy | Yes | 2.8 | White | Woman | Upper | Yes | 21 | 17 | 2 | Yes | No |
| Fran | Yes | 2.8 | White | Woman | Middle | Yes | 20 | 27 | 4 | Yes | No |
| With academic multiplex ties: | | | | | | | | | | | |
| Natalie | Yes | 3.8 | White | Woman | Lower | Yes | 24 | 10 | 2 | Yes | One |
| Daniel | Yes | 3.8 | White | Man | Lower | No | 31 | 16 | 2 | Yes | Multiple |
| Jason | Yes | 3.7 | Latino | Man | Lower | Yes | 28 | 29 | 4 | Yes | One |

| | | | | | | | | | | | |
|---|---|---|---|---|---|---|---|---|---|---|---|
| Michelle | Yes | 3.7 | White | Woman | Middle | No | 23 | 13 | 2 | Yes | Multiple |
| Ruth | Yes | 3.7 | White | Woman | Middle | No | 27 | 19 | 3 | Yes | Multiple |
| Juan | Yes | 3.6 | Latino | Man | Lower | Yes | 25 | 16 | 2 | Yes | One |
| Wendy | Yes | 3.3 | Black | Woman | Middle | No | 21 | 18 | 3 | Yes | Multiple |
| Liz | Yes | 3.3 | White | Woman | Lower | No | 27 | 13 | 2 | Yes | Multiple |
| Abby | Yes | 3.2 | White | Woman | Upper | No | 27 | 18 | 3 | Yes | Multiple |
| Whitney | Yes | 2.8 | White | Woman | Lower | Yes | 26 | 30 | 3 | Yes | Multiple |
| Jim | Yes | 2.8 | White | Man | Middle | Yes | 26 | 30 | 3 | Yes | Multiple |
| **Academic multiplex ties, lacking segmented academic involvement:** | | | | | | | | | | | |
| Noleen | Yes | 3.8 | White | Woman | Middle | Yes | 23 | 11 | 3 | No | Multiple |
| Kathryn | Yes | 3.7 | White | Woman | Upper | No | 28 | 40 | 2 | No | Multiple |
| Brandi | Yes | 3.5 | White | Woman | Middle | Yes | —* | 5 | 2 | No | One |
| Melanie | No—transferred | 3.4 | White | Woman | Upper | No | 27 | 19 | 2 | No | Multiple |
| Molly | Yes | 3.2 | White | Woman | Middle | No | 23 | 21 | 2 | No | Multiple |
| Gina | Yes | 2.8 | White | Woman | Upper | No | 26 | 30 | 3 | No | Multiple |
| Emily | No—transferred | 2.8 | White | Woman | Middle | Yes | —* | 18 | 2 | No | Multiple |
| **Lacking both academic multiplex ties and segmented academic involvement:** | | | | | | | | | | | |
| Kirk | No | 3.7 | White | Man | Upper | No | 30 | 12 | 2 | No | No |
| Margaret | Yes | 2.6 | Black | Woman | Middle | Yes | 25 | 14 | 2 | No | No |
| Julia | Yes | 2.5 | Latina | Woman | Middle | Yes | 19 | 24 | 3 | No | No |

*Note:* See table 0.2 notes for discussions of socioeconomic class, first-generation college students, and ACT scores.

* Brandi and Emily reported that they did not take either the SAT or the ACT. I was not permitted access to MU records to be able to confirm this.

from lower-class backgrounds balanced their academic and social lives with *both* segmented academic involvement *and* academic multiplex ties. When friends helped in both these ways, compartmentalized networks helped students cope with racial- and class-based social marginality, unlike the samplers discussed in the next chapter. This is another example of how networks matter for students' experiences and have the potential to decrease existing inequalities. In the following sections, I discuss how Mary was academically and socially successful with a compartmentalized network, while Julia was less successful and lacked academically focused ties.

## Mary's Story of Clustered Friendship Ties

I met Mary at her sorority house. As I walked up to the house, I was struck by its pristineness compared with the fraternity houses where I had recently been interviewing. The house was decorated inside and out with lights, garlands, and wreaths for Christmas. Mary and I walked through several large formal rooms before entering a smaller study filled with fuchsia overstuffed chairs and a couch, a large TV, and a few computers on a table. We both sat on the couch to begin the interview. At the time of our interview, Mary was in her second year at MU. Mary was typical of the compartmentalizers in many ways: she was white and middle class, she had a 3.5 GPA and a 28 on her ACT, and she had 17 friends, grouped into two clusters. She was also a member of a Greek organization, as were half of the compartmentalizers. Her sorority was historically white.

Like most participants, Mary placed herself close to the middle of the academic-social scale. She self-identified as slightly more social: a "6" out of "10." She explained, "If I had the option to study or go out to dinner with a friend, I'd make sure I could go out to eat and then have a little time to study." She also used an example from the week before our interview to explain her "balance." Her sorority formal was last Friday and she had a "big test" on Thursday. On Wednesday, she still did not have a dress for the formal, so she and her friend drove an hour from campus and spent the day shopping to find her dress. They got back late, so she stayed up late that night studying. She said that it "worked out, but I put the dress before studying." Her sheepish tone made it clear that she was not exactly proud of this decision. Nevertheless, she felt that she was thriving at MU.

Mary named 17 friends, but said that if she expanded her definition, she could mention about 100 more (20–30 from home and the rest from MU). As shown in figure 4.1, her network was compartmentalized into two clusters of friends: those from home (on the right-hand side) and those

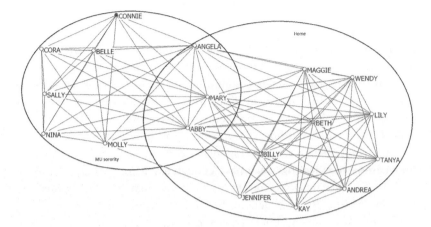

4.1. Mary's friendship network

from MU (on the left-hand side). Abby and Angela, who are friends from elementary school and junior high who also attend MU, bridge the two clusters. Her network included 35 percent friends from home who attended MU, 30 percent other friends from home, and 35 percent friends she met at MU. Her friends were very similar to her as far as race and gender: she had around 90 percent white and female friends.

Mary said that when she first arrived on campus, she had "a lot of problems just adjusting to everything." She felt that MU was really different from her "small high school," which had three to four hundred in her graduating class, because in high school "I knew everyone and I had a close group of friends. And as I walked to class, I knew everyone." When she entered MU with seven thousand other first-year students: "I walk to class and I feel like nothing, like really insignificant. It was really hard for me to adjust. . . . I didn't know how to get involved. I wasn't meeting the people I wanted to meet. And it was really frustrating because I didn't know how I was going to do it. Honestly, it was rushing [the sorority] that kinda got me through that and over that and happy." She commented that she did not feel comfortable on her dorm floor last year, noting that "we're all really different" and that most of them "came here already knowing so many people that they weren't out to try to have new friends." Instead, her house helped her find her place socially and academically. Mary explained that because of her sorority, "I feel part of the school. I feel very involved, part of something." Most of the friends she met at MU were members of her sorority. Mary said that she thinks that the route she took—joining a sorority—is not right for everyone, but it definitely helped her. She mentioned several times that everyone needs to find their place. She argued that students can do academics anywhere, but why would they choose MU if not for the social experience that it offers.

Mary did not have academic multiplex ties; instead, her different groups were academically involved in different ways. Mary described some academic emotional support from a group of close friends. She explained how friends "keep you motivated, . . . involved, and more like always thinking about school." She discussed how her friends do not "give me advice. I don't think they feel like they have enough say to say what they think I should do. They're supportive, at least. They're like, 'I'm failing business so I'll be right with you whenever I drop out.'" Mary seemed to be joking with the last comment, but it conveyed to me that her friends were not overly serious about their academics. Rather than instrumental and intellectual engagement, emotional support was the main academic help that her friends provided.

Other peers who were acquaintances provided academic competition and instrumental support. Mary studied with academic acquaintances, they shared notes, and they quizzed each other before exams, but she did not do these things with her friends. She described these academic acquaintances as "more people that I've just met or lab partners who you're stuck with and have to work with." They also inspired competition that encouraged Mary to do better: "you can study with them and just keep up with [what's] going on [in class] and they motivate you. When they ask you what your score is, you don't want to say it's bad or whatever." While Mary's academic acquaintances were a source of academic competition as well as instrumental help, her friends were not. Mary felt that her friends did not increase her knowledge: "Classes, you learn facts, you learn chemistry. I don't learn chemistry from my friends; we don't really talk about that much. Class is more something you put up with, more than something you enjoy." Mary achieved the balance between academic and social life discussed in chapter 2 by having different groups involved in different aspects of her life. Generally, she saw friends as important for social life. However, one cluster of her friends provided some emotional support regarding academics. Acquaintances, rather than friends, provided instrumental support. This network configuration allowed Mary to be socially successful, feeling like she had "found my place" at MU, and also academically successful, graduating with a 3.5 GPA. Mary's experience of having different clusters of friends who are socially and academically involved in different ways, without academic multiplex ties, characterizes about one-third of compartmentalizers, as shown in table 4.1.

## Julia's Story of Clustered Friendship Ties

I met Julia, a third-year, middle-class, Latina student, at the main library for our interview. As we rode the elevator up to the room where we would do the interview, I noticed her gray hooded sweatshirt with "HARVARD" printed in maroon on the front. From that, I expected her to be more academically than socially oriented, but she described the same balance as most students I interviewed (as discussed in chapter 2). In fact, Julia earnestly told me that her personal motto is "study hard, party hard."

Throughout her interview, it was evident that she had partied hard during her first three years at MU, but I struggled to see that she had also studied hard. Her grades reflected my perceptions: she graduated, but with a GPA of 2.5, in the lowest 12 percent of my sample. Julia is a compartmentalizer who found high social success but relatively low academic success at MU.

Her friendship network contained the multiple clusters characteristic of compartmentalizers. When I asked her to describe her friendships, she replied: "Definitely I would say I have different groups of friends. . . . I pretty much would divide it into my sorority sisters and everybody else. Honestly, my sorority sisters do come first, I will say, they do and I'm closest to them." Julia joined a Latina sorority, which is much smaller than the historically white sororities and fraternities, such as Mary's. Julia's sorority had 11 members, and she included five of these—Jennifer, Claudia, Deirdre, Anica, and Solana—on her friend list. They are central in the cluster on the left-hand side of Julia's network, shown in figure 4.2. Also within this cluster are several Latino men—Daniel, Oscar, and Tomas—who joined a "brother" Latino fraternity, affiliated with her sorority, at MU. On the upper-right side is a smaller cluster composed of friends Julia met the summer before college through Team Up[2]—Kiku, Sydney, India, Suki, Erica, and Elizabeth. Erica and Elizabeth also worked with Julia at an on-campus food court. Julia also maintained several friendships from her first-year dorm (bottom of fig. 4.2). Two MU friends—Crystal and Melissa—bridge two clusters but are not involved in the organizations central to these clusters. Her network also includes two friends from home—Angela and Yesenia—who did not know anyone else in her network. As this shows, her network is not as neatly divided into groups as Mary's; however, unlike

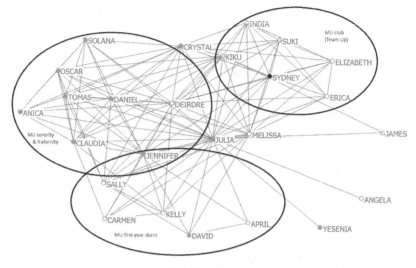

4.2. Julia's friendship network

the networks formed by tight-knitters, it does not consist of one cohesive group, nor is it a mostly disconnected collection of friends, as exhibited by samplers' friendships. Julia's network is compartmentalized into three clusters.

Julia struggled academically and her network lacked an academic cluster and academic multiplex ties, as the bottom row of table 4.1 shows. Julia gave and received some academic emotional support but not instrumental help or intellectual engagement. She also did not discuss academically oriented acquaintances like those whom Mary mentioned. Julia appeared largely on her own in terms of academics.

Unlike most of the tight-knitters discussed in the previous chapter, Julia described little race-based social marginality on campus. However, she did comment that she felt more "connected" to friends who shared her ethnic background, given that they were a minority at MU. Because they shared a common experience of "being a Hispanic girl" growing up, "there is a certain connection between us that no one else can share." Julia characterized her Latino/a friends as those "I can really be comfortable" with and "I can relate to." The cluster of her Latino/a friends, labeled as "MU sorority and fraternity" on her network in figure 4.2, provided her with social support facilitating the transition to MU.

Although Julia's friends did not provide instrumental help or intellectual engagement, they provided implicit emotional support for academics by understanding what it was like to be an MU student. Julia explained, "[I talk to] sorority sisters, friends, and roommates [about] things that happen in class, professors I hate, things I hate, things that people did stupid in class, stupid comments made. Not academics, like gradewise, like, 'Oh my gosh, I'm flunking this class.' Not that. But just day-to-day life of going through classes—yeah, I would say I share that." Julia also indicated that she does not take classes with her friends, saying, "I don't think that you need to have your friend in your class; you know, I'm a big girl, I can go to my own class." Though Julia emphasized how she can talk to her friends about anything, she was equally emphatic in emphasizing how she does not discuss academic problems or grades with them. In terms of academics, Julia keeps it to herself:

JM: Do you ever study together?

JULIA: No, no, I really wouldn't.

JM: Not even different subjects at the same time?

JULIA: No. Seriously, I study by myself. It's pretty much on our own time. . . . [If] there's activities going on or certain things and I can't do it, they're very understanding of that. . . . I saw it more with my friends Sally and Melissa telling me to stay in and study. I could honestly think, definitely, those two say, "No, that's not good; you better stay in and study." If I'm like, "I have a test. Should I go out?" It's like [they'd say], "No, I think you should stay in and study." I'm like, "Oh, okay."

Typical of many of the samplers described in chapter 5, Julia depicted academics as an individual endeavor. In this way, Julia differed from most compartmentalizers, whose friends were regularly involved academically either as academic multiplex ties or as clusters who provided different types of help, as shown in table 4.1.

Julia also struggled to balance so many clusters of friends. In addition to her part-time job, she regularly spent time with all three clusters in her network, leaving little time for academics. Without academic multiplex ties or a cluster of friends to share her academic interests or focus, Julia struggled academically. She ended up in one of the "easy majors" created for the party pathway at large public universities, described by Armstrong and Hamilton (2013), which was a mismatch with her expectations to support not only herself but her family, including younger siblings, after college. Julia graduated, but with a low GPA that would hold her back from future opportunities, such as graduate school, that are based on grades.

## Who Are Compartmentalizers?

Most compartmentalizers were white women (85% are white and 79% are women) and middle class (55%). They were from more privileged class backgrounds than tight-knitters, with fewer lower-class (18% vs. 41%) and first-generation college students (36% vs. 73%). They also stand out from the tight-knitters and samplers in terms of Greek affiliation: about half were in sororities or fraternities, with most of these in historically white organizations (10 of the 33 compartmentalizers). Of the five students of color who were compartmentalizers, all but one (Margaret) were in Latino or multicultural sororities or fraternities, all but one were employed (also Margaret), and all but one were first-generation college students (Wendy). Nearly 40 percent of compartmentalizers were in romantic relationships (similar to tight-knitters), nearly half lived on campus (also similar to tight-knitters), and nearly 40 percent were employed (similar to samplers), working an average of 19 hours per week (similar to tight-knitters). The compartmentalizers were also similar to samplers in terms of their ACT scores (averaging 26 and 25, respectively) and grades (averaging 3.3 in both groups). As these numbers show, compartmentalizers were similar to at least one of the other network types in most respects; however, they were more likely to be white women, from privileged class backgrounds, and affiliated with a sorority or a fraternity.

## The Structure of Clustered Networks

Compartmentalizers' discussions of belonging, comfort, and support typically mapped onto the clusters in their networks. Most of the compartmentalizers discussed having at least two places where they felt they belonged, with at least one of those places located on campus. Mary described the sense of belonging on campus as occurring within her historically white sorority, and Julia, within her Latina sorority. Other compartmentalizers found it through other clubs, their dorms, a sport, their majors, or occasionally friendships not connected with an institutionalized group. For example, Abby described her network as consisting of three clusters: "I have my group from freshman year, I have my karate group, [and] I have my sorority." Compartmentalizers often separated friends from home and those at MU into distinct clusters, such as in Mary's network in figure 4.1. Typically, among compartmentalizers' friends, "a few of them have met each other," as Jenny explained, so these groups are not completely separate. My results support other network research that has found that friendships are often formed through organizations (McPherson, Popielarz, and Drob-nic 1992; McPherson and Smith-Lovin 1987; Small 2009b) because fo-cused, joint activities—"foci," to use a sociological term—put people into contact with each other (Feld 1981). More so than among the tight-knitters or samplers, foci structured compartmentalizers' networks.

The structure of this network type differs from those of samplers and tight-knitters not only in terms of the number of friendship clusters but also in terms of two mathematical properties introduced in chapter 1: den-sity and betweenness centrality. Density is the proportion of ties present out of possible ties. Compartmentalizers have middle-density networks, meaning that approximately half of their friends know each other. To be more precise, compartmentalizers have networks where one-third to two-thirds of their friends know each other, which results in density scores of 0.34–0.64 (from a possible range of 0–1). Betweenness centrality is a mea-sure of how central a person is in a network in terms of how many others in the network are connected only through that person. Compartmental-izers were between tight-knitters and samplers in normalized betweenness centrality scores,[3] as well as in density scores. These scores confirm that most friends in tight-knit networks are connected to each other, samplers' friends are often connected only through the interviewed students, and compartmentalizers played a moderately central role by connecting friends from different clusters but not friends within a cluster.

## Segmented Academic Involvement

Most compartmentalizers had clusters of friends who provided different types of academic support. Such segmented academic involvement charac-terizes 23 of the 33 compartmentalizers—those in the top two sections of table 4.1. With segmented academic involvement, students have separate groups of friends who provide instrumental, intellectual, and emotional support for academics. Sometimes my respondents' friends provided one type of academic support and acquaintances provided others, as happened for Mary. These students do different things with different groups and get different types of support from them, similar to the mothers Small (2009b) studied. For example, Whitney's network, shown in figure 4.3, was divided into her work friends (she worked as a resident assistant in the dorms), her friends from home, and the friends of her ex-boyfriend (who lived in a residential honor's college with most of his friends). Whitney exchanged academic support and discussed intellectual issues with her work friends, and she discussed intellectual issues with her ex-boyfriend's friends, while

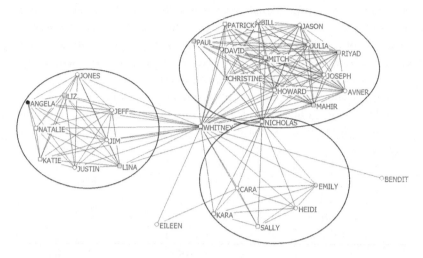

4.3. Whitney's friendship network

her friends from home were mostly uninvolved academically. Jenny also described three groups who played different roles in her academic life: sorority sisters provided emotional support; people in her classes provided instrumental help; and friends from home were mostly uninvolved academically, providing social support only. Other compartmentalizers had a cluster of friends, rather than acquaintances, who provided instrumental help. For example, Heather told me that she would turn to a group of friends before her professor with questions about class, and they prepared her course schedule for her because Heather had a "crappy" adviser. Heather's actions would appall many of the samplers discussed in the next chapter, who felt that friends could hurt them academically with "bad advice." In sum, segmented academic involvement involves of multiple groups that each provide different types of support or involvement.

Compartmentalized networks can enable students to navigate the obligations of their multiple friendship groups, even when they conflict with each other or with their own beliefs. For example, Jenny's friendship clusters were academically involved in different ways, as discussed above. And she was able to draw on these benefits to maintain her social ties with her sorority sisters by being social with them on her own terms. Jenny explained, "Everybody comes to our apartment before the parties. So I'll be kickin' it with them before the party, and then I'll be like, 'Okay, you all have fun [out at the party].' And I'll stay home and just study." Jenny would again hang out with them when they returned to her apartment after the party. This arrangement allowed her to have social time with this cluster of friends and to minimize how they distracted her from schoolwork. Compartmentalization provides the flexibility to avoid unwanted group obligations, which contradicts what Balázs Vedres and David Stark (2010) find for individuals who occupy more than one group, which they refer to as a "structural fold." Vedres and Stark (2010, 1174) determined that "structural folding is disruptive"—that is, groups break up more often when their members belong to multiple groups. In contrast, I do not find compartmentalizers' membership in multiple groups to be disruptive to the groups or to the individuals. I find that being in a structural-fold position by belonging to multiple groups allows compartmentalizers the flexibility to party when they want to party and study when they want to study.

### The Desire for Intellectual Discussions

Some compartmentalizers with segmented academic involvement discussed problems associated with social clusters that began to dominate their networks. For example, Greg responded to my question about whether he talked about interesting ideas from readings or from classes with his friends by saying, "No! [*laughs*] I wish I did. Honestly, I wish people challenged me intellectually. It bothers me [*laughs*]." Greg contrasted this with his friends from home, with whom he did have these intellectual conversations: "One thing I've been really disappointed about at MU is that people here don't tend to stay in tune with what's going on in the world today, and they don't tend to challenge me intellectually. . . . That's definitely one of my top three disappointments at MU, because some of my friends from back home are so smart and, like, we have such intelligent conversations. . . . I don't feel challenged intellectually here; it bothers me." Students' desires for more intellectual discussions with friends, while rare, were expressed more frequently among compartmentalizers than among samplers or tight-knitters. Having intellectual discussions with a best friend or a cluster of friends in the past seemed to highlight for compartmentalizers how this type of academic support was missing from their current clusters of friends. They felt their clusters were overly focused on social life. The experiences of other MU students who had intellectual conversations with friends, however, highlights that such conversations were not absent at MU as some compartmentalizers, such as Greg, believed.

### Academic Competition and Greek Organizations

As mentioned in chapter 2, competition is the least common of the strategies of integration students used to involve friends in academics. It is, however, noticeably more common among compartmentalizers than among those with other network types, particularly among compartmentalizers with segmented academic involvement who are in historically white sororities and fraternities.

Research and popular culture both characterize sororities and fraternities as drawing students away from academics,[4] and students certainly brought up how features of their environments contributed to friends as a distraction. Existing alongside this distraction, however, was the possibility of positive competition. For example, Caitlin described her sorority in terms of their academic success on campus: "We're known as being nerds on campus. . . . [W]e had the highest GPA on campus. All my friends are like, 'Oh my gosh, what a bad stereotype,' and 'That's not fun!' But I really did join the house partially because of academics, just because I thought it would challenge me. You have to hold a certain GPA [to be a member]. . . . And the fact that it does have a higher GPA, that does challenge me more." Vanessa, a member of another sorority, also discussed the competition she felt among members: "In this house, there's a lot of smart girls, so I feel like the more I'm with them and study with them, the more competitive I am. If they're doing well, I'm going to do well." Grades were a frequent comparison point, not only among sorority women. Daniel discussed grades with fraternity brothers who were his friends as a sort of friendly competition: "We definitely talk about grades. And we'll check the computers together and make fun of each other if someone does worse. We definitely are competitive in the grades, actually. But I guess that's okay." Competition fostered by comparing grades may be one way that sororities and fraternities promote academic achievement.

Although I am not able to show directly whether the competition that compartmentalizers experienced had a positive impact, it is notable that they frequently mentioned it. While academic competition was not an everyday occurrence among most Greek-affiliated students, it does provide some balance to memoirs and journalistic accounts that claim that social status and bonding are more important than attending class among sorority and fraternity members (Lohse 2014; Robbins 2004). In fact, over half the compartmentalizers in historically white sororities and fraternities specifically mentioned competition among their friends in the house as encouraging their academic success. All these students had networks with segmented academic involvement.

## Academic Multiplex Ties

The other important feature of compartmentalized networks was whether they contained academic multiplex ties. Table 4.1 shows that about one-third of compartmentalizers (12 of 33) had segmented academic involvement and academic multiplex ties. This path was the most common among black, Latino, and lower-class students. A smaller group of compartmentalizers (seven of 33) who were all white women lacked segmented academic involvement but engaged in a particular combination of emotional and instrumental support in academic multiplex relationships. These women referred to friend relationships as "moms." I explain both of these patterns below.

### Race- and Class-Based Social Marginality

While black and Latino tight-knitters typically found social support to deal with race-based social marginality in their full network, black and Latino compartmentalizers typically found this support within a cluster of friends.[5] For example, Wendy, a black compartmentalizer, responded to my question about what has been most helpful for her socially at MU by saying, "Having these types of groups that I can connect with—these support systems." When I asked her to elaborate, she responded. "Race plays a lot in that, . . . feel[ing] like, Why am I even here at this university? There's nobody like me here." She discussed how specific groups of friends have helped her with these feelings of social marginality. Wendy discussed not only social support but academic emotional support related to being one of few black students on campus and in particular classrooms, such as a chemistry class; for example:

> Minority students anywhere at any university, you already feel marginalized by being a minority in college, which is a pressure that's already on your shoulders from day one. You add that to whatever your major may be, depending on the level of difficulty. Being a biology major, for instance, which is not likely to see any minorities in that field, it's hard. [*laughs*] It's really hard on a day-to-day basis, and to have people, other minorities, lift you up into, like, "We can do it," like, "We can become doctors. We can be surgeons. We can complete and finish this exam," is encouraging. That's encouraging.

Wendy had a diverse friendship group and she received social support and academic emotional support from multiple clusters of friends. Yet two clusters of friends, both composed of students of color, helped her deal with race-based marginality on campus. This was typical of the students of color who were compartmentalizers. Even Julia, the Latina discussed at the beginning of this chapter who experienced less race-based social marginality than most students of color, relied on a cluster of Latino friends for social support.

Compartmentalizers from lower-class backgrounds discussed friends as helping them deal with class-based marginality. For example, Whitney believed that most MU students spent "outrageous" amounts of money. She said that she felt isolated in her first-year dorm until she found friends who could relate to her financial obligations. She described how, the night before our interview, she was up late talking with a group of friends about how "my dad lost his job and then we had no money and I had to sell my car so that I could stay in school," a situation that she felt most MU students could not relate to. Natalie was from a small working-class city near MU, the first in her family to attend college, and one of two from her circle of hometown friends who attended college. Echoing the findings of other research on working-class students (Kaufman 2003), Natalie discussed how attending college could be a barrier with her friends from home. Through the Team Up program, which was for students from underrepresented groups, Natalie formed a group of friends with whom she felt she could connect, "like you're on the same page." Natalie and Whitney relied on their friends for both social and academic support.

It is notable that among compartmentalizers nearly all students of color and lower-class students crafted the most complex pattern—that is, networks with both segmented academic involvement and academic multiplex ties. Even with the challenges of managing these multiple clusters (described earlier), students expressed how college was easier because of their friends' support. Both the multiple types of support from different clusters of friends and the more in-depth involvement from at least one cluster played important roles in students' descriptions.

### Friend "Moms"

As shown in table 4.1, all the compartmentalizers with academic multiplex ties who did not have segmented academic involvement were white women. Their academic multiplex ties were unique in that they combined academic emotional and instrumental support. Several women students described these friend relationships as like "moms," as Emily explained:

> I'll walk in my room and my friend will be like, "Oh, okay so I just failed my math quiz," and I'll be like, "Oh my gosh! Me too!" And then like sometimes we'll say good luck to each other if, like, we're going to a test, and we'll ask each other, you know, "How'd you do on that test?" . . . We look out for each other like, "Didn't you have to do that homework assignment or something?" So, I mean, we talk about academics but it's more of like in a mom sort of way, like, "Make sure you do your homework" kind of thing.

Like a mom who provides instrumental support in terms of reminders and emotional support in terms of good wishes and checking to see how it went, Emily's friends provide both instrumental and emotional support for each other. Later in the interview, she described more things that they did for each other as "moms":

> We always tell each other to go to class. We're always just like, "It's an hour. Just go. It's not that hard. When you get back you can take a nap if you're tired." . . . We always remind each other like, "You just wasted three hundred dollars by not going to that class," or stuff like that, like, "You paid for that class. Go." So, yeah. We encourage each other to go to class all the time. We even have to wake each other up sometimes. Like, I have to wake up Gina like every morning. I just go knock on her door superhard. She's like, "What?" I'm like, "Go to class!" She's like, "Okay." I'm like her mom every morning.

Emily and her friends provided instrumental reminders about attending class to each other and also checked in with each other, providing emotional support. This occurred within a cluster of friends rather than in a compartmentalizer's full network. These discussions show a collective understanding of motherhood as aligned with the middle-class notion of concerted cultivation, where mothers must develop their children and keep them on track (Lareau 2003).

Women commonly combine instrumental and expressive support in the "mom" friend role discussed by Emily. Not surprisingly, men never used the language of being each other's "moms"—or "dads." As explained elsewhere in the book, men engaged in some of the types of instrumental and emotional support common in the mom role. Men, however, engaged in fewer reminders, including reminding each other to attend class and complete assignments. The types of academic involvement in the mom role require more emotional investment and result in less academic benefit for the person providing it, thus perpetuating gender inequalities.

## Lack of Segmented Academic Involvement and Multiplex Ties

As shown in the bottom rows of table 4.1, only three students lacked both segmented academic involvement and academic multiplex ties. Margaret and Julia, the compartmentalizers with the two lowest GPAs, who both clearly struggled with academics, did not have any academic multiplex ties, and they also did not have an academically focused cluster or receive different types of academic help from different groups of friends. The only other compartmentalizer without these ties was Kirk. Kirk was an exception in other ways as well. He did not receive much of any type of support from friends. He saw academics as mostly on himself, as most samplers do. He talked about it little with his friends; in fact, he spent little time with friends from what I could tell. As a stereotypical "grind" (Horowitz 1987; Moffatt 1989), Kirk saw himself as having a "bad balance," as discussed in chapter 2, by being overly focused on academics. Kirk saw this as a necessity for acceptance into medical school.

All three described themselves as academically self-sufficient and not relying on friends for help with academic matters. Margaret was one striking example. Although early in our interview, Margaret commented that "it really does help to have people around you that have the same mind-set as you do," she disclosed that she seldom talked to anyone about academics:

MARGARET: I really don't talk about [academics], unless it's something just so major, so tragic that happens, then I'll talk about it. But if it's just little every-day, petty stuff, I just keep that to myself. I know everybody else has problems too, so why do I feel the need to express all my problems when I know other people have problems too. . . . I'm pretty self-sufficient, keep to myself as far as problems and stuff like that.

JM: So, not even just talking about problems but just academics in general, do you—?

MARGARET: Like I said, unless it's something major, just I really don't feel the need to talk about it.

JM: So it's not a topic of everyday conversation?

MARGARET: No. No.

Later in the interview, she elaborated:

JM: Do your friends try to get you to go to class when you don't wanna go? Or do you try to get them to go if they don't wanna go?

MARGARET: No. We look at it as we are grown women. If you make the decision not to go, that's on you. So it's not like I'm gonna sit here and babysit you. . . . We're grown women. I don't need you telling me what to do. If I ask you, you can give me advice, you can kinda help me. But don't tell me what to do because I'm just gonna rebel, you know? You're not my mom!

Like Julia and Kirk, Margaret kept academics to herself. She viewed academics as a personal concern, not something to involve her friends in. I also provide this example because her ending comment "You're not my mom!" is in stark contrast to the more common combining of instrumental and expressive support in the "mom" friend role used by many white women compartmentalizers who had academic multiplex ties but lacked segmented academic involvement, as discussed in the previous section.

## Pressures from Compartmentalized Networks

In many ways, segmented networks seem to be the easiest network type for balancing academic and social life. Most compartmentalizers are socially and academically successful. Even the two compartmentalizers with the lowest GPAs—Margaret and Julia—found a place to belong on campus and graduated. The main problem with segmented networks, however, is the cost of managing multiple friendship groups.

In order to maintain their membership in the friendship group, students needed to spend time with the group. Less investment, however, was required for friendship groups from home than for those at MU. Students were expected to maintain occasional contact with friends from home via phone, e-mail, or text, but not the weekly, or even daily, contact required of friends who lived near them. This meant that students with multiple clusters of MU friends were the ones who felt the most strain. Network researchers discuss how dense networks and multiplex ties can be draining for people (C. Fischer 1982; Hirsch 1980; Kuwabara, Luo, and Sheldon 2010; Verbrugge 1979); I similarly find that segmented networks can pose a strain when they place competing expectations on people. Jim provides one example:

If I have an exam the next day and, you know, Molly calls me and is like, "Hey, you know, let's study together." Knowing that we're really not gonna get a lot of studying done, but I'll still say, okay, you know, and go over to her room or she'll come over to my room and we'll study a little bit, but not sufficiently for that exam, where even after I leave, I'll have two or three more hours of studying to get done. I just kind of wasted that time hanging out with her. But that kind of goes back to friendships being really important to me. It's kind of a thing, not [being] paranoid at all, but just the fact that I'm worried that if I don't hang out with my friends enough, that they're gonna stray away from me. And I've seen that with my friends from home that didn't come to school here. We lost contact because we don't hang out nearly as often. And I'm worried that some of my good friends now who I can see myself being friends with for life, that will happen as well if I don't hang out with them as much.

As Jim puts it, his friendships are important to him, so he spends time with friends even when he knows he has academic work because he worries about losing these friendships. This seems to be a particular concern for compartmentalizers. Because compartmentalizers have to balance multiple friendship groups, they feel more pressed for time to spend with each group.

Students also described strains tied to their identity when it emphasized how they differed from most of their friends in some way. For example, Melanie discussed how being from out of state made it difficult to form the type of network she saw among her MU friends:

I have a lot of different groups of friends. Back home, from high school, I had *a* group. [Then,] college, it's so spread out that you meet people from your [dorm] floor, and then you meet people from your classes freshman year, and then I joined a sorority. I came from out of state so I didn't know people and so it's been a little frustrating like being at a state school . . . just because people are coming from high schools around here that like they know kids and so they've already got that base. And I feel like my friends are just random people that I've really connected with.

Melanie was leaving MU after the semester that I interviewed her, but not because of academic troubles. She was academically driven and focused (with a 3.4 GPA), majoring in business. However, she did not feel that she fit in socially, particularly in terms of being from out of state and ending up with a roommate from a nearby city who came to college with a group of high school friends. These social problems, along with family problems—her parents divorcing and her mom diagnosed with cancer—made Melanie unhappy and led to her decision to transfer. Without a group of friends, even a cluster, that they felt similar to, a few compartmentalizers felt strains on their identities.

## Conclusion

Compartmentalizers' friends' academic involvement follows four patterns, as shown in table 4.1. The first pattern is segmented academic involvement without academic multiplex ties. This pattern is more common for students with a distinctly social cluster and those with membership in historically white sororities and fraternities. The second pattern is for compartmentalizers to have segmented academic involvement along with academic multiplex ties. All the compartmentalizers from lower-class backgrounds and nearly all the students of color fit into this second pattern. This is the most complex pattern, and it supports success for compartmentalizers from more disadvantaged backgrounds. Third, some compartmentalizers had individual friends who were academic multiplex ties but only one cluster involved in any sort of academic help—that is, they lacked segmented academic involvement. This pattern occurred among white women who acted as friend "moms" by providing each other with academic emotional and instrumental support. Finally, three compartmentalizers lacked both academic multiplex ties and segmented academic involvement. The two compartmentalizers with the lowest GPAs were missing both of these types of academic involvement. Although they graduated from MU, these students struggled academically. Without the help of friends, students had to be extremely internally motivated, as was the case for Kirk.

In order to maximize their academic and social success, students in compartmentalized networks should be mindful of the number of clusters in their network. As the number of clusters increased beyond two, students felt more time pressure. They found it harder to maintain the social ties to each of their groups and to keep up with their schoolwork. If students are balancing multiple groups, they might consciously prioritize which groups (and activities) should get the bulk of their time, to ensure that important friendships and academics do not suffer. They also might introduce specific friends to each other across clusters, because cultivating some ties across clusters might result in fewer clusters and make it easier to balance their relationships.

Parents, administrators, and faculty members should recognize that students spend much time with their friends, and they should not devalue this social time. They also should recognize that compartmentalizers can do well academically with one cluster of friends who are not academically focused. Unlike samplers, their friends provide them with general social support that promotes social success. And, unlike tight-knitters, having friends who are academically unsuccessful or unfocused is not associated with low grades as long as they have segmented academic involvement or academic multiplex ties. For these reasons, compartmentalized networks are often the safest. Administrators can also support clusters of friends by building study spaces that are enticing and plentiful. Students enjoy spending time with their friends, and by offering appealing places where students can engage in academics with a group of friends, administrators encourage students to cultivate academically focused friendships.

Overall, compartmentalized networks make it easier to balance academic and social life for most students than do the other network types. Because their networks are segmented, compartmentalizers are able to get their academic and social needs met, typically by separate clusters. Compartmentalized networks are not without problems, however. Multiple clusters can be difficult to juggle. Friendships demand time and energy, and compartmentalizers spread these across multiple clusters. Although having separate academic and social clusters can help compartmentalizers get these multiple needs met, it also takes effort to maintain these clusters. Speaking about individual friendships rather than networks, Georg Simmel (1906, 458) refers to friendships based on one dimension as "differentiated" and explains that differentiated friendships "demand that the friends reciprocally refrain from obtruding themselves into the range of interests and feelings not included" in their relationship. Extending this to the clusters I found in compartmentalizers' networks, which are also based on distinct interests, Simmel's writings suggest that one challenge of this type of friendship is in maintaining each of these clusters. Fulfilling different needs for different groups not only takes time but also can take a toll on individuals' sense of self, particularly when they feel that their academic and social goals do not match those of any of their clusters. Because their networks contained clusters, however, most compartmentalizers were better able to find a place—sometimes multiple places—at MU, an experience lacking for most samplers, who are the focus of the next chapter.

# FIVE

# Samplers

Few of samplers' friends know each other.[1] The relationships—or, more precisely, lack of relationships—among their friends distinguish samplers from compartmentalizers and tight-knitters. Samplers have approximately the same number of friends as the compartmentalizers, but most of samplers' friends remain unconnected from each other. Samplers tend to make one friend at a time at various times and places, like clubs or organizations, and maintain that individual friendship. For compartmentalizers and tight-knitters, sometimes a relationship would begin that way but then they introduced their friends to each other, resulting in a cluster. There are fewer clusters among samplers' friendship networks. As I will show in this chapter, these differences in friendship structure have important implications for students' social and academic experiences.

Samplers often appeared successful academically and socially, but paradoxically they often experienced academic and social isolation. Of the 12 samplers I met at MU, all but one graduated and all but two had GPAs of at least 3.2, which is a B average. Samplers were involved in college by traditional measures: they belonged to clubs[2] and named many friends. Their friendships, however, did not alleviate their isolation. Many samplers characterized their friendships as "disappointing" or described a "distance" between them. Samplers typically felt alone and as if they did not belong, often but not always because of racial isolation. Nearly every sampler experienced high levels of social marginality, despite their involvements.

Samplers tended to be academically independent, if not isolated, rarely seeking help for their academic work from friends. In turn, samplers' friends provided little instrumental help, limited and implicit emotional support, and limited intellectual engagement. Although samplers were successful, they expressed a high degree of academic independence, stating, for example, that "academics are all on me." Because they did not rely on their friends for much academic help, they had few academic multiplex ties. Unlike tight-knitters and compartmentalizers, for whom there is a division between those with higher and lower levels of academic success, samplers were much more uniform. Consequently, I highlight only one student (Martin) at the beginning of this chapter in order to describe the common pattern among samplers of high levels of academic success yet academic and social isolation.

## Martin's Story of Loose Friendship Ties

I interviewed Martin at his on-campus job at MU's media center, where he checked out equipment to students as we talked over the course of two days. He was a senior, involved in several academic clubs, including the student paper and television station. Martin rated himself as in the middle of the academic-social scale, balancing academic and social life. He also was a black man from a lower-class background and the first in his family to attend college.

Martin is a typical sampler. He did well academically, later graduating with a 3.2 GPA, and was involved on campus, but he felt that he did not quite belong anywhere. Martin listed 16 friends, which are shown in figure 5.1; however, his friends did not create a sense of belonging for him at school. Although most of his friends knew at least two other friends, his

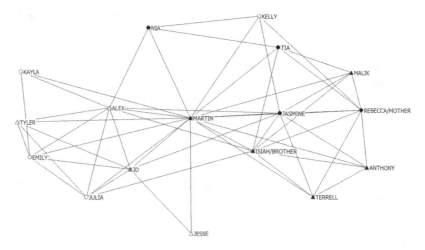

5.1. Martin's friendship network

network was not densely connected or clearly divided into communities. He told me that he made friends easily: "I have so many different interests. I mean I'm not just interested in one or two things. . . . I do many random different things and that leads to me meeting many random different people." He went on to say, "I'm not antisocial. I'm not a social butterfly either. I can walk into a room where I don't know anybody and walk out knowing five people, but that's still no guarantee that any of them will become any more than associates in a couple days. . . . I feel like the Batman almost. I can swoop in, make the best of the situation, and swoop right back out and be the same as when I went in." As "Batman," Martin was able to appear as if he fit in as he went about his day on campus, but he did does not feel "at home" anywhere. Like other samplers, he picked up a friend or two in many different organizations and activities throughout campus. In this way, he had a collection of friends but not a supportive community.

Although he was academically successful, his friends generally were disconnected from academics. For example, in response to my question about whom he talked to about academics, Martin said: "Nobody really. Well, I talk to Herb but that's [it]. . . . I like it when I can sit around with people and talk about Middle Eastern politics or other obscure subjects like Iceland [or] the Andy Warhol invasion. . . . I like talking to people who enjoy knowing stuff—people who don't automatically write things off as stupid or silly or unnecessary." Herb, the only person with whom he said that he discussed academics, was not someone he considered a friend; thus, Herb does not appear in his network (see fig. 5.1). Martin enjoyed having intellectual discussions but had them more often with acquaintances rather than with friends: "One of my favorite things to do is to do what I am doing right now [in the interview]. Like I said, I like knowing things, and thus, I like talking to people who like knowing things because that means they will gladly tell me what they know. They will argue with me. They will fight about stuff, and the intellectual discourse is very stimulating. You learn stuff when you do that and I like learning stuff." One might have expected his job, which was on campus and connected to his major and hobbies, to provide opportunities to connect him with like-minded peers, but he did not consider these students his friends. In contrast to compartmentalizers and higher-achieving tight-knitters, who engaged in many academic activities with their friends, Martin clearly stated that he was on his own academically; it was an individual endeavor:

JM: Is that the only way you see your social life affecting your academic life?
MARTIN: Pretty much. I mean, because my academic life is my own decision and

my social life is a combination of my decision plus the decisions of other
people that eventually affect me.

He valued his academic independence because it made any success his success alone, but this mind-set left him academically disconnected.

Despite his Batman-like ability to make friends anywhere, Martin generally felt marginalized, if not isolated, at school. His friends did not seem to
help ease this sense of isolation, likely because his relationships with them
were one-on-one. He described how he felt disconnected from other black
students because of his interests and major: "It's really hard for me to find
people that are doing the same thing that I'm doing, especially black people. There aren't any black people doing the same things I'm doing. I don't
know any other black people who are telecommunication majors." He also
felt disconnected from his family, neighbors, and black peers from home:

> Most the people I grew up with have no clue what I do, or if they do have
> a clue, they think, "Oh that's great! You're gonna be big someday. You're
> gonna be famous! You're gonna be on TV." Most of them, they are business
> majors, English majors, physical recreation majors. The more I grow up, the
> more I find out that I didn't really have a lot in common with people I grew
> up with anyways except the fact that we were usually all the same place, at
> church or at school or whatever. . . . Sometimes that's the only thing you
> have in common with them is that they're black.

As this quotation shows, Martin felt race-based isolation and academic isolation. He did not find it hard to meet other students who shared his racial
identity but did find it challenging to find those who shared his interests,
despite his involvement in several clubs and an on-campus job related to
these interests. The race-based marginality he experienced came through
even more strongly in a story he told me about running into a friend between classes the previous week: "[My friend] is funny. He went off on a
tangent. He says, 'You know, I gotta come to my white school, do my white
homework with my white professors in my white class. Go home and do
the white homework and bring it back to the white school the next day.'"
Martin connected with his friend's sentiments: "Yeah and not even being
racist at all, but sometimes it's just the sense of belonging. The familiar
isn't there or the—everybody needs a dose of familiarity every now and
then. I mean, when you don't get it, you kinda go nuts." This was the only
friend Martin connected with in this way. Martin's sense of marginality and
lack of belonging also came up in some of his responses to the last ques-

tions I asked during the interview, when he described himself as the biggest obstacle to and yet the most helpful for his social life. Given the marginality he felt, it may be surprising that Martin graduated from MU with a 3.2 GPA and was attending law school when I spoke with him five years later (more on this in chapter 6). However, this pattern of academic success and social marginality was common among the samplers.

## Who Are Samplers?

Samplers tended to do well academically but felt socially marginalized or at least that their friends and peers provided them with little social support. As I mentioned earlier and expand on in the next chapter, all but one of them graduated, usually with at least a B average. In other words, they ended up being successful, but their friends did not help. Importantly, their friends also did not stand in their way.

I spent quite a while trying to figure out what made the samplers different. They experienced marginalization, including race-based isolation similar to tight-knitters. They were similar to compartmentalizers in terms of who was in their network (samplers vs. compartmentalizers: 60% vs. 65% MU friends, 33% vs. 36% friends from home, and 5% vs. 2% friends who are family members). I wondered if it was a personality difference: were samplers just more extroverted, focused, career driven, or achievement oriented? In each way I tried to measure this, no differences among the three network types emerged.[3] In sum, as suggested by the average ACT scores, samplers did not seem to be more driven or have higher prior performance, on average, than the other two network types.

Samplers were similar to the compartmentalizers and tight-knitters on most background characteristics; however, they differed in a few potentially important respects: samplers were more likely to live on campus than compartmentalizers and tight-knitters (75% vs. 48% and 55%), were less likely to be in a sorority or fraternity (17% vs. 48% and 32%), and worked more hours if employed (24.5 vs. 19.4 and 17.7). They were also significantly less likely to be in a romantic relationship: only one sampler (8%) was in a romantic relationship, compared with 40–50 percent among the other network types. Of the three network types, samplers were the most diverse of the students with whom I worked at MU. Half were women; one-third were white, one-third were black, and the remaining one-third were Asian, Indian, or Latino. The diversity was even more apparent when considering the race, gender, and class backgrounds of the 12 samplers. Of the six women, three were white (two upper class and one middle class), one was black and lower class, one was Indian and middle class, and one was Latina and an upper-class, first-generation college student. Of the six men, three were black and first-generation college students (one middle class and two lower class), one was Latino and a lower-class, first-generation student, one was Indian and upper class, and one was white and middle class. Samplers' friends were also more diverse: only 54 percent of samplers' friends were the same race as the sampler, and 56 percent were of the same gender, compared with 70–80 percent among compartmentalizers and tight-knitters. Although the number of organizations they joined and the specific organizations did not differ from tight-knitters and compartmentalizers, samplers collected, or "sampled," one friend from each organization, which seemed to add to their friendship diversity.

## The Structure of Samplers' Networks

I have a lot of friends. I make friends easily. . . . I wouldn't say I have any best friends or, like, superclose friends right now. At this point, I just have, like, general friends. People who I meet through programs really, like student government and [the program for first-generation students], and classes. [I've met] a lot of people through [my major].

—Amanda

Amanda's statement describes the general structure of samplers' networks. As she puts it, she has friends whom she met through organizations and classes, but these friendships are separate from each other. This can also be seen in her friendship network illustrated in figure 5.2. Amanda's network density of 0.14 reveals the sampler structure well because samplers have friends who often do not know each other.

Whereas tight-knitters' friends almost all knew each other and compartmentalizers' friends clustered in two to four groups, samplers tended to have friends who knew few of their other friends. As Richard put it, "a handful of people know other people I hang out with." Even when some clusters of friends appeared, such as the ones visible in Martin's network (see fig. 5.1), the majority of friends were unconnected to each other. This occurred even when samplers were friends with compartmentalizers and tight-knitters.[4] Javier referred to the lack of connection among his network as "lots of different groups of friends. . . . I'm not just limited to one group of friends." One reason that samplers have a variety of friends might be their open orientation toward meeting people. Javier, for example, discussed how "I didn't lock myself in to" the friends that he made at the be-

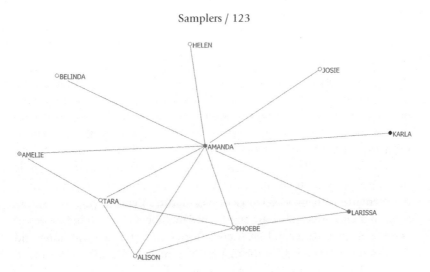

5.2. Amanda's friendship network

ginning of the year in his dorm. He noticed that most of his "dorm friends" hung out only with each other, whereas he constantly sought to expand his network. Similarly, Steve noticed that other students went everywhere with the same few friends: they "can't go anywhere by themselves," whereas "I came to meet new people." He asked rhetorically, "Why do I want to stay with you all my four years?" As Amanda put it, "I'm always looking for something to join . . . [and] I'll make a point to talk to somebody by the end of the meeting." Although I do not list "networking" as a separate category of how students' friends are involved academically, samplers more heavily participated in what many people tend to think of as networking behavior. I do not call it "networking," because samplers are not being strategic in cultivating connections that might help them professionally. Samplers, however, frequently search for new connections, and this "sampling" shapes their network structure.

Mathematically, samplers' networks can be distinguished from those of tight-knitters and compartmentalizers based on their low density and high betweenness centrality. Briefly, density is the proportion of ties present out of possible ties, and betweenness centrality is a measure of how many people are connected to each other only through a specific person.[5] Samplers have low-density networks, where fewer than one-third of their friends know each other (specifically, 8%–33% of samplers' friends knew each other). Samplers also have high betweenness centrality scores, showing that they are often the only connection, or one of the only connections, between their friends.[6]

In some ways, their networks can be considered a less connected version of compartmentalizers' networks. This is shown mathematically in modularity scores, which are similar for samplers and compartmentalizers.[7] The structure of the networks of the two samplers with the least dense networks clearly differs from that seen in the networks of compartmentalizers: these two samplers' sociograms look like daisies, with connections primarily out from themselves to their friends, as shown in Amanda's network in figure 5.2. The sociograms of the other 10 samplers show not only this daisy-like pattern but also some of the clusters that are evident in compartmentalizers' networks. For example, Martin's network (fig. 5.1) shows some tighter connections among family members (his mother, Rebecca, and his brother, Isiah) and his friends from home (Jasmine, Anthony, and Terrell), on the right side of the figure, and among some MU friends (Alex, Emily, Julia, Tyler, and JD), on the left. Even these more connected groups, however, are missing many ties. Martin also had several friends (Jesse, Nia, Kelly, and Kayla) who had few ties to any other friends in his network. Consequently, only 32 percent of the possible ties among his friends were present. In sum, samplers have low-density networks in which most of their friends remain disconnected from each other.

## Sparse Networks and Social Marginality

As shown in table 5.1, all but one sampler felt socially marginalized at MU. Although they had friends and all but one were involved in campus organizations, most samplers experienced social marginality, often but not always based on racial isolation. While tight-knitters also experienced marginality, they found support through a cohesive friendship group. In contrast, samplers experienced marginality but remained isolated. Javier explained, "Sometimes I feel like I'm not a person. Depending on who I'm with, I'm acting. I'm acting out a character that I should act out with that one person." With one-on-one, rather than group-based, friendships, Javier felt pressure to reinvent himself with each friend. Doing so, he believed, would help him maintain each relationship. The downside was that he felt that it took a lot of energy to maintain these distinct personas with each of his 45 friends. And it left him feeling fragmented and "disappointed" in his relationships and himself.

Like Javier, most samplers discussed difficulties in developing genuine connections with their peers. They also felt they were dissimilar to their peers, as Matthew, a white student, explained, "I feel slightly distant from them, probably because what I don't like is talking about myself the

**Table 5.1** Selected characteristics of samplers

| Name | Graduated from MU | GPA | Race/Ethnicity | Gender | Class | First-Gen. | ACT | Years at College* | No. of Friends | No. of Clubs | Social Marginality | Academic Multiplex Ties |
|---|---|---|---|---|---|---|---|---|---|---|---|---|
| Deb | Yes | 4.0[†] | White | Woman | Upper | No | 26 | 1 | 38 | 8 | No | Multiple |
| Jocelyn | Yes | 3.7 | White | Woman | Upper | No | 23 | 1 | 7 | 0 | Yes | One |
| Matthew | Yes | 3.5 | White | Man | Middle | No | 27 | 4 | 25 | 3 | Some | One |
| Amanda | Yes | 3.5 | Latina | Woman | Upper | Yes | 23 | 2 | 9 | 9 | Yes | No |
| Riyad | Yes | 3.5 | Indian | Man | Upper | No | 31 | 2 | 22 | 3 | Yes | No |
| Steve | Yes | 3.4 | Black | Man | Middle | Yes | —[‡] | 3 | 17 | 4 | Yes | No |
| Nicole | Yes | 3.4 | White | Woman | Middle | No | 28 | 2 | 15 | 3 | Some | No |
| Martin | Yes | 3.2 | Black | Man | Lower | Yes | 30 | 4 | 16 | 3 | Yes | No |
| Richard | Yes | 3.2 | Black | Man | Lower | Yes | 25 | 4 | 19 | 6 | Some | No |
| Javier | Yes | 2.9 | Latino | Man | Lower | Yes | 19 | 2 | 45 | 3 | Yes | Multiple |
| Lisa | Yes | 2.1 | Black | Woman | Lower | No | 17 | 4 | 10 | 6 | Yes | No |
| Akira | No | —[§] | Indian | Woman | Middle | No | 26 | 1 | 11 | 3 | Yes | No |

*Note:* See table 0.2 notes for discussions of socioeconomic class, first-generation college students, and ACT scores.

* This corresponds to how long they have been at MU with two exceptions: Richard was at another college for 2.5 years and had been at MU for 1 year when I first interviewed him; Javier was at another college for 1 year and had been at MU for 1 year when I first interviewed him.

[†] This GPA was from Deb's first semester. This is the only GPA information that I have for her.

[‡] Steve did not remember his ACT or SAT scores.

[§] I interviewed Akira during the final-exam period of her first semester at MU. She did not yet have final grades and I was not able to gather later GPA information from her.

whole time. . . . I feel some distance between me and other students. . . .
I think maybe I've matured in a way more than they have, not to say that
I'm more mature than they are, just that I have more experience or they
are still developing a lot of their beliefs." Although Matthew struggled to
find the words to explain why he felt the "distance" between himself and
other students, he brought up this feeling multiple times during the interview. Jocelyn, another white student, described people she met at MU,
even those she considered friends, as "disappointing." Despite advice from
her sister, who also attended MU, Jocelyn originally ended up in one of the
"party dorms" similar to that described by Elizabeth Armstrong and Laura
Hamilton (2013), full of what Jocelyn characterized as "in-style girls," who
were focused on fashion and partying. This dorm was not a good match for
the level-headedness that Jocelyn desired among her friends. After much
legwork, she found a new room in a new dorm. However, she felt disconnected from the students in her new dorm because they were "very, very
different from each other" and they generally were not "social." Even her
next-door neighbor, who had been friendly to her, was not a genuine connection. Jocelyn's closest friend was her older sister.

Disappointment with college friendships and a lack of belonging were
also apparent among other white samplers, including Nicole, who explained why she decided to join a sorority:

> I didn't really want to go through [sorority] rush, really. And my mom asked
> me just to try it, just the first part, and she said she'd pay . . . and then my
> roommate was doing it and . . . my whole floor was doing it, so that was defi-
> nitely peer pressure there. . . . In high school I was on the volleyball team, so
> that was like a place to belong. And when you come to a school this big, it's
> hard to feel like you belong anywhere. So I guess that was a factor in it too,
> just wanting like a group to be in, I guess.

Although her sorority gave her "a group to be in," she still did not feel as
if she belonged. She viewed her sorority sisters as generally superficial and
was "disappointed" with the depth of these relationships. Joining a sorority widened her social circle but not with the kind of friends that Nicole felt
that she could talk to about herself, to cross "the line" into talking about
"family things or feelings," as she explained to me. She talked to her sorority friends about "more casual stuff." Nicole answered my question about
the biggest obstacle in achieving what she would like by saying, "probably
just my own reservations about making friends. . . . I'm my biggest obstacle." While samplers blamed themselves or their peers, I found that their

network structure, specifically the lack of relationships among their friends, greatly contributed to, or at least reflected, their social marginality.

For all the nonwhite samplers, their sense of marginality was partially based on their race. This comes through clearly in Martin's story at the beginning of this chapter. Akira, an Indian student, articulates this rather thoughtfully: "I think friendships sometimes, a lot of times, go on your skin color. As you can see [pointing to the tables of students sitting around us in the library], African Americans hang out with African Americans, whites hang out with whites, and then, you got your people in the middle who aren't either [black or white], [like] me. . . . So I think sometimes your race can also play the role in, like, your friendships and stuff—what you choose and who your friends are." I then asked her whether she would like more Indian friends here at MU. She replied, "Oh yeah! I just met a girl name Julie downstairs, through my dad, actually [laughs]. . . . She's really nice too, but like, she's busy 'cause her major's like chemistry or micro-biology, so she's busy all the time. I talked to her a couple of times, but I wouldn't really consider her a friend yet, just kind of acquaintance—like, 'Hey, how are you?' Stuff like that." Her parent's connections from another state helped Akira find another first-year Indian woman living in her dorm; however, Akira did not (at least yet) feel as if they had connected. She described several failed attempts to connect with peers individually and through campus organizations, including a sorority, and again brought up race: "I think your race probably plays the biggest role on who your friends are and who they're not. Just like, Greeks [sorority and fraternity members] are mainly Caucasian people—you don't really see any other type of race going into that type of thing really." Javier sums this up nicely: "people can come together no matter, like, what their ethnicity or culture . . . [but] peo-ple can also pull apart because of ethnicity and culture." In other words, sometimes differences don't matter and sometimes they do.

Some students described gender, religion, or values as shaping the race-based marginality they felt. Steve, for example, discussed his isolation as a black male student:

STEVE: I haven't really found a best male friend here yet. And I don't think I will.
JM: You don't think you will?
STEVE: Uh-uh.
JM: Why not?
STEVE: I don't know. It's kinda—it's kinda hard. I wouldn't say hard, 'cause I can do it if I wanted to, but it almost seems like males have just a different attitude—and I guess I could have it myself—that I can do stuff alone or

it's hard to get in a circle with men. I notice more so in black men that they don't sit close to each other. [If there were] three people, one would sit right here, one would sit right there, and one would be right there [pointing to chairs with other chairs in between]. It's like, why [are] you so far apart? And it's just like—I guess they don't wanna be close. They feel it's gonna make them lose some of their masculinity or something like that. So that's why it's hard for me to get in with some of these guys.

Steve's network included four black men friends from home, one black woman friend from home, and twelve black women friends from MU. The men knew each other, but most of the women did not. As with the other samplers, Steve had friends but longed for more meaningful relationships. He had not made the deep friendships with other black males at MU that he had hoped for, and he found it challenging to maintain close relationships with his hometown friends, who were a four-hour drive away. Similarly, Riyad described values and religion—particularly being raised a Muslim—as an added layer in the race-based divide separating him from his peers:

JM: What would you say has been the biggest obstacle for you in achieving what you'd like socially in college?
RIYAD: My background. Most definitely my background.
JM: What do you mean by your "background"?
RIYAD: We don't drink or smoke or date, so it makes it hard for you to blend in on this sort of campus. . . . You should avoid being in situations where you're around people that are drinking, and it's very hard to do that here—especially in the dorms. So, my biggest obstacle is just basically the conflict between what's going on around me and the way I was brought up. . . . It's religious and cultural. . . . I know which way to follow, but it's like you're always in conflict with what's around you, which is very hard because at some point you just give up.

In the year that I interviewed him, Riyad found that navigating this "conflict" had intensified because his roommate was a partyer and "part of the problem." The previous year, he had felt as if he could more easily "blend in" as far as his values were concerned. When I spoke with him, he felt on the verge of giving up. Some tight-knitters and compartmentalizers brought up similar concerns but found groups of friends with whom they could discuss these experiences. Samplers did not. Samplers who were students of color not only felt socially marginal but also experienced their marginality as tied to their minority identity.

Students who experienced only "some" or no marginality (see table 5.1) generally believed that specific organizations helped them. While it would be easy to say that these specific organizations were the key, it is notable that other samplers also participated in these organizations but did not find the same social support. Still, I briefly discuss the exceptions. Their experiences are nicely summarized by Deb's account of the benefits of the intensive summer program[8] that she attended with other incoming first-year students prior to fall semester:

DEB: At first I really didn't wanna go [to the intensive summer program] because you had to give up three weeks of your summer, you had to move in early, and I was nervous. But looking back on it, it was probably the best decision I could've made because I knew the campus before anybody on my floor. The first week that people on my floor were trying to find one friend, I already had people that I was constantly hanging out with that I was really close with. It just made me feel more welcome in the community, for the fact that I feel part of it for longer. The first month, I didn't feel like a freshman for the fact that it wasn't brand new, which made me feel a lot more comfort-able. . . . If I had tests, I'd been more concentrated on the test 'cause I was comfortable because I took tests, I took notes, I went to class for [the inten-sive summer program]; it was an actual course so I knew what to expect. While some people were nervous about it, I was more comfortable.

JM: So it helped you socially but academically too?

DEB: Yeah. Like, I could tell that most teachers would give you Scantron [mul-tiple choice] tests if it was a large lecture hall; like, some would give you written [essay] tests if it was a smaller classroom. I was able to judge more of what to expect of the level and size and the teacher and stuff.

Deb discussed how she felt "a lot more comfortable" and "more welcome in the community" because of the relationships she had already built and the familiarity she had with the college environment. This comfort was missing for most samplers, who experienced social marginality on campus. This isolation was similar to that experienced at one time by many tight-knitters. However, the tight-knitters found that their friendship groups pro-vided them with support and a sense of "home." Most samplers' friend-ships did not resolve this lack of belonging. Also suggesting that samplers' marginality was tied to the campus environment is that most samplers did not remain samplers after college. Of the four samplers whom I interviewed again in 2009, three had become tight-knitters and one remained a sampler. Constructing these sparse networks did not appear to be the effect of a stable personality trait or friendship preference among samplers.

## "Academics Are All on Me"

Nearly all samplers experienced academic success: most had relatively high GPAs and all but one graduated from MU. These typical markers of academic success hide the fact that samplers' academic experiences were also quite different from those for the other network types. Although it is possible that social isolation caused samplers to keep academics private, the experiences of tight-knitters suggest that this is not likely. Tight-knitters experienced social isolation, but half of them—generally, the higher-achieving ones—incorporated friends into their academic lives in multiple ways.

One trait that distinguishes samplers is their academic independence. Rather than relying on friends for instrumental help, emotional support, or intellectual engagement, samplers relied on themselves. Amanda described academics as "more of a personal journey. I've never really learned anything with somebody." Riyad referred to himself as "academically self-sufficient," commenting, "Well, I mean there's always gonna be somebody I can blow off to, but I tend not to rely on other people for help, just because I like to know where I stand in the class as a result of my own work rather than everyone in the group working together and me [saying,] 'Oh, okay, that makes sense,' but I really didn't learn it. It made sense because the answer was laid out to me." Both Amanda and Riyad believed they learned more by themselves. Like Martin, Riyad argued that learning by himself was better because it more accurately marks what he knows. Academic self-sufficiency was also tied to motivation, specifically the belief that it was one's own decision whether to attend class or complete an assignment. Most samplers believed it was not friends' place to give academic advice, as Akira explained:

[My friend] Marion constantly sleeps in, but I'm not gonna tell her, like, "Don't go to class" [or] "Do go to class," just because she pays for it. She knows better to go to class, and they know better that I paid for mine. . . . We don't ever like, "Oh, you need to go, you need to go," because we're all grown up, we're eighteen, we know we should know better. You pick whether you go to class, you don't go to class, you party, or don't party. I think we're very mature and just like, "You do what you wanna do. I'm not gonna force you to do anything you don't wanna do."

Although a similar sentiment was expressed by the least successful compartmentalizers—such as Margaret, discussed in the previous chapter—it was typical of samplers. Most samplers saw academics as an individual endeavor, whereas this belief was held by a minority of compartmentalizers.

Samplers' discussions about competition also show how they engage in academics largely on their own. Academics are "private," as several students described it, often refraining from sharing their grades. For example, Nicole did not talk to friends about grades: "I talk about my grades to my parents and no one else because I don't like the extensive competition that comes with talking about grades with friends. . . . I don't like talking about things that invoke kind of a competitive—when you are in the same class with somebody and you did better than them on a test, or worse [laughs]." Riyad shared this sentiment: "When I do poorly on a test, I withdraw. I don't wanna be around people because a lot of times the people around me, some of them are in the same classes and they do consistently well, so it's kind of like twisting the knife. . . . For me I think that's [grades are] private." Riyad was more direct than other students in explaining that he kept his grades to himself because he did not want to feel worse than he already did about his grades. He had a 3.5 GPA, which was well above average, so I did not suspect that he received "bad grades" too often. Nonetheless, this was his reasoning for keeping grades private.

The only sampler who discussed competition as a way to integrate friends into academics, as discussed in chapter 2 as friendly competition around grades, was Javier. Javier discussed how people in his classes, some of whom were friends, compared grades to motivate each other: "People in my classes that have the same major, they're like, 'Oh, you're trying to become an accounting major too? Oh, how'd you do on that Accounting 100 class?' 'Oh, I got a 100 percent on my test!' Like, 'Oh, really?' You just find similarities in your major, and then you can kind of compete and that'll make you do better in your academics." Even Javier, however, discussed academics as primarily individual: "I really recognize that I really am alone. All alone. That's not a big problem for me. I don't mind. I kind of like that." He discussed how difficulties at home impacted his grades negatively: "At first I didn't realize it, but . . . these problems I'm facing, it's the main reason why I say I can't get As." Javier saw friends as motivating him at times to do better but still saw academics as primarily his responsibility. Like other samplers, he felt "all alone" when it came to academics.

## Few Academic Multiplex Ties

As the earlier discussion of Martin shows, samplers rarely engaged in emotional support, instrumental help, or intellectual engagement with the same friends. In other words, samplers rarely had academic multiplex ties. This is shown in the last column of table 5.1. Unlike the situation with the tight-knitters, among samplers academic multiplex ties are not absent mainly among those with lower achievement but are rare altogether. It is notable, however, that three of the four samplers with at least one academic multiplex tie have the highest GPAs. Although it is possible that social isolation caused samplers to keep to themselves academically, the experiences of tight-knitters suggest that this is not likely. Tight-knitters experienced social isolation, but over half of them had academic multiplex ties. Social isolation drove many tight-knitters to connect with others, resulting in both social and academic support; it did not have the same effect for samplers.

In the next sections, I discuss each of the missing components of academic multiplex ties. Samplers typically have friends who provide little instrumental help, limited and implicit academic support, and restricted intellectual engagement.

### Little Instrumental Help

Samplers typically discussed few ways that their friends gave instrumental help with academics. This is tied to their belief that academics were personal. For example, Matthew responded to my question about whether he studied with friends by saying, "No, no, *very* distracting, very much so." Amanda was typical in her response to my question about how her friends were involved in her academic life:

> I'd say they're not [involved]. The only way they're involved is through being in the same class with me. That's about it. I don't study with people ever. I don't really ever try to get help from other students unless it's like a direct, random thing like, "Oh well, did you understand that question?" But if I don't understand a concept, I don't go to a student. I just don't trust other students to help me. Because I know if I'm having problems, I'm probably not the only one, so I try to avoid, you know, miscommunication in regards to subjects, and I don't want to be messed up academically because I rely on someone else.

My next question was whether she relied on friends to help her pick classes. She interrupted me, exclaiming, "Absolutely not!" Rather than seeing friends as offering instrumental help, Amanda saw this as a burden. Not only were these friends a burden in terms of taking up time in their frequent requests for help, but they could hurt students' academic performance if they offered wrong advice, which Amanda believed was likely. She called these friends "moochers" and discussed how they could distract students from academics: "Moochers are not good for you. People who are only your friend when they want something, questions answered, or when they [*high-pitched silly voice*] 'don't understand the concept. I don't get it! Could you explain?' . . . And I'm like, just read the book or do what you were assigned to do. I'm like, 'Did you read?' And they're like, 'No.' Okay [*laughs*], 'Go read!' So people like that." It was not that samplers never engaged in instrumental help with friends, but that these experiences were infrequent. For example, when I asked more specific questions, Amanda, who above said, "I don't study with people ever," discussed asking friends to proofread her papers or critique her art projects, particularly if they were in her class and knew the guidelines for the project. Nicole similarly described proofreading papers for her roommates "a couple times." Javier discussed how his friends sometimes provided instrumental help, most commonly through doing homework together. He noted, "I study a lot and when I'm by myself it's a lot easier to get distracted." He then told me about "this one time when I was studying with a friend. . . . I was on one side of the bed; he was on the other. He was doing some homework. I was reading. And I noticed I wasn't distracted because I was like, oh, he's busy, I've gotta do this." This example, however, suggests that studying with friends is not a common occurrence for Javier. Like most samplers, he discussed friends mainly as a distraction, "someone who can bring me down."

Deb is the clearer exception since she discussed multiple ways that multiple friends provided instrumental help for her and for each other. Her discussion of instrumental help from friends is similar to that of many compartmentalizers. For example, when I asked how Deb's friends were involved in her academic life, she replied: "Actually they're in the same classes, so we work together on projects, [and] we consult each other for advice, with like a paper that we have to write. We're more than willing to proofread other people's papers and stuff like that. . . . Helping Andrea study for a math test or teaching her how to do a problem—she can turn to any of us and we'll be more than willing to help. Same with anybody on the floor; we just help each other out." Deb discussed how her friends studied together if they were in the same classes, and they studied side by side, often while watching TV if they were not studying the same thing. She gave an example of the latter from the previous night. Her friends were watching a baseball game on TV because "Laura's really into the Cardinals": "Anna was doing her [business homework], I was doing my English, Andrea was doing math, and Laura was watching the game. We can be all in the same room and we can talk once in a while, but we're all doing our own individual homework."

Most samplers, however, described little instrumental help from their friends. The samplers did well academically but not because of regular help from friends with studying, editing papers, or tips for which classes or professors to take or avoid. Samplers' friends provided little instrumental help, and samplers provided little instrumental help in return.

### Implicit Academic Emotional Support

Some samplers reported that friends provided no emotional support for academics, while others described mainly implicit support. Few samplers described explicit and regular academic support from their friends. Nicole's explanation was typical: "I stress out a lot about school, and when I talk to friends, I feel like they're just like, 'Oh, just don't study,' and I don't want to hear that, so I talk to my parents the most about that." Nicole lacked emotional academic support from friends and instead received this support only from her family. Steve similarly said that his main source of academic support was his family. In response to my question about whether his friends encouraged and supported each other, Steve replied: "More so, I'm the giver." Later, when he described himself as "giving all the time," I asked, "So you don't feel like you get a whole lot of support and encouragement academically back?" Steve replied, "Not really. But I really don't strive for it. It's like because I know I'm doing it myself. I got my parents to fall back on [and] my brother and sister. I want it but at the same time I don't really need it." Although Steve seemed to be trying to downplay his disappointment, it was clear that he wished for more support from his friends. With friends, his support was one-way.

Other samplers discussed getting some emotional support from friends, but this support was more implicit. For example, Matthew described the support that his friend Marilyn provided: "When Marilyn came into my life, it opened up a new door. . . . She helped me realize . . . [that] she worked hard all the time, and I'm like, yeah, I might as well work hard all the time too. . . . We just kinda kept each other accountable academically." Similarly, Richard felt that his friends provided some encouragement, particularly Heather and John. However, Richard described this support in a strikingly different way than the higher-achieving tight-knitters and even many of the compartmentalizers did: "The people I hang around with now, most of the people, it's kinda like we encourage each other. Maybe not even verbally, just through one another's actions. Most [of] the people I know are involved in extracurricular activities, we work, and we still hang out and have fun. But then we still do well in school. So that's kinda like it's a reciprocal encouragement to do better. . . . Just being around people who always want to do their best and be the best. That rubs off on you." The implicit support that Richard described as "encouragement to do better" and that Matthew received by being friends with Marilyn is better than no support, but it still left them feeling isolated and alone.

The two samplers who had multiple academic multiplex ties—Deb and Javier—were the only ones whose friends provided explicit support. Deb described her friends as involved: "[My friends] they encourage me and make sure I get my homework done, and they always wish me luck on tests. We know when each other's tests are, [and] we'll wish each other luck and help them study even if we're not in the same class." Javier described this type of direct support from one friend: "He doesn't really help me, but [he's] like, 'Oh, man, go get your homework done. Do your homework. Go get it done. Come on. Let's go do our homework together.'" Both Deb and Javier had some clusters of friends, although the ties within these clusters were not as dense as for compartmentalizers and tight-knitters. Their academic multiplex ties and emotional support were within these low-density clusters. As these examples suggest, not all samplers were devoid of any emotional support from friends, but most samplers had friends who provided little support for academics, and what support they did receive was mostly implicit.

### Intellectual Engagement with Certain Friends

In general, samplers seemed to desire intellectual discussions but did not find these within their friendship networks. Amanda's response was typical. When I asked whether she talked about intellectual matters or "interesting issues" with friends, she responded, "Not in-depth," clarifying, "As a general thing, no." She discussed intellectual issues most often with her mother: "I'll talk to her about things like that. She's actually the person that I talk to the most about intellectual matters. We can argue any point and we don't even argue about it. We discuss things a lot. We talk about everything." Similarly, Jocelyn described talking about ideas mainly with her dad and her sister Paige, who also attended MU: "They're the most intelligent people that I have really good discussions with." Lisa also discussed intellectual ideas with her sister but not with other friends.

As mentioned earlier, Steve described himself as unable to find supportive black male friends. Among other things, he desired intellectual engagement and had difficulty finding peers, not just black men, who wanted to engage in intellectual discussion. Steve typically would try to engage others in such conversations by asking, "'Have you ever wondered why certain people do this?' And then I'm like, 'Okay, I learned this in that class,' just to hear what they got to say about it." He noticed that his efforts were not often reciprocated or even appreciated: "I can't stand when people just give me a yes and no answer. And that makes me so mad. . . . [Recently, I asked a peer], 'How you enjoying the class?' And she was like, 'Fine.' I'm like, 'Fine? Can you say why is it just fine?' Then I have to follow up: 'Oh, so what in particular do you like about the class?' I have to keep making these follow-up questions going. Come on." Steve moaned that "some people don't think that deep." He explained, "I'm always listening to people, what they [are] saying in the conversation so I can just join in on a smart conversation, but only happened . . . twice [at MU]. So I haven't found that." Both of these "smart conversations" happened in the food court where he chose to hold our interview. One of these conversations was about "slave labor overseas" and the other was about "checking the racial box—should they have it on applications or not."

Most samplers described one friend (occasionally a few friends) with whom they could discuss intellectual ideas. They also discussed wanting more of these relationships and more of these discussions. Nicole was typical in both respects: "I wish people did that more too. Because I feel like in my religion class, I find a lot of interesting things, and I like to tell people about them, but sometimes I don't always think people are as interested as I want them to be [laughs] but I do like talking about things from classes, and I do like hearing about things from other classes." Nicole later commented that being able to "talk about your ideas and intellectual things" is "a very important part of a friendship." She lacked this among her sorority sisters, as discussed earlier. She also belonged to a writing group, which provided her with an outlet for discussing her writing, but it served that one narrow purpose. The limited intellectual purpose of her writing group was revealed as she talked about her friend Jessica, who was a member: "I don't know her very well—um, just, it's interesting. The relationship with her is very interesting because I would say hi to her if we were passing on the street for sure, but when we're in writers group, I feel like we talk about *such* personal things and that when you pass someone on the street, you seem like you would talk more, but it's just like when you're out of that setting, it's different." While Nicole seemed to feel enriched by the intellectual engagement within her writing group, this was limited to two friends, Jessica and Amber, who were part of the writing group. She did not engage in intellectual conversations with other friends, despite wishing for this to happen.

Two students described having more regular intellectual conversations with a greater variety of friends. Riyad discussed how his friends have "huge intellectual conversation[s]. One time, we had a conversation that went from abortion to rights of the dead to religion to—it just was all over the place." Javier noted that hearing different perspectives from friends "changes me intellectually. . . . It opens up my perspective about something. Friends definitely help intellectually because each person has a different view about things. When you hear it, you learn it, and you're like, 'Oh, I never seen it that way.'" With the exception of Riyad and Javier, most samplers did not feel that they had especially deep or meaningful conversations with multiple friends. And, with the exception of Deb, samplers desired more of these relationships.

## Conclusion

At first glance, samplers seemed to be models of college success. Upon closer examination, however, most experienced both academic and social isolation. Their academic success was achieved largely on their own, and they lacked academic multiplex ties, which facilitated academic success in other network types. More importantly, they tended to feel socially marginalized on campus despite having friends and being involved in several campus organizations. On the one hand, this shows that friends are not necessary for academic success. On the other hand, this raises the question, could samplers be even more successful if they allowed their friends to be friends with academic benefits?

Perhaps being a sampler is a temporary friendship type for some students. Deb and Javier, the samplers with multiple academic multiplex ties, might have been transitioning into more compartmentalized networks. Both were finishing their first year at MU when I interviewed them and, more so than other students, appeared to be gaining distance from some friends while deepening ties within some emerging clusters. That developing cluster for Deb seemed to be with several women on her dorm floor. For Javier, the developing cluster seemed to be with members of the Latino fraternity that he was in the process of joining. Perhaps if I had interviewed them the following year, they might have had different network structures centered on common activities—what sociologists refer to as "foci" (Feld 1981)—and Javier would have found friends who helped him overcome his feelings of academic, social, and race-based isolation. Such change was not under way for other samplers, however, including Lisa and Martin, who were in their final year before graduating from MU.

My observations about samplers point to some implications for campus administrators and researchers. As mentioned in the introduction, over half of students surveyed at 139 colleges reported feeling "very lonely" in the past 12 months (ACHA 2010). Clearly, this is a problem. Administrators and researchers should not overlook samplers' experiences of social marginality, despite their academic success and their appearance of social success. Administrators can play valuable roles in helping these students connect with others in meaningful ways. To facilitate such connections, colleges should continue to support a range of student clubs and organizations where students can share academic and social interests.

Parents played a larger role in the lives of most samplers than they did for compartmentalizers and tight-knitters. With the exception of Matthew and Javier, who both had strained relationships with their parents, the other samplers all reported parents providing both instrumental help and emotional support regarding academics. On the one hand, it seems positive that samplers received support from someone and that their parents were able to provide it. On the other hand, because they received this support from their parents, they may have been less willing to reach out to friends. In this way, their parents may resemble the hovering "helicopter parents" that characterize this generation of young adults (Howe and Strauss 2007) and should instead strive to give their children the space to turn to friends for support.

Beyond campus administrators and researchers, students who are samplers may be able to take some steps themselves to influence their sense of belonging. First, while recognizing that academics are under their control, they do not need to approach their studies alone. They should understand that friends can be valuable sources of help and that they can draw on these sources by asking friends to study with them or talk about ideas from class together. Second, students might be able to actively create a supportive community, or a couple of supportive communities, of friends. This community does not need to be a unified network, like those of tight-knitters, or even a strong subset of their network, like those of compartmentalizers, but having a small group of friends who provide emotional support, intellectual engagement, and instrumental help is advantageous and would reduce their feelings of marginalization and isolation. Because not all samplers felt socially marginal, the samplers' network structure is not incompatible with a sense of belonging. Samplers can achieve both academic and social success.

Both these solutions focus on changing the content of networks, but changing the structure would also help samplers find a "home" among their friends. Samplers could do this by introducing their friends to each other, inviting a friend from their network to an event that the friend normally would not attend, or asking to meet a friend's friends.[9] These solutions have the possibility of creating more of a compartmentalized network, which are typically more supportive of students' social belonging. This was missing for most samplers, such as Martin.

Samplers' experiences advocate for an expanded definition of success in college. While academic success, especially graduating from college, is an important measure, administrators and researchers should not focus exclusively on this goal. Instead, we should be looking at more holistic measures of social and academic success. Education researchers were on the right track when they proposed to measure academic and social integration or involvement; however, even by these measures most samplers would be seen as successful (see Astin 1993; Kuh et al. 2005; Tinto 1993, 2012).[10] Samplers would likely be seen as socially integrated, for example, because they have friends and are involved in campus clubs or organizations. Samplers' discussions of obstacles to their social and academic success typically revealed their experiences of marginality better than asking them directly. Tracking samplers over time also gives hope to those interested in improving students' college experiences. Being a sampler does not seem to be a stable personality trait or a friendship preference but rather is associated with isolation in a particular place and time. After college, most samplers were no longer samplers, finding social support among either a cluster of friends or their network as a whole.

# SIX

# Friendships after College

I feel like my friendships have matured into a new type of relationship [after college]. Things for which I counted on my friends in college often seem trivial. . . . Now, however, my friends and I provide support for each other when making career decisions, counsel each other when marriages turn sour, and care for families and homes when loved ones are on their deathbeds. The bonds that have developed with many of my adult friends run much deeper than those with my college buddies.

—Krystal

What happens to students and their friendship networks once they leave college? Like Krystal, many students, even those who experienced supportive relationships during college, noted that life after college brought changes and new depth to their friendships. This chapter follows up with my participants five years after the original interviews.[1] No longer students but young adults, most participants had been out of college for 1–4 years and were 23–27 years old. In this chapter, I discuss what young adults saw as the most important transitions in their lives, how their friendships changed, and how their friendships during college affected their current lives.[2] I find that network type during college influenced young adults' friendships after college in terms of their structure, content, and composition. For example, samplers experienced the largest changes in their friendship networks, while those who had been in tight-knit networks kept more friends (particularly those who had provided academic benefits during college) over time than did people with other network types. In the following sections, I discuss the three students mentioned in the introduction and at the start of chapters 3–5—Alberto, the tight-knitter; Mary, the compartmentalizer; and Martin, the sampler—focusing on changes in their friendships and lives after college.

## Characteristics of the Young Adults in My Sample

Before going into the patterns by network type, I begin by describing similarities among participants in my sample in order to contextualize them among young adults in general. My participants were undergoing many of the financial and family transitions associated with emerging adulthood (Arnett 2004). In terms of romantic relationships, about a quarter of participants described themselves as single, half were in a serious relationship (including cohabiting or being engaged), and the other quarter were married.[3] No one was divorced. Only 6 percent had children.[4] Aside from the lower-achieving tight-knitters, who are discussed later, most of my participants graduated from college within six years of entering.[5] Twelve percent had earned master's degrees and another 8 percent were working on graduate degrees when I interviewed them.

In terms of income, participants earned $20,000–$30,000, on average, and no participant made over $100,000.[6] These figures are lower than average for college graduates (Cataldi et al. 2014).[7] Participants were working in a range of occupations, including teacher, cashier, community organizer, bartender, police officer, and registered nurse. Two were unemployed. About 40 percent were employed in jobs that typically required a four-year degree or higher, and another 20 percent were attending graduate or professional school. More participants reported taking out student loans to fund their education than is average for federal student loans at MU (76% vs. 39%).[8] The average loan debt among debtors, however, was quite similar, averaging $21,000–$22,000 in both my sample and among graduates (Reed 2008).

Another similarity across network types was the lack of assistance from friends in getting a job. In contrast to Mark Granovetter (1973) and other researchers who found that weak ties—that is, acquaintances—matter more than strong ties, such as friends, in the job search, I do not find patterns by network type in either acquaintances or friends helping young adults find jobs. Similar to Richard Arum and Josipa Roksa's (2014) research on young adults two years after college graduation, my research indicates that very few young adults found a job through friends.[9] Arum and Roksa (2014, 73) attribute this low number to the fact that "many of their college friends were in the same boat—having a difficult time finding work"—and speculate that friendships may be more important later in life. Future research that includes friendship network type and follows participants over the life course could test these possibilities.

## How Friendships Changed

I began the follow-up interviews by asking young adults what they believed was the biggest change in their lives over the last five years. They mentioned geographic moves, new jobs, religious conversions, romantic relationships beginning and ending, illnesses, deaths in their families, and increased responsibility associated with family and professional transitions, such as getting married, having children, being a homeowner, and working full-time. A few launched into discussions of how these factors changed their friendships, such as Gina, who noted that her work obligations made it hard to hang out with friends as she did in high school and college. However, even if they did not bring up their friendships immediately, nearly all young adults in my sample discussed multiple aspects of their friendships that had changed since college. In this way, their discussions fit with research noting that "[t]he whole realm of peer relationships represents the biggest adjustment during the first year out" (Clydesdale 2007, 95). Although that research focused on the first year after high school, the same thing could be said about the period after college. Friendships changed.

One area of significant change is the number of friends reported. Young adults' networks grew larger after college, increasing from 18 to 24, on average. While this growth might seem unexpected given the peer-centered experience at residential colleges like MU, I found that the transitions mentioned earlier not only changed networks but also expanded them. The variation in network size was also larger than during college, ranging from seven to 87 friends. Most young adults, however, listed between 13 and 24 friends, and there were no significant differences across race, class, or gender.[10] As mentioned in chapter 1, differences in how researchers collect friendship data make comparisons across studies and the life course difficult.

A second change involves who is in the network. Most generally, there was a large turnover in who was in the network, consistent with previous work measuring networks over time (Feld 1997; Wellman et al. 1997). On average, I found that 25 percent of students' friends remained over the 5-year period; this is consistent with the 20 percent continuity reported over a 10-year period among young adults (Wellman et al. 1997)[11] and the 54 percent continuity reported over a five-month period during men's first year in college (Feld 1997). Young adults varied considerably in how many friends remained, with one student (Justin) keeping 88 percent of his friends and another (Adrianna) keeping none. I also found that after-college networks included fewer friends from MU than during college, changing from 65 to 39 percent, on average. This is not surprising given research showing that foci of activity (such as attending the same college) shape social networks and that life transitions disrupt these foci and, consequently, the networks associated with them (Feld and Carter 1998). Therefore, leaving MU would likely lead to fewer MU friends. Because little research examines network change over time, my findings add important insights regarding how they change. Importantly, as discussed below, I found that network structure helps to explain why certain individuals kept a fewer or a greater number of friends.

Although the number of friends from MU decreased, family was more often included after college. The proportion of family members in networks increased from 2 to 6 percent, with the largest change for tight-knitters, for whom family members went from zero to 10 percent of their networks, on average. From his research on adults, Claude Fischer (1982) concluded that "stage in the life cycle" was one of the most important determinants of the number of family members in people's networks, and Peter Marsden (1987) found that the proportion of family members in discussion networks was lowest in the early thirties and higher among younger and older respondents.[12] Perhaps since the transition to college involves breaking with parents, family members are less likely to be in students' networks but are included after college, when young adults have established more independence.

A third change is that networks became slightly less dense, with less variation in density.[13] During college, slightly more than one-half of students' friends knew each other, whereas after college, this number dropped to slightly less than one-half of friends (from 56% to 46% density). The change I found was much less dramatic than that in another study of adults' networks over a 10-year period, which found a density decline from 35 to 13 percent (Wellman et al. 1997). Rather than just noting the general change in density over time, however, I focus on how density changes according to network type (discussed below).

There were also some differences in how young adults defined friendship during and after college. Trust and closeness were central, but after college closeness came up in a slightly different way—in terms of emotional support and shared interest. Other differences, however, were more noticeable. Reliability came up frequently in the after-college interviews. Young adults noted that the importance of having "someone they can count on," the ability to depend on these people for different types of problems and situations. Continued communication also played a central role in defining someone as a friend after college. Most young adults noted that in order to maintain a friendship, they had to stay in touch with friends in some way. For example, Brittany explained:

> I guess friendship was so easy in college because you are around that person . . . in the same city and . . . [sorority] house. Friendship was more effortless. . . . Now, I see who my true friends are because they're the ones [who] continue to keep in contact. . . . [There were] friends that I had in college that I had expected that we'd always be friends. And through whatever reason, neither one of us has kept in contact like I thought we would. Because it is—it takes effort to keep in contact. . . . With as many life changes that we've had since college, I think that those friends that kind of deal with you through the highs and lows are the ones that you know will be there for the rest of your life.

Brittany discussed how the geographic and professional changes in her life and her friends' lives tested their friendships. The ones who reliably provided support and stayed in touch were the ones who would continue to be friends "for the rest of your life."

How they stayed in touch with friends also changed over time. While much contact occurred face-to-face in college because friends often lived with or in close proximity to each other, after college more contact occurred via phone calls, e-mail, and Facebook. Typically, they would also discuss the importance of face-to-face contact, which was easier and more regular among friends still living nearby. Many participants discussed the value of traveling to spend time with friends, either going to where their friends were (as Martin did) or getting together at MU or another central location (as Alberto did). Most young adults used multiple methods to stay connected to each other.

Friendship networks changed little, however, in terms of their gender and racial composition, with about 70 percent same-gender friends and same-race friends, on average, at both points in time. Individual students' networks also changed very little; the average change in racial composition was zero, and the average change in gender composition was 5 percent more same-gender friends after college. Because research shows that structural diversity predicts racial homophily of friendships (M. Fischer 2008), students at colleges with different racial compositions may have different points at which they hold steady over time.

As this discussion shows, the young adults in my study displayed many similarities in their backgrounds and in their experiences of friendship. There are many other ways, however, that experiences diverged by network type. Perhaps surprisingly, networks after college differed more by network type than by other transitions; for example, while one study found that the four respondents who got married or divorced experienced almost completely different ties during the decade of the study (Wellman et al. 1997), I found that the networks of my six married respondents (19% of my sample) differed little from those who did not marry (81% of my sample).[14] Next, I will describe what changes came about for tight-knitters, compartmentalizers, and samplers.

## Alberto's Friendships after College: Tight-Knitters

When I interviewed Alberto (the upper-class Latino man with a tight-knit network whom I discussed in chapter 3) for the second time, he had been out of college for four years. Alberto's achievements matched his goals better than most of my participants' achievements matched their goals. During college, he told me that he hoped that in five years he would have a master's degree and live in New York City; in four years he had earned a master's degree and was moving to New York City the week after our interview to start a new job. He had achieved both goals. When I asked him about the biggest change since our last interview, he immediately mentioned a long-term romantic relationship that had ended. He was clearly sad about this, but he discussed how his friends had been helping him through this tough time. His friends provided social support by "understanding me at my worst and best."

Despite this loss and some changes in whom he considered friends, Alberto had maintained a tight-knit friendship network. During college, Alberto was a tight-knitter with one cohesive group of 14 friends. After college, he still had one tight-knit group surrounding him, but he added several pairs and individual friends who were loosely connected to the main group. Keeping a tight-knit group but adding friends increased the size of tight-knitters' networks substantially over time (from 13 to 21, on average, as shown in table 6.1). Alberto's after-college network included 37 friends. Figure 6.1 shows his large cohesive group on the right-hand side of his network, centered on friends he met at MU (six of these friends remained

**Table 6.1 Characteristics of after-college networks by during-college network type**

| | Tight-Knitters | Compart-mentalizers | Samplers | Overall Sample |
|---|---|---|---|---|
| **After-college network characteristics (in 2009):** | | | | |
| Number of friends | 21 | 25 | 17 | 24 |
| Friends from 2004–5 (%) | 30 | 23 | 23 | 25 |
| MU friends (%) | 50 | 31 | 33 | 39 |
| Friends who are family members (%) | 10 | 6 | 5 | 6 |
| Same-race friends (%) | 81 | 75 | 53 | 73 |
| Change in same-race friends, 2004–9* | –4 | 0 | 7 | 0 |
| Same-gender friends (%) | 70 | 73 | 56 | 71 |
| Change in same-race friends, 2004–9* | –3 | –8 | 1 | –5 |
| Density score | 50 | 42 | 50 | 46 |
| Change in density score, 2004–9* | –32 | –5 | 30 | 9 |
| Betweenness centrality (normalized) | 0.25 | 0.32 | 0.26 | 0.28 |
| **Reflections on college friendships (in 2009):** | | | | |
| Importance of friends for academic life:[†] | | | | |
|   Very important (%) | 38 | 17 | 0 | 21 |
|   Somewhat important (%) | 13 | 28 | 0 | 18 |
|   Not important (%) | 50 | 56 | 100 | 60 |
| Believed friends provided academic emotional support (%)[‡] | 63 | 44 | 0 | 42 |
| Survey questions about changes in friendships over time:[§] | | | | |
|   Believed spends more time with friends now than in college (1–5) | 1.6 | 2 | 2.4 | 1.9 |
|   Believed has more friends now than in college (1–5) | 2.5 | 3 | 3 | 2.9 |
|   Believed has completely new friends now (1–5) | 2.6 | 3.3 | 3.6 | 3 |
| N** | 10–14 | 18–23 | 4–5 | 32–47 |

* Change variable. A positive score means an increase over time (i.e., more same-race or same-gender friends in 2009 than 2004, or a higher density score in 2009 than 2004), and a negative score means a decrease over time (i.e., fewer same-race or same-gender friends in 2009 than 2004, or a lower density score in 2009 than 2004).

[†] This is coded on the basis of responses during the follow-up interviews.

[‡] This is coded on the basis of responses during the follow-up interviews.

[§] The next three questions were answered with numeric responses (1–5) on the web survey. Higher scores indicate stronger agreement with the statement, lower scores indicate greater disagreement, and a score in the middle (3) indicates no change.

** Number of friends and the three questions assessing changes in friendships over time were collected in the follow-up survey, and N is 14 for tight-knitters, 21–22 for compartmentalizers, 5 for samplers, and 47–48 for the overall sample, which includes participants without network data during college. The other variables are based on questions collected in the follow-up telephone interview, and the N is 10 for tight-knitters, 18 for compartmentalizers, 4 for samplers, and 32–38 for the overall sample.

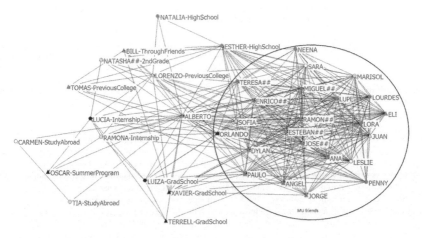

6.1. Alberto's friendship network after college

from the original interview, marked by ## in the sociogram). His close-knit group of friends stayed in touch through not only phone calls, e-mail, and Facebook but also planned events, parties, and trips. The month before our interview, many of these friends traveled to MU—which is a four-hour drive from where Alberto was living at the time—for an annual sporting event. On the left-hand side of figure 6.1 are loosely connected friends he met at other places, such as graduate school, studying abroad, high school, and the previous college he attended. Of the loosely connected friends, only one (Natasha) was on his original friendship list.

Like Alberto, after college tight-knitters tended to keep one large cohesive group in their network and add some friends (typically pairs or individuals) who were not closely connected to their main group. In terms of density scores, table 6.1 shows that tight-knitters averaged 50 percent density after college, meaning that half of their friends knew each other. In comparison, during college, their average density was 86 percent, meaning that over five-sixths of their friends knew each other. While the density scores changed over time, the structure of the network—one tight-knit group—remained for all except three tight-knitters, as shown in table 6.2.[15] Two became compartmentalizers, with two to three clusters of friends, and one—Erica, the tight-knitter with the lowest density (0.21)—became a sampler.[16] Most tight-knitters, like Alberto, had middle-density networks after college; rather than consisting of multiple clusters (like compartmentalizers), however, these networks had one tight-knit group and some loosely connected friends.

Table 6.2  Network type during and after college

| | During College | | |
| --- | --- | --- | --- |
| After College | Tight-Knitters | Compartmentalizers | Samplers |
| Tight-knitters | 7 | 0 | 3 |
| Compartmentalizers | 2 | 18 | 0 |
| Samplers | 1 | 0 | 1 |

*Note:* During college, network density was the most important measurement I used to categorize students as tight-knitters (network density of 0.67–1.0), compartmentalizers (0.34–0.64), and samplers (0.08–0.32). After college, I rely on density along with modularity and betweenness centrality scores to place young adults into the three network types. Of the 7 tight-knitters who remained tight-knitters, 3 would be categorized as tight-knitters just by their density scores (0.67–0.90), and the other 4 had middle densities (0.39–0.50) but their network structure most resembles that of tight-knitters with a few disconnected individuals. Of the 18 compartmentalizers, 14 would be categorized as compartmentalizers just by density score (0.34–0.65), and the other 4 had low densities (0.26–0.32) but their network structure most resembles that of compartmentalizers with two to four clusters. Of the 3 samplers who became tight-knitters after college, 1 would be categorized as a tight-knitter just by density score (0.77), and the other 2 had middle densities (0.41 and 0.46) but their network structure most resembles that of tight-knitters with a few disconnected individuals.

If we look at network composition, the race and gender of Alberto's friends changed little. His network was only slightly more diverse after college, changing from 86 to 73 percent same-race friends and 57 to 49 percent same-gender friends. As shown in table 6.1, this similarity in race and gender of friends between college and postcollege is common among most participants regardless of network type, pointing to the long-term consequences of patterns from college.

Like other tight-knitters, Alberto had many friends who attended MU. As shown in table 6.1, tight-knitters kept more friends over time (averaging 30% same friends over the five-year period vs. 23% in the other network types) and had more MU friends (50% vs. 31%–33%) in their postcollege networks than the other network types. Tight-knitters also had more family members in their networks than the other network types (averaging 10% family members vs. 5%–6% in the other network types). Alberto's after-college network contained substantially more MU friends than average.[17] One reason was that he remained active in a graduate chapter of his fraternity. This activity was much more common among members of minority Greek organizations, such as historically black and Latino fraternities and sororities, than among historically white ones (Berkowitz and Padavic 1999; Torbenson and Parks 2009). At least once a month, Alberto participated in community service or social events with his fraternity's graduate chapter in the city where he lived. Most of his MU friends, however, became his friends after college. Alberto experienced more change in who remained a friend than most tight-knitters.[18]

As discussed in chapter 3, Alberto's friends were very involved in academics during college. Rather than relying solely on what participants told me about this during college, in the follow-up interviews I asked them to revisit how their friends were involved academically and how important this involvement was for them. When I asked Alberto about this in the follow-up interview, he agreed that his friends were very involved academically and that this helped him academically. Other tight-knitters stated this more emphatically, including Sean, who commented, "I would not have graduated MU if it wasn't for them [my friends]. I just wouldn't have. In order to survive, I realized the importance of surrounding yourself with other people." The academic benefits of tight-knitters' friends is also affirmed in the survey results. When I asked about the "importance of friends for academic life," 38 percent of tight-knitters said that friends were very important, compared with 17 percent of compartmentalizers and zero samplers (see table 6.1). Friends played the biggest academic role for tight-knitters and the smallest academic role for samplers.

Alberto also clarified that the most important thing that his college friends did for each other academically was provide "support." While they helped each other instrumentally, the academic emotional support was most important to him. Alberto explained how it was helpful, "in times of high stress like midterms and finals, being able to call up some of these friends to just kind of get my mind off of things." He also remembered his friends encouraging him with words and by their actions. For example: "There were times when a friend might not have had much of anything to do but may have stayed up in the library with me till four or five in the morning just doing nothing but just kind of hanging out with me so I didn't fall asleep or not be as productive." Although this type of help may seem trivial, it was memorable to Alberto. The friends who provided this type of help during college all remained in his network four years later. Academic emotional help, thus, was memorable, and friends who provided it forged enduring ties with tight-knitters.

Academic multiplex ties (i.e., the friends who provided multiple forms of academic assistance: academic emotional support, instrumental help, and intellectual engagement) not only were associated with academic success during college but were also more likely to remain friendship ties after graduation. Nearly all the friends whom Alberto kept were those who were academic multiplex ties in college; this characterizes six of the seven

Table 6.3   Selected characteristics of higher-achieving and lower-achieving tight-knitters'
after-college networks

|  | MU Friends in 2009 (%) | Same Friends over Time (%) | Total Participants |
|---|---|---|---|
| Higher-achieving tight-knitters | 61 | 40 | 4 |
| Lower-achieving tight-knitters | 43 | 24 | 6 |

friends appearing on both his friendship lists. This shows the lasting importance of academic multiplex ties. Examining differences among tight-knitters further confirms these patterns and their meaning. As discussed in chapter 3, higher-achieving tight-knitters, like Alberto, were more likely than lower-achieving tight-knitters to have academic multiplex ties. Dense networks were academically powerful when they contained academic multiplex ties. Friendships were also more likely to last when they were based on academic multiplex ties. This is apparent for individual friendships. It is also shown in table 6.3: higher-achieving tight-knitters keep more friends over time and have more MU friends in their after-college networks than do lower-achieving tight-knitters. This is another way to show the lasting value of academic friendships.

Lower-achieving tight-knitters were the least likely to graduate among any of the network types in my sample. Over 90 percent of samplers and compartmentalizers graduated, and all the higher-achieving tight-knitters graduated, whereas fewer than half of the lower-achieving tight-knitters did so. Certainly, the background of these students played a role in terms of the lower graduation rates in general for black students, lower-class students, and first-generation students (Baker and Vélez 1996). I argue, however, that networks mediated this effect. Students from more disadvantaged backgrounds reported more struggles with paying for college. Their friendship networks spent time trying to help each other cope with these financial problems, which meant less time spent studying. For example, Mya described how "[a] lot of my friends encouraged each other to try your best, but we all had financial problems as well as just trying to study and just trying to make sure we graduated." Mya did not graduate. Students from more disadvantaged backgrounds are often less academically prepared, and homophily processes tend to bring them together into friendship groups. As discussed in chapter 3, some lower-achieving tight-knitters were in networks where their friends lacked the skills and knowledge to help one another. In these cases, tight-knit networks did not have the resources to pull students up academically. While these networks may have provided social support for students during the college years and beyond, they provided little academic help. In sum, friendship networks are not the only factor that led to lower-achieving tight-knitters' low GPAs and low graduation rates, but they seem to play a role. At the least, they did not provide the academic help found in the networks of higher-achieving tight-knitters.

In sum, Alberto's tight-knit network supported him academically and socially during college. It also supported him after graduation. Many of the specific people in his network changed, but it retained its tight-knit structure and provided many of the same benefits for him. The cohesive ties tight-knitters crafted during college generally resulted in less change in their networks, more MU friends after college, and a higher degree of social support than the other network types provided.

## Mary's Friendships after College: Compartmentalizers

When I caught up with Mary (the middle-class white woman with a compartmentalized network whom I discussed in chapter 4) in 2009, she was living in a nearby state and starting her third year in a physical therapy PhD program. Mary described her biggest change during this five-year period as geographic. For her, the four-hour distance to her graduate school, both from her home and from MU, was an enormous change.

During college, Mary struggled to describe what made someone a friend, explaining that the friends she made at MU were people who seemed "really friendly" and with whom she "got along." In the follow-up interview, she described a friend as "[s]omeone I can rely on, someone that I have a lot in common with, someone that I know I would have kind of like a deep relationship with someone that would be around for a long time." Rather than a definition based on friendliness, friendship now meant common experiences and goals and depth of their relationship. Similar to the changes described by Krystal at the beginning of this chapter, Mary's definition of friendship had clearly matured. Mary also discussed having less time for friends but being closer with her friends now than she had been at MU.

Mary's network structure had changed even less over time than Alberto's. After college, Mary remained a compartmentalizer. Her network had a density of 40 percent, meaning that slightly fewer than half her friends knew each other (her density during college was 59%).[19] Figure 6.2 shows three clear clusters of friends with few connections between them. During college her clusters were friends from home and friends at MU; after college the two largest clusters were friends from home (on the left-hand side of fig. 6.2) and friends from graduate school (on the right-hand side), with a small cluster of friends from MU (at the bottom). Mary maintained different types of communication with different clusters. With Mary's graduate school friends, it was face-to-face, when they saw each other in classes and intramural sports; with her MU friends, it was through Facebook; her friends from home were a mix: some she primarily contacted through phone calls or saw face-to-face, and others primarily through Facebook. As during college, compartmentalizers tend to engage in different activities with their different groups of friends. Their clusters are also organized around different activities, or "foci" (Feld 1981). For example, Mary's three clusters are friends from home, MU, and graduate school. Others are not centered on school; Jason's network, for example, has two clusters: a group of friends from work and another composed of family members and neighbors.

Compartmentalizers kept fewer friends from MU and fewer friends over time than tight-knitters. Mary, however, kept more friends over time than was typical for compartmentalizers.[20] Among the 20 friends she named, nine had attended MU (interestingly, most of them were also friends from home), and seven were her friends during my first interview with her. Like Alberto, the race and gender composition of Mary's network remained fairly similar over time, with around 90 percent same-race friends and same-gender friends both during and after college. While there were some changes in her friendships, Mary's experience was largely one of similarities over time.

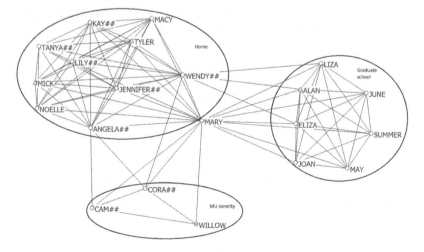

6.2. Mary's friendship network after college

Like most compartmentalizers, Mary's organizational involvement during college was apparent in her after-college network. During college, Mary discussed how her sorority helped her feel as if she belonged at MU. She found her friends through her sorority, similar to other compartmentalizers whose clusters centered on organizations. After college, she noticed that she had become closer with friends she had prior to MU and kept in touch with only three women from her sorority, despite that being her main source of support during college. In my follow-up survey, she wrote:

> Looking back I'm surprised on some friends I've kept from college and others who have faded away. I could not have guessed those who I would be closest with now when I was still in college. It's been hard moving to a city far away from anyone I was close with in college, and considering most of those friends are in the same cities, I feel I've lost touch more than others. At the same time I've grown closer to friends I've had since elementary or high school, and I feel those are the people I will always be in touch with and closest to.

While four hours did not seem far to move for Alberto, who maintained his tight-knit network over that distance, it seemed enormous to Mary. She kept only three friends from her sorority, citing the four-hour distance as the main barrier to their continued connection. With other clusters of friends to rely on, Mary did not have as much incentive to maintain the ties. For Alberto, losing his tight-knit ties would mean losing his friendship group.

In college, Mary's primary organizational commitment was her sorority. After college, it was a Bible study group and intramural sports at her graduate school. She characterized both as social organizations. Her Bible study group "helped me branch out and meet new people" since moving to a new city. She described intramural sports as "stress relief [and] fun," explaining that "we get carried away with school. And we use that as kind of an outlet. To make us do something else besides study. We get to that point where we just get bogged down." Rather than describing friends in general as a break from academics, as discussed in chapter 2, Mary characterized her interactions with friends in sports as this break from academics, which provided important "stress relief" from academic pressure. Participants who were not in graduate school described friends as "stress relief" from work or family obligations, suggesting that this strategy of integrating friends applies in more than just the college context.

As an undergraduate, Mary said that emotional support from a group of close friends was the main way her friends were involved academically. It was other peers who generally provided instrumental help, such as studying together or sharing notes. Her after-college reflections confirmed these observations. She reflected that "overall, my closest friends probably were not that important [academically]." Her friends were "more of a social thing" and "not focused on academics quite as much." She did not have any academic multiplex ties in college, so the friends she kept were not related to whether they provided multiple forms of academic assistance. Even in graduate school, she failed to form academic multiplex ties. The types of academic involvement among her friends still seemed segmented.

Compartmentalizers who had academic multiplex ties during college, however, found these relationships supportive during college and likely to last. For example, after college, Liz, who had academic multiplex ties with a cluster of friends during college, reflected on these ties: "I would still say they were important definitely because it was a support group. We got through it together. Yeah, they definitely were important. I couldn't have made it through college without them." After college, she remained friends with these four people and described them as "dependable" and "someone who I can count on." Such reflections suggest that not all clusters of friends during college were equally likely to remain in students' networks after college or to be important ties. Academic multiplex ties and those who provided emotional support during college were most long lasting and important to young adults.

In sum, like most compartmentalizers, Mary had a compartmentalized network both during and after college. Although the clusters changed, Mary still found support in multiple friendship groups. Her graduate school friends supported her academically, and her other clusters were exclusively social in focus. Mary did not keep as many friends or as many MU friends over time as Alberto. Losing friends was not as consequential for Mary, whose compartmentalized network gave her other groups to fall back on, as for tight-knitters (like Alberto) who had one group providing all the support.

## Martin's Friendships after College: Samplers

During my follow-up interview with Martin (the lower-class black man who sampled friendships and had a loosely connected network that I discussed in chapter 5), he was attending law school. Martin was pleased with this decision, despite the fact that this career path was very different from what he predicted during college: "I want to do hard-hitting journalism,

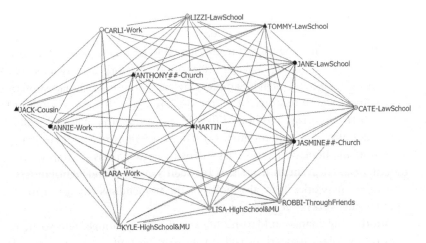

6.3. Martin's friendship network after college

expose scandals, and be a watchdog for the state" or "producing platinum albums and writing lots of music, winning Grammy's and getting lots and lots of money." After graduating from MU, he moved to four different states, each time for a job or graduate school. He picked up a couple of friends in each of these moves, similar to the strategy he used during MU of sampling friends from various parts of campus. This variety can be seen in figure 6.3, as the labels after his friends' names indicate where they met.

Martin's network changed drastically after college in terms of structure and content. In 2009, he named 13 friends, only two (15%) of whom were on his first list and another two (15%) of whom attended MU. His density was 77 percent, which would place him as a tight-knitter. His new network contained more than twice as many ties among his friends as his network during college, when his density was 32 percent. Figure 6.3 shows that the structure of his network resembles that of the tight-knitters discussed in chapter 3: he was surrounded by one cohesive group of friends.

Like Martin's, samplers' networks changed over time. While samplers' average density during college was 24 percent, meaning that one-fourth of their friends knew each other, their average density after college was 50 percent, meaning that half their friends knew each other. Only four of the samplers completed the density portion of the follow-up interviews, so my findings are more tentative for this group. Nonetheless, three of the four show a consistent pattern of one tight-knit group. Two also include some additional disconnected friends or smaller clusters. For example, Steve's and Lisa's networks look quite similar to Alberto's, having one large tight-knit group with a few pairs of friends and disconnected friends. Jocelyn was the only sampler who maintained the loosely connected sampler structure, collecting friends from many different settings with few ties between them. Samplers' average after-college network density was the same as tight-knitters' (50%). Samplers and tight-knitters also had similar betweenness centrality scores (0.26 and 0.25, respectively) and modularity scores (0.11 and 0.16), and both differed from compartmentalizers' scores (0.32 centrality and 0.21 modularity). The similarities in visual structure as well as mathematical properties—density, betweenness centrality, and modularity—all point to likenesses between samplers' and tight-knitters' postcollege networks. They also point to the tremendous change in most samplers' networks over time.

Another big change in Martin's life was that he no longer felt isolated. Martin's tight-knit network provided him with support for the race-based isolation that he still experienced. For example, he brought up how "a black man is something I will never be able to escape. I have no choice. I have no choice but to be that. . . . For example, being black is the first thing everybody sees. They see that before I open my mouth." He discussed such experiences with groups of his friends. During the interview, he described developing new friends, more friends, and more supportive friendships after college. Martin blamed the size of MU for making it hard to connect with others. His experiences, however, suggest that it was less the sheer size of the school that mattered than the lack of opportunities for regular contact with the same students. At law school, where there were 250 students in his class (vs. 7,000 at MU), it was easier to connect with other students: "You sit around every day together; . . . you're going to socialize with those people as well [as take classes together]. I mean, whether you intend to or not." It was not, however, just his friends from law school who he felt supported him. Martin also received support from his network as a whole.

Not only his network type but how he defined friendship changed over time. During college, Martin offered an unclear description of what made someone a friend. He directly acknowledged this during the interview: "Sometimes I have trouble with defining exactly what a friend is because there are two or three people that I talk to regularly about myself but then with everybody else I know we're usually talking about them or about something else." After college, he crisply distinguished levels of friends. He explained what separated the 13 friends he named from the "numerous others" whom he would consider less close friends: "If I called and said, 'Hey, can you help me with something?' or 'Hey, I'm coming to visit, will you be in town?' They'll say, 'Yes.' And they'll be happy to see me." In the later interview, Martin also discussed the challenges that the label "friend" posed, commenting that most people do not explicitly and reciprocally name their friends. He remarked, "Those you consider a friend may not consider you one, and vice versa." He continued: "People's definition of 'friend' can vary from person to person as well. Like some people think they know who you are. And they talk to you on occasion and call you a friend. But you'll never be their best friend. Some people have actual best friends, and they're just acquaintances to everybody else." As this quotation makes clear, Martin was quite reflective about what makes someone a friend for him and in acknowledging that his definition was not shared among his peers. He spoke about graduation and geographic changes as tests for his friendships,[21] specifically stating that his friendships have changed substantially since the first interview and predicting that they "will change again in five years. I think as you go, you acquire your friends through different things." His serious and reflective perspective on friendship was also shown in a question he posed during the follow-up interview: "Have you ever considered that by asking these questions and forcing people to revisit, not so dark but dusty, corners of their own lives, that you might actually be helping people rekindle old friendships?" It is possible that some of the changes in samplers' networks over time came from a maturing of their views of friendship during this five-year period.

During college, Martin experienced academics as all on himself. He agreed with this description in his after-college interview, responding to the question about how important his friends were to him academically by answering, "Almost zero." He elaborated, "I tended to study alone. It was no fault of theirs but mostly the fault was mine." Although his friends did not help him, they also did not impede him academically. He explained, "My feeling about that is they only get in the way if you let them. . . . You can control that." As typical for samplers during college, Martin approached academics independently, with friends neither helping nor hindering his academic success.

Similar to how the support that tight-knitters felt during college came through even more strongly when I spoke with them after college, samplers' isolation during college became more apparent over time. For example, when we talked after college, Jocelyn told me: "I was miserable in college. In the dorms it was very much like high school. And after the dorms I really didn't have very many friends here. [MU was] socially disappointing." Like other samplers, Jocelyn did not believe that her friends provided academic emotional support during college, whereas 63 percent of tight-knitters and 44 percent of compartmentalizers said that their friends supplied such support in college. Although the number of samplers is small (four participants in follow-up interviews), it is striking that all the samplers described their friends as not important academically, and none described their friends as providing emotional support. This highlights their academic isolation even more starkly than my discussion in chapter 5, which was based on my perceptions of them during college. Perhaps because of this isolation during college, samplers saw more changes in their friends over time than did tight-knitters.

Unlike most young adults, Martin's network became less diverse as far as race and gender. In some ways, this is not surprising since he had 50 percent same-race and 50 percent same-gender friends during college (in other words, his friendships could hardly become more diverse). After college, he had 82 percent black friends and 31 percent men friends. He was also atypical among young adults in having only 15 percent MU friends in his network (vs. 39% overall).

Samplers' romantic relationships also differed from those of tight-knitters and compartmentalizers. During college, only one of the 12 samplers was in a romantic relationship, compared with 40–50 percent of the other network types. After college, none of the samplers were cohabiting, engaged, or married, and only one sampler was in a committed relationship, compared with 70 percent among my other respondents. The friendship network of the one sampler who was in a committed relationship did not significantly differ either after college or in its changes over time from those of the other samplers.

In sum, like other samplers, Martin's network changed considerably and these changes tended to be positive for him. Martin went from being academically successful but socially isolated in college to thriving academically and socially after leaving MU. He continued to craft a network by sampling friends from multiple locations and contexts; however, rather than keeping these friends separate from one another, he now had a closely connected network in which most of his friends knew each other. Surrounded by this cohesive network, Martin found social support.

## Conclusion

In sum, this chapter shows that the friendships students developed in college had an impact on their lives after graduation. Relationships among students' friends during college shaped many features of their postcollege friendships, including their structure, the proportion of MU friends in their network, and the probability that they would remain friends. This chapter also shows that there was less variation in after-college networks than in those during college. During college, I found three network types. After college, samplers' networks changed the most, and compartmentalized networks remained common, particularly for students with compartmentalized networks during college. However, samplers and tight-knitters converged into one network type, which closely resembled the tight-knit networks found during college, but added some friends who were less closely connected to the main group within the network. These networks differed from those of compartmentalizers, who even as young adults tended to have two to four clusters of friends that were more balanced in size. These findings contrast with those of the only other study I could find assessing density changes over time, which concluded that network density declines over time and that dense networks are rare (Wellman et al. 1997). I propose that differences in network structure as well as point in the life course might account for this discrepancy between findings. Perhaps a compartmentalized or a tight-knit structure is more common following college, when young adults are focused on their careers.[22] Future research could assess the extent to which these network types match those of students at other colleges and of individuals at other points in the life course.

In terms of content—that is, the support and academic involvement, or lack thereof, within these networks—samplers also experienced the largest change. While students in all network types experienced some loneliness in college, samplers' friendships did not craft a sense of belonging. Samplers' college networks left them feeling isolated. In contrast, after college most samplers had networks that provided meaningful social support. These changes over time suggest that the college setting rather than some constant personality trait or friendship preference distinguishes samplers from the other network types.[23] In terms of friends' academic involvement during college, students' after-college reflections confirm two patterns. First, tight-knit networks provided more academic emotional support than other network types. This support was mentioned more frequently by tight-knitters than by compartmentalizers or samplers. Second, academic multiplex ties—that is, relationships providing multiple forms of academic assistance: emotional support, instrumental help, and intellectual engagement—were important relationships. Across network types, academic multiplex ties were more likely to remain in students' networks than ties that did not provide multiple types of academic help. They were most common among higher-achieving tight-knitters. Not only do such relationships help students academically and socially during college, but they also are relationships that last.

In terms of composition, there was substantial change in specific friends but not much change in the racial and gender composition of friendship networks. Young adults experienced much change in who their friends were, keeping only one-fourth of their friends over this five-year period, even when the structure of their network (as was the case for compartmentalizers and many tight-knitters) remained similar. Young adults also had fewer MU friends in their networks after college. These changes were less drastic for tight-knitters than for compartmentalizers and samplers. There was much less change, however, in the racial and gender composition of friendship networks. The racial and gender makeup of their networks remained stable for most young adults as they transitioned to life after college.

Network type, however, had little impact on whether networks became more diverse over time with respect to friends' race and gender. In contrast, I find that friendship diversity during college is strongly related to friendship diversity after college. This finding also fits research showing that more general social attitudes are formed during college and remain stable for 25 years (Newcomb 1967) and even 50 years after college (Alwin, Cohen, and Newcomb 1991). Also confirming the importance of diverse interactions during college are a few students who discussed seeking out or particularly enjoying diverse work environments because of the diverse friendships they had during college. For example, Jasmine said that she chose "the company I work for because it wasn't just all white and I'm the only black person or all black and I feel like I got to change my ways." In contrast to research on the link between diverse interactions prior to college and during college, which is mixed (e.g., cf. M. Fischer 2008 and Harper and Yeung 2013 with Hall, Cabrera, and Milem 2011), the small body of research on the transition after college shows that patterns from college are more lasting.

As discussed in previous chapters, college context likely affects students' friendships. This can be seen through the importance of student organizations, particularly sororities and fraternities, and dorms, particularly first-year dorms, in remaining influential in shaping clusters or pairs of friends in young adults' after-college networks. Structural diversity also seems to matter. It seems likely that a campus environment that is more racially diverse would promote more racially diverse student friendships both during and after college. Future research with friendship data over time at multiple institutions could test this hypothesis. This research could pay special attention to schools with particularly high and low levels of diversity. James Moody's (2001, 699) research, which looks at middle school and high school students' five closest friends of each gender at the school, finds that "in schools with low heterogeneity race is simply not salient, while the salience of race appears to level off (and even drop slightly) at the highest levels of racial heterogeneity." Mary Fischer (2008) found a similar relationship among colleges: in schools with less racial diversity, students have fewer cross-race friendships. My findings point to the lasting effects of structural diversity on friendship diversity, providing more support for the long-term benefits of increasing racial diversity on campus.

These findings about network structure, content, and composition offer some suggestions for students, their parents, administrators, and faculty. First, steps should be taken to make the campus environment more supportive for all students, particularly for samplers, who lack a social support system in college. Samplers' experiences of social and academic isolation that were not eased by their friendships during college show that not all friends come with social support or academic benefits. The range of connections samplers had in their networks indicates that they were not alone; however, they typically felt alone because these connections were not supportive. The supportive networks that they crafted after college show that their college networks did not doom them to being lonely. Their postcollege experiences point to unfulfilled opportunities to connect them with others at MU. After college, samplers shifted to recognize rather than distance themselves from the potential power of friends for academic and social support. Perhaps this shift could happen earlier in a college culture that more strongly values relationships. This view has recently received backing through the research of Daniel Chambliss and Christopher Takacs (2014, 5, emphasis in original), who conclude: "The *people* (friends, acquaintances, teachers, staff) whom a student encounters matter more than the *programs*." My research adds to their findings by showing how specific types of people—friends—and the connections between them help students thrive in college. Colleges promote supportive friendship networks by bringing people together where they can form these meaningful relationships. As Chambliss and Takacs (2014, 161) note, the solution is not just to create more programs but to design programs, dorms, and other aspects of college to help "motivated students meet each other." Hosting discussions or dinners, for example, around interests shared by a group of students could help them craft meaningful bonds that would become supportive networks.

Second, my finding that academic multiplex ties are more likely to offer the most support and to last offers additional evidence for the importance of students' engagement of friends in academic life in multiple ways.

These ties can be formed when students themselves value them and seek to involve their friends in academics in not just one way but more holistically in instrumental, emotional, and intellectual ways. Faculty members can cultivate academic multiplex ties in classrooms; for example, faculty can incorporate group work into their courses and encourage students to study together and work together on homework. Academic multiplex ties can also be fostered by administrators through their support for academic clubs and attractive study spaces where ties can be developed and nurtured.

Third, my finding that friendship diversity during college is associated with friendship diversity after college provides additional evidence for those who believe that colleges have a role in cultivating students' openness to diverse perspectives. Friendships can have important implications not only for individuals but also for the type of society we wish to be. Research shows the benefits of diverse interactions and connections for individuals and society (Gurin 1999; Gurin et al. 2002; Hurtado 2007; Locks et al. 2008). For example, in her testimony to the US Supreme Court, Patricia Gurin (1999, 1) describes how "patterns of racial segregation and separation historically rooted in our national life can be broken by diversity experiences in higher education." To increase friendship diversity, faculty can set up group work that brings students together across differences (including race, gender, and social class), and administrators can set up roommates and floor mates in on-campus housing to increase interaction across differences. Both these suggestions are on the level of interactional diversity. Structural diversity also matters. My findings, coupled with research showing that students have fewer cross-race friendships when the campus has less racial diversity (M. Fischer 2008), suggest that increasing racial diversity on campus would likely lead to more racially diverse friendships during and after college. I expand on these suggestions in the next chapter.

multi-plex =
    multiple social context ties.

# SEVEN

# Conclusion

At the end of my interviews with students during college, I asked what advice they would give a first-year student who wanted to be successful at MU. Although we already had been talking for nearly two hours, students typically became exceptionally animated and serious as they answered this question. They would pause briefly before answering and seemed uncharacteristically mature as they advised this fictitious incoming student. I was also surprised by how closely their advice fit with that of numerous student affairs professionals and education researchers (e.g., Chambliss and Takacs 2014; Chickering and Reisser 1993; Kuh et al. 2005; Tinto 1993, 2012). It also fits with the advice that I offer in this book.

The most frequent advice, mentioned by over three-quarters of participants, was to "get involved." Students' suggestions included the following: "definitely get involved [in] any way, shape, or form" (*Molly*), "find something you like and get involved almost immediately" (*Lisa*), "try to get involved in different organizations, really try to get out there and meet people" (*Carlos*), and "get involved with a couple different things, [but] not too many" (*Michelle*). Most other suggestions dealt with balance, specifically how to have fun but also stay on top of schoolwork; for example, Logan advised, "get your work done during the day and party at night, for sure," and Martin suggested, "know when to shut your door and know when to walk out of it." Their advice echoes many of the findings in this book. It shows how important students felt it was to find their place on campus. It also shows the role of campus organizations in helping students find their place. And, most importantly, it shows that friends can both help students succeed in college and get in their way.

In this book, I demonstrate for the first time how university students form different types of friendship networks and use them in different ways to manage their academic and social lives—ways that affect their lives after graduation. I find that most students, men and women, spent a good deal of time with friends and defined friendship as based on trust, closeness, and similar interests. On average, three-fourths of students' friends were same-race and two-thirds were same-gender, yet some students had quite diverse networks. Most students also discussed pursuing balance between academic and social life in college. They provided cautionary tales of others who were imbalanced, and they discussed ways that their friends helped them achieve balance and the possibility that friends would distract them academically. Nearly all students integrated their friends into their academic lives and kept them separate at times.

I identify three network types: tight-knitters, who have one densely woven friendship group; compartmentalizers, who have two to four clusters of friends and move effortlessly between these groups; and samplers, who make individual friendships in a variety of places, with the result that their friends are less connected to one another. As summarized in table I.1, these network types are associated with different academic and social experiences during and after college.

Tight-knitters reported tremendous social support from their networks. Academically, tight-knit networks were also powerful, but they could either pull students toward school or distract them from it. Friendships in tight-knit networks were also more likely to last throughout the five-year period of my study than were those in the other network types. This was particularly true for friends who provided academic emotional support and those who were academic multiplex ties.

Compartmentalizers, on the other hand, received more moderate levels of support for academic and social life from their friendship networks. Compartmentalizers from more privileged backgrounds who experienced more ease in the college environment were able to balance academic and social life *either* by segmenting academic involvement in their multiple clusters of friends or by having at least one academic multiplex tie. Compartmentalizers who were students of color or from lower-class backgrounds, however, found more academic and social success with *both* segmented academic involvement and academic multiplex ties.

While many tight-knitters and compartmentalizers found that their friends helped them thrive in college academically and socially, samplers achieved academic success independently. Importantly, samplers' friends did not distract them from academics. They did not help either. Samplers' friends also did not provide much social support to help them thrive on campus. After college, however, most samplers found social support in more tightly connected networks. Compared with tight-knitters and compartmentalizers, samplers experienced the most change in their networks over time.

By mapping students' networks and taking seriously students' accounts of their experiences, I find that friendship and its benefits are not the same for all students or all their friends. My focus is not on determining *how much* influence networks have on students' academic and social outcomes compared with other, more traditional explanations, such as family background or prior school experiences, but to show *how* friendships matter academically and socially. Future research using representative samples could better tease apart whether people's networks are causing these outcomes or mediating them and to what extent people self-segregate into different kinds of networks on the basis of constraints versus agency. This book is a first step toward documenting the ways college friendship networks matter academically and socially, as well as how they might matter differently for different groups.

In the previous chapters, I made suggestions related to specific findings, including for each network type. Administrators, policymakers, and faculty, however, will likely not know the network type of particular students. Even if they did, the most practical solutions have the potential to improve the experiences of students regardless of network type rather than targeting one network type. In this chapter, I offer suggestions aimed to help all students thrive academically and socially. I also discuss the theoretical implications of my findings with the goal of improving research and students' experiences.

## Practical Implications for Colleges

Since academic life and social life are connected in many ways, perhaps the most important thing colleges can do is to show they support students' social ties as well as their academic success. One way to do this is to encourage multiple communities on campus where students can "get involved," to use the language of many of my respondents. If college administrators follow best practices, which encourage "multiple and varied initiatives" (Milem, Chang, and antonio 2005, 19), students with a variety of interests should be able to find a "home" or niche in some area of campus. The goal is not just to create more organizations. After all, MU had over four hundred organizations on campus, and the students I met were involved in many of them. Yet some failed to find a place where they felt supported. Three factors seem particularly important in deciding in which communities to invest resources: (1) members should have regular contact with each other, (2) members should engage in a collaborative project together, and (3) a strong status hierarchy between communities should be avoided.

### Regular Contact through Shared Physical Space

Groups whose members come in regular contact with each other facilitate a greater sense of community (Chickering and Reisser 1993). This contact can be achieved in many ways, such as formal meetings, social events, study groups, and living together. Regular contact is easily facilitated by residence halls since students enter this space daily. However, as discussed by Daniel Chambliss and Christopher Takacs (2014), some residence hall designs foster more interaction than others and these may not be the designs most desired by students. Shared bathrooms, common lounges that are useful, and common eating areas bring people in close contact with each other. Residential sororities and fraternities typically have many of these features, which may be one reason that they create a strong sense of community among members. Nonresidential organizations can encourage this as well by holding regular functions, including meetings, social events, and academic activities.

Space is an important consideration here. Its importance can be seen in the contrast between two academic programs for underrepresented students at MU. Team Up helped many tight-knitters find friends, and students consistently told me stories of how this program helped bring them to college and keep them in college through its financial, academic, and social resources. The Team Up office had a large physical space in a central location on campus, and students told me how they would go there between classes to use the informal study space, to hold meetings, and to meet up with friends. Successful Scholars was a similar program but received more mixed reviews from students, who generally found it more helpful for the financial resources that it offered than for academic help and assistance in meeting others on campus. The physical space devoted to Successful Scholars was limited, consisting of offices for the staff but no space for studying or socializing. Martin explained how lack of access to space for socializing made it hard for students to connect with others:

> I've been here for four years. I don't know any of these people [other members of Successful Scholars]. . . . I go in there and visit the [Successful Scholars] office every now and then, but there's no space there for anybody to just sit [and] get to know [another member]. . . . You know when you walk

in a library and see somebody reading a book that you're familiar with and you bolden yourself up to stop and ask them a question. That sort of thing doesn't happen for the Successful Scholars program because there's no space for it to happen. I mean we're all forced to sit in a class, but we all hate it, do projects we all thought were stupid, and then after that we're so glad to be released, we kind of just don't give it a second thought anymore.

Martin noted that the class required of Successful Scholars brought people physically together but did not permit them to get to know each other—a point that ties to my second recommendation for communities on campus.

My findings confirm the importance of "safe havens," such as cultural centers for racial minority students (Jones, Castellanos, and Cole 2002), by showing that friendships formed at these sites provided important social support, but the academic consequences of these friendships were more ancillary and thus less consistent. Efforts to improve students' campus experiences should focus not on dismantling safe havens, as some critics have suggested (see Hefner 2002), but on helping friends who meet through these organizations to provide each other with academic help and support, in addition to the social support they already offer.

One trend that puts all three of my recommendations into practice is the current interest in learning communities, freshman interest groups, and living-learning centers (LLCs). There are many different models, but what they share is students living together and taking at least one class together. As Arthur Chickering and Linda Reisser (1993, 399) put it, "Most of us know from experiences with out-of-town workshops, retreats, or excursions that staying together in a communal setting fosters a unique kind of bonding." Although not focused on friendship, research shows that students in LLCs have greater academic and social involvement, greater interaction with peers and faculty, and greater academic gains than students in traditional residence halls (Pike 1999), and researchers refer to LLCs as providing "a ready-made friendship support group" (Grigsby 2009, 68). Students frequently join LLCs in their first year of college, which is when students start cultivating the friendship networks that sustain them throughout college. Therefore, it stands to reason that LLCs greatly influence the networks students form. Because I found students in LLCs exhibiting each of the three network types, there is no reason to believe that LLCs would necessarily lead to one type of network. Future research using a representative sample could better assess these patterns. Nonetheless, LLCs have the potential to craft communities that support students' academic and social success.

Dartmouth College, where I currently teach, recently announced a new design for student housing. Modeled after the house system at other campuses, including Harvard University and the University of Chicago, first-year students will be randomly assigned to one of six housing clusters on campus, each with a faculty adviser living there. The academic calendar at Dartmouth is sufficiently flexible to enable students to study abroad and complete internships during any of the four quarters, but one consequence is that students presently shuffle from dorm to dorm throughout their four years. Dartmouth administrators hope that this new residential design will improve the sense of community on campus. While students will not necessarily take classes with others in their clusters, it seems likely that their shared physical space over the four years will make it easier for students to regularly connect with each other and to academically and socially thrive in college.

### Collaborative Projects

Collaborative projects bring people together into communities. These projects go beyond requiring people to share the same physical space and require them to work on something that is of interest to them—for example, a social or cultural event, a community service opportunity, or a research report. In describing the "optimum development" of communities, Chickering and Reisser (1993, 398) point to the importance of offering "opportunities for collaboration and shared interests, for engaging in meaningful activities and facing common problems together." This means not just giving students a task to do together but empowering them to work on something together. These opportunities can be transformative, as in the "validating experiences" described by Patrick Terenzini and colleagues (1994). Students themselves often see what is missing from their college experience: for example, Martin saw the lack of physical space for social bonding in Successful Scholars, and Alberto saw the unmet needs of Latino men and worked for two years to found a chapter of a Latino fraternity. Martin's observation was not transformed into a collaborative project, whereas Alberto's efforts created both his tight-knit, supportive network and institutional change. While students can initiate and craft collaborative projects that support their social and academic success on campus, they cannot do it all on their own. The college can promote their success by providing them with recognition, encouragement, and resources, such as physical space.

### Multiple Campus Communities and Greek Life

Ideally, campuses would have multiple communities equally valued in the student culture. Many campuses with a strong Greek life, such as MU, have a dominant pathway where joining a sorority or fraternity is seen as attaining a higher status. This is evident in the large midwestern campuses studied by Mary Grigsby (2009), Jenny Stuber (2011), and Elizabeth Armstrong and Laura Hamilton (2013) and in the small liberal arts college studied by Stuber (2011). Similar to students on other campuses, MU students perceived a hierarchy, with historically white sororities and fraternities above minority sororities and fraternities and other organizations, and a hierarchy within historically white organizations. In this way, MU's status hierarchy more closely resembles that found in elementary school (Adler and Adler 1998) and middle school (Eder, Evans, and Parker 1995), where there is often one vertical status hierarchy, with "popular" students on top, than that found in high school, where subcultures proliferate horizontally and offer students more options to fit in (Milner 2006). Campuses without strong Greek life, such as Hamilton College, a liberal arts college in New York, seem to be better at providing multiple alternatives for students (Chambliss and Takacs 2014). It is not that Greek life cannot be one of these options or that all options need to be equal but that there should be several options; for example, when student activities at Hamilton College are mapped into core and periphery, some Greek organizations, majors, student organizations, and sports teams appear in the core and some appear in the periphery (Chambliss and Takacs 2014). Certainly, students enter college with preferences for particular types of activities (Armstrong and Hamilton 2013; Stuber 2011). Students, however, often do not hear about many of the options that are available. I agree with Stuber (2011) that spreading the word about the many organizations that exist on campus would be a low-cost and relatively easy intervention for institutions. Campuses could harness technological advances to do this electronically and to capitalize on the excitement of students who are involved in these organizations to highlight these options.

While some researchers, faculty, and students have advocated getting rid of the Greek system, I stop short of that here because of the sense of belonging it can provide students. At Dartmouth College, faculty overwhelmingly voted to phase out the Greek system in November 2014, and the student paper published a front-page headline, "Abolish the Greek System," supported by the editorial board, during homecoming weekend

2014, when many alumni were in town. Such arguments are supported by research showing higher rates of sexual assault and alcohol abuse among members (Armstrong, Hamilton, and Sweeney 2006), less openness to diversity among white members (Pascarella et al. 1996), and lower academic outcomes for members (Arum and Roksa 2011; Astin 1993; Blimling 1989; Charles et al. 2009; Pascarella, Edison, and Whitt 1996; Pike and Askew 1990; Pike 2003). Research on Greek life, however, is not all negative. Some studies, for example, find no effect of membership on academics (Hernandez et al. 1999; Pike 2000) but do find that membership increases the sense of community and social integration with the campus (Lounsbury and DeNeui 1995; Pike and Askew 1990). Specific chapters, particularly those that are part of historically black and multicultural organizations, can be positive forces on campuses, actively working to lessen racial divisions on campus, engaging in community service, and developing personal and professional skills (Berkowitz and Padavic 1999; McCabe 2011; Torbenson and Parks 2009). Researchers and journalists recognize the potential of strengthening other options, such as allocating resources to minority Greek organizations and the residential college system, as one way to reform the Greek system (Armstrong and Hamilton 2013; Robbins 2004). And this ended up being the approach taken by the administration at Dartmouth College, rather than eliminating sororities and fraternities as suggested by the faculty and by the student paper. Hopefully, bolstering these other options will draw on the regular contact occurring through Greek organizations to build a more inclusive and supportive campus community.

### Online Classes

Some of my respondents saw classrooms as a place to meet friends and nurture supportive relationships. This is less likely to happen in online classes, where there is less of a built-in community. Online classes and MOOCs—massive open online courses—have increased over the past decade (I. Allen and Seaman 2013). Best practices for online classes for instructors and students focus on students' engagement with the material and with the professor (Vesely, Bloom, and Sherlock 2007). Rarely are such discussions concerned about the engagement between students, yet alone between friends. Certainly, thoughtful pedagogical practices can be used to connect students with each other, which I will discuss more below in my advice to faculty. As institutions increase online education, particularly through MOOCs, crafting a sense of community between students should not be ignored.

### Roommate Assignments

Colleges should be conscientious in assigning roommates and floor mates in residence halls. Colleges differ in whether they let first-year students choose where they live (either in terms of choosing particular roommates or on the basis of broader interests, as in the LLCs mentioned earlier), assign roommates randomly, or assign roommates on the basis of survey results. MU allowed students to choose their roommates and dorms, matching only those who did not express a preference. Like the research cited by Anna Altman (2014) in a recent *New York Times* article, I find that students remained friends with their first-year roommates and floor mates at a rate greater than chance. However, rarely were these cross-race friendships. On its face, random assignment seems like an ideal way to promote diverse interactions and help students get to know someone new. However, on predominantly white campuses, random roommate matching may help white students feel more comfortable with diversity but would not have the same effects for students of color, who already interact regularly with white students and would miss some of the support they provide each other for race-based experiences. In their study of a university similar to MU, Armstrong and Hamilton (2013, 236) also argue that random matching would not work on "a homogenous campus, as full integration would mean that students of color would be isolated in entirely white living situations." For these reasons, randomly assigning roommates can have great benefits when accompanied by structural diversity but may not always be best, particularly for students of color. At predominantly white institutions like MU, colleges could create community for all students by organizing residence halls around common interests and identities while also promoting a range of campus organizations so students are not isolated if they do not fit into their residential community. Administrators should also be cautious that students' choices do not turn overly social, such as in the "party dorm" studied by Armstrong and Hamilton (2013). With only moderate amounts of structural diversity, campuses could follow the lead of Davidson College, where nearly all students choose random assignment and are carefully matched to a roommate and floor mates with the goal of crafting communities with a mix of common interests and diverse ties.[1] Such careful placement poses greater challenges in cohorts of seven thousand (typical at MU) than in cohorts of five hundred (typical at David-son). My research, however, shows that such decisions are consequential for the friendship networks that students form, which in turn shape their academic and social success.

## Campus Diversity

Increasing diversity on campus would also increase diversity in students' networks during and after college. And if increasing diversity resulted in a better campus climate, it could also change students' network structure, such that there would be fewer samplers and tight-knitters or tight-knit networks would center on other dimensions besides race. Efforts should focus on structural diversity—that is, diverse enrollments or numerical diversity at the institutional level—along with informal interactional diversity and classroom diversity (Gurin et al. 2002). Although the climate is generally better for students of color at campuses with structural diversity (Hurtado and Ruiz 2012), recent news stories have demonstrated that structural diversity is not enough: campuses with more diverse enrollments can remain chilly climates for students of color (DeFrancesco 2014; Vega 2014). Research shows that diverse connections have benefits for individuals and for society, such as the ability to participate in a diverse democracy (Gurin 1999; Gurin et al. 2002; Hurtado 2007), a sense of belonging (Locks et al. 2008), complex thinking, cultural and social awareness, and concern for the public good (Hurtado 2007). Some research shows that white students gain more than students of color from informal interactional diversity in terms of critical thinking skills (Loes, Pascarella, and Umbach 2012) and "postcollege cross-cultural workforce competencies, including pluralistic orientation" (Jayakumar 2008, 631).[2] Both white students and students of color, however, gain from interracial interaction (see review in Hurtado 2007), and evidence on this point has appeared in court cases examining affirmative action (Gurin 1999). For example, white students and students of color who had positive interactions with diverse peers report a greater sense of belonging to their college or university (Locks et al. 2008). Although evidence is mixed on whether diverse interactions in high school lead to diverse interactions in college (e.g., cf. M. Fischer 2008 and Harper and Yeung 2013 with Hall, Cabrera, and Milem 2011), my findings add to a growing body of research showing that patterns in college matter for later friendships (Gurin 1999), thus providing more evidence for the long-term benefits of college diversity.

Given rising college costs and slashed budgets, I focus on ways to strengthen community that are fairly low cost. These suggestions are based on my research at one large, public, predominantly white university and on discussions by other scholars. I speculate about how institutional context matters, but we need much more research attending to the ways that students' experiences might differ at other institutions, including more diverse ones, smaller ones, and commuter campuses.[3]

## Practical Implications for Faculty

My advice for faculty follows the same thread as that for institutions and that offered by students. Faculty should show they support students' social ties and design opportunities for students to get to know each other. Supporting social ties can be as simple as recognizing that students spend much time with their friends and not devaluing this social time. Faculty, particularly those in an advising role, could ask students how their friends help them academically and how their friends might stand in the way of their academic success. Doing so may show students that their professors recognize that social, as well as academic, life is an important part of college. It also may help students to reinforce strategies that are working well for them and to replace those that are potentially harmful. Students may not recognize that they are leaning on friends for emotional support regarding academics, for example, which can be particularly powerful within tight-knit networks.

In the classroom, faculty can support these actions by helping students to get to know each other through meaningful group work. Faculty could increase their use of cooperative and problem-based learning.[4] A meta-analysis of over three hundred studies shows that cooperative learning cultivates academic and social success through increased academic engagement and relationships with other students (Johnson, Johnson, and Smith 1998). Assigning groups should be done deliberately. If students themselves pick the groups, then there is a greater chance of reinforcing existing ties and divisions. Instructors should attempt to construct groups where everyone has something to contribute and make this decision explicit to students.[5] Meaningful group work can be used not only in face-to-face classes but also in the growing number of online classes on college campuses. Community is not impossible in online classes, but it is something that takes concerted work to achieve.

Faculty can also assign and support students in collaborative projects. One of the most transformative educational experiences I had involved a group research project my final year at Tulane University. As a culminating experience in women's studies, my professor had designed a group project in which my classmates and I would investigate women's work in nearby casinos. During our planning meetings, my classmates and I discovered that we all lacked the strong friendships with other women that we expected to find in college, especially as women's studies majors. We wondered how widespread this experience was on campus. Thanks to our professor's flexibility in changing our topic and expanding this one-term class into a two-term class, we were able to explore this alternative project. Not only did we end up with hands-on research experience and a final written report, but we also found the friendships we felt we were lacking.

## Practical Implications for Students

As I mentioned at the beginning of this chapter, students provided thoughtful advice for their peers, particularly in terms of encouraging involvement on campus and balancing academic and social life. I agree that students, regardless of network type, should strive to "get involved" on campus in multiple communities to find a niche or "home." Students should be involved—but not overscheduled. My findings also suggest that the multiple communities students seek should tap into both academic and social aspects, enabling them to balance these competing goals.

More simply, I would encourage students to value friendships. Even the most successful and balanced students claimed that they—at least sometimes—kept their friends separate from academics. The strong claims from students that they separated their friends from academics seemed to be reactions to their awareness that friends can be academic distractions. This is true. Students, however, gained many academic and social benefits from integrating their friends and their academics. Mentors and friends can serve as powerful models for how to do this. Specifically, peers and friends who either shared students' goals, motivations, and behaviors or served as models for these characteristics were incredibly helpful in supporting students' efforts for balance. With such models, students were not left figuring this out through trial and error—"falling on my face flat on the floor," as Sean put it.

When I present this work, student audience members have often come up to me to express the disappointment that they felt in not having one tight-knit friendship group. A single friendship group works well for some students but not for all. As this book makes clear, there is no single friendship type that is best for all students, but students can make their friendships work to their benefit. Students will likely find themselves in at least one of the network types discussed here. Recognizing the type of network they have will enable students to take some steps to make the most of their friendships. Tight-knitters should be particularly conscious of who they surround themselves with, as their friendships have the most power to either pull them up or drag them down academically. Compartmentalizers should check to make sure they are receiving social support and academic help from friends, whether in the same cluster of friends or in different clusters. More clusters are not necessarily better, as managing spending time with all of them can drain the energy students have for academics and other goals. Samplers can work to create a sense of support within their network. They can continue to seek out multiple communities on campus, checking (similar to compartmentalizers) to make sure they are not stretched too thin. Samplers also would do well to recognize that although academics are under their control, they do not need to approach their studies alone. Friends can be valuable sources of help, and they should seek out friends for intellectual discussions and academic help and encouragement.

My final suggestion to students relates to the importance of academic emotional support and academic multiplex ties. These ties helped students to thrive academically and socially in college and were more likely to remain in their networks five years later. These ties also helped students cope with race- and class-based marginality, facilitating a sense of belonging on campus. Students could ask themselves whether they have ties that provide both social support and multiple types of academic support. If not, they might work to actively create a supportive community of friends. This community does not need to be a unified network, like that of tight-knitters, or even a full cluster, like that of compartmentalizers, but having a group of friends who provide social support and a group that provides academic emotional support, intellectual engagement, and instrumental help is advantageous and would reduce their marginalization and isolation. Offering support to others often provides a powerful model for others to return that support. The norm of reciprocity appears in literature and social science throughout history (see review in Gouldner 1960) and in more contemporary social psychological and network studies (e.g., DePaulo and Fisher 1980; Homans 1958), pointing to others' desire to return help that we provide them.

## Practical Implications for Parents

I also want to briefly touch on implications for parents of college students or soon-to-be college students. The most important thing that parents can do is to support their children in both academic life and social life. Students spend much time with their friends, and parents should not devalue this social time, recognizing that time with friends is not always wasted time. Parents could also help students to figure out which network type they fall into and to draw on the strengths and guard against the downsides of that type.

While parents should certainly support their children, they should also guard against providing so much support that students do not turn to their friends. Rather than being "helicopter parents" and helping their children figure out every little thing about college—what courses to take, what clubs to join, whether to become Greek, whether to study abroad, and such (Howe and Strauss 2007)—parents should give their children space to figure these things out for themselves. Perhaps this will encourage students to turn to classmates, roommates, and dorm mates for advice, thereby cultivating more friendships. This may be particularly true for samplers, who seemed most dependent on their parents for academic advice and support.

## Theoretical Implications

Researchers need to pay more attention to friendship because there is much we do not know. Many gaps exist in our understanding of this topic within sociological research generally as well as within research specifically on higher education. Education researchers consistently find that social and academic integration are important in college, yet rarely do they focus on friends as distinct from peers and investigate *both* their benefits and their costs. Even in network research, many questions remain about friendships generally and specifically how they function for college students and young adults.

### Network Analysis

Most broadly, my findings speak to sociological theories of how people are connected to each other, responding to calls for more research on relationality and relationships in sociology (Emirbayer 1997). In answering this call, I found some surprises. By combining rich data on students' experiences with network measures, I discovered that density is not just a scale from low to high but a typology with three distinct types. Network researchers frequently use density, betweenness centrality, and modularity to assess network structure, but rarely do researchers have qualitative data with which to understand what happens in networks with particular structural characteristics. Using mixed methods, I add context and process to findings about how density, betweenness centrality, and modularity matter, identifying three types of network structure.

By identifying three "ideal types" of friendship networks—tight-knitters, compartmentalizers, and samplers—my research adds empirical evidence to theories positing particular types of relationships. For example, in discussing the change to "modern" society, Georg Simmel (1906) notes that friendships transformed from being tightly cohesive and narrower to "differentiated," meaning that individuals have only one type of connection to a friend, whether through religion or as part of an intellectual community. Both friendship types are evident in my sample of students from one college: the former characterizes tight-knitters and the latter characterizes compartmentalizers. Simmel ([1908] 1971), moreover, discusses high levels of homogeneity in the cohesive groups, which I find among many but not all the tight-knitters. My findings also contradict network researchers' assertion that dense networks are not the norm (C. Fischer and Shavit 1995; Haynie 2001; Schreck, Fisher, and Miller 2004; Wellman et al. 1997). This is true only for white students; most black and Latino students have tight-knit networks. One interesting expansion on the work I present in this book would be to map out networks in a representative sample to find out which patterns are more common, among what groups, in which institutional settings, and at what points in the life course. My research provides a first step toward mapping out "ideal types" of friendship structure.

On the basis of my findings, I would caution against claims that tight-knit networks are negative per se. Friendship is what researchers refer to as a strong tie, a connection that is emotionally intense, reciprocal, and intimate and involves time spent together (Granovetter 1973). A long line of research, dating back to Mark Granovetter's work, has focused on the importance of weak ties for many types of outcomes, particularly getting a job. Although I do not systematically measure weak ties, the interviews allowed me a glimpse into whether students had many weak ties or were more insular. Most tight-knitters had ties outside their group, weak ties that were not friendship ties. Therefore, conclusions such as "isolation in a tight-knit, exclusive group can be detrimental" and advice such as "Don't put all your eggs in one basket" (Chambliss and Takacs 2014, 165) do not make sense for most students.[6] Because tight-knit networks helped many students, such as Alberto, thrive socially and academically at MU, Chambliss and Takacs's advice needs more contextualizing.

It may also be surprising that the social capital flowing within networks can be negative not only academically but also socially and that its negative effects differ by network structure. My finding that friends do not always have academic or social benefits adds to research showing that networks and the social capital that flows through them are not always beneficial (Bourdieu 1986; Portes 1998; Putnam 2000). I find that the two main negative effects of social capital are what Portes (1998; Portes and Sensenbrenner 1993) refers to as excess claims to group members and constraints on individual freedom that can limit access to outside contacts. Because college students value a balance between academic and social life, the excess claims they face revolve around academic and social aspects. Network members spending too much time together on social aspects of college have too little time for joint academic involvement. This occurs somewhat differently for each network type. For tight-knitters who are students of color, providing each other with social support to counter negative experiences on campus takes time and energy from their joint academic involvement. In other words, friends end up supporting each other socially with little time to be involved in each other's academic lives. Tight-knit networks restrict individual freedom, provide social support, and circulate information well, as prior research asserts (e.g., Coleman 1990; Haynie 2001; Portes and Sensenbrenner 1993; Wellman and Gulia 1999), but these effects are not always academically positive. Some research has found that people with less dense networks experienced the positive effects of emotional support (Hirsch 1980), satisfaction with socializing (Hirsch 1980), and mental health (C. Fischer 1982), but I find that although samplers had mostly positive academic outcomes, they had less positive social ones. Moreover, samplers' low-density networks did not help them thrive academically or socially, although their friends also did not pull them down academically, as was true for some tight-knitters. Thus, they do not face as many constraints on individual freedoms.[7] Samplers gain fewer benefits from their friendship networks but also face fewer of the negative effects. Theoretically, this shows that the positive and negative effects of social capital are stronger in more dense networks and weaker in less dense networks and have the greatest impact on those who are more central in their networks (as measured by betweenness centrality). By focusing on network structure, my findings advance social capital research by documenting not only its negative effects but also how negative effects are magnified in some network structures and reduced in others.

The strategies of integration and separation discussed in chapter 2 can not only serve as a handy checklist for students but also help researchers better understand the mechanisms through which peers affect one another. A growing body of research, particularly in economics, shows that peer groups influence individuals academically (e.g., in terms of grades and test scores) and socially (e.g., in terms of drinking and criminal behavior) (see review in Sacerdote 2011). While my research does not settle the self-selection issue these researchers grapple with, the strategies of integration and separation I identify provide details about how such academic benefits of a specific group of peers—friends—may occur. These mechanisms, moreover, operate differently according to network structure, as chapters 3–5 show, suggesting the need for data on friendship networks over time, which can both address the self-selection issue and measure network type.

### Sociology of Education

My findings have implications for educational research in several areas. By highlighting close connections between academic and social life, these findings reorient educational scholarship that tends to focus on either one or the other. They also confirm that social and academic integration are important and cannot be measured by a single indicator. Network analysis, however, provides another tool with which researchers can assess the extent to which students are socially integrated. Samplers, in general, do not thrive socially, and their disconnected networks provide one piece of evidence for this.

Close attention to the ways that network structures vary by students' race, gender, and class provides important insights into the mechanisms that perpetuate stratification. Perhaps surprisingly, I find that friendship both contributes to racial, gender, and class inequalities in higher education and can be helpful in ameliorating them. For example, two recent books both titled *Degrees of Inequality* argue that the US "system of higher education not only fails to mitigate inequality but it exacerbates it, creating a deeply stratified society" (Mettler 2014, 24), with Suzanne Mettler (2014) focusing on class and Ann Mullen (2010) on how class and gender influence where a student attends college and what she or he majors in. Others frame this problem around how students learn little in college (Arum and Roksa 2011), how public colleges do a better job of meeting the educational needs of privileged than of less advantaged students (Armstrong and Hamilton 2013), and how there are racial gaps in students' academic outcomes at selective colleges (Charles et al. 2009). I find that friendships can both enable and constrain these educational inequalities. Friendships can elevate the academic achievement of students of color, as they did for Alberto and other high-achieving tight-knitters. While I find that many students of color face microaggressions and race-based isolation in college, in some cases the "minority" identity is a positive factor because it brings students together academically and also helps them craft supportive networks. This places white students at both an advantage and a disadvantage. They benefit from white privilege without recognizing it (also see Feagin, Vera, and Imani 1996), yet they see students of color benefiting from connecting and joining "special" groups for students based on racial or ethnic background. Friendships can also harm students academically, as they do for low-achieving tight-knitters, and socially, as they do for samplers. In terms of gender, scholars have documented many ways in which women exceed men in educational outcomes (e.g., DiPrete and Buchmann 2013) and have argued for the educative value of women's friendships (Martinez Alemán 1997, 2000, 2010). My research, however, which compares men's and women's friendships, does not find that women's friendships contribute to their educational advantages. If anything, men gained an advantage from their girlfriends' academic instrumental and emotional support. Similarly, class differences in students' friendships are not as vast as recent research implies (Armstrong and Hamilton 2013; Stuber 2011) and are most stark in compartmentalized networks. Education scholars should pay more attention to friendships for their ability to reduce and increase multiple types of educational inequalities.

My findings also add to research on inequality in higher education by attending to the intersection of race, class, and gender. Although scholars argue that race, class, and gender inequalities, among others, cannot be understood separately (e.g., Collins 1990), rarely do scholars have the data that allow them to explore students' experiences across the intersection of these three inequalities. While race generally provides the starkest contrasts in the outcomes and experiences of my participants, I find that gender and class also affect how and whether friends provide academic and social benefits.

In sum, paying more attention to friendship is important for several reasons. I argue that friends help and hinder individuals academically and socially and that academically supportive friendships have lasting impacts academically and socially. Friendships also contribute to the reproduction and disruption of racial and class inequalities, such as the gaps in graduation rates. By better understanding friendship, we can assist students and institutions in drawing on the strengths of friends and avoiding the pitfalls they may present. Paying more attention to friendship helps us better understand college life and how networks influence life after college. It also helps us to address the criticism that higher education is failing our youth and to offer meaningful solutions.

## ACKNOWLEDGMENTS

I have spent much of the last 12 years researching and writing this book. This process has been an intellectual journey, and I have a range of people to thank who helped me in various ways throughout this journey. I particularly wish to thank Donna Eder for her unwavering support for me and this project and for her example of leading a "balanced life." I also offer a special thank-you to my amazing editor, Elizabeth Branch Dyson at the University of Chicago Press, who believed in this book and provided sage advice at critical points.

I appreciate the many people who read drafts of the full manuscript, including anonymous reviewers at the University of Chicago Press and participants in my Manuscript Review Seminar sponsored by the Nelson A. Rockefeller Center for Public Policy and the Social Sciences: Denise Anthony, John Campbell, Deborah King, Adam Kleinbaum, Kathryn Lively, Scott Pauls, Eric Ramsey, Bruce Sacerdote, Andrew Samwick, and Chris Wohlforth at Dartmouth and my outside reviewers, Claudia Buchmann and Camille Charles. Many other people have read or listened to papers or chapters over the years: Amanda Koontz Anthony, Elizabeth Armstrong, Richard Arum, Marc Dixon, Emily Fairchild, Laura Hamilton, Reese Kelly, Bernice Pescosolido, Brian Powell, Doug Schrock, Jenny Stuber, other faculty and students at Dartmouth College, Florida State University, Indiana University, University of California–Davis, and Davidson College, and attendees at the annual meetings of the Sociology of Education Association and the American Sociological Association. I also thank my writing group members, who read many drafts of chapter introductions and listened to many weekly goals: Celeste Campos-Castillo, Charlene Cruz-Cerdas, Joe DiGrazia, Jason Houle, Yvonne Kwan, Kim Rogers, Kristin Smith, and Emily Walton.

This project benefited from generous financial support during data collection, analysis, and writing from many sources: the National Science Foundation, the Association for the Study of Higher Education and the Lumina Foundation, Alfred Lindesmith-Elizabeth Ione Mullins Fellowship at Indiana University, First Year Assistant Professor and Sociology Department Research Grants at Florida State University, and Walter and Constance Burke Research Initiation Award and funding from the Nelson A. Rockefeller Center for Public Policy and the Social Sciences at Dartmouth College.

A number of undergraduate and graduate students have provided help along the way—transcribing interviews, entering data, analyzing data, conducting literature reviews, and checking references—Emmanuel Blankson, Eugene Cho, Stephanie Cimino, David Cordero, Gina Greenwalt, Kristin Hauge, Morgan Matthews, Emily Meanwell, Sarah Milligan, Kate Moore, Abraham Pena, Dana Rasmussen-McComb, Colleen Reilly, Tiffany Stephens, Lindsey Trimble, Carmen Von Rohr, Lisa Warner, and others I may have forgotten to name. I especially want to thank Orit Fisher, Amanda Koontz Anthony, and Brandon Jackson for help with collecting the follow-up data while they were graduate students at Florida State University.

I thank the many friends with academic benefits that I've had over the years, especially Sarah Smith Rainey, Alicia Suarez, and Emily Fairchild. I feel indebted to the other women's studies majors at Tulane, who encouraged my interests in women's friendships through our senior project, especially Amy Bergholtz, Marta Cuboni, and Kathleen Farmer Williams, and our professor, Beth Willinger, who supported our curiosity.

I also thank my family, who have stood by me and listened to me talk about the book throughout the decade that I've been working on it— Marilyn, Mark, Maureen, Marvin, and Andrew McCabe and Deb and Alex Vida—and my partner, Jeremy Vida, who cooked many meals and corralled children so that I could have "just a few more minutes" to write. I hope that our children, Kallen and Cole, will find friends who support them in the many ways that I discuss in this book.

A final thanks to all those who, as students and young adults, generously shared their stories with me and answered my many questions about their friendships. Without them, this project would not have been possible.

I began this project interested in students' friendships, particularly in how women's and men's friends supported them academically. As I got into the field and talked with students, I realized that the issue was much more complex. The experiences students shared with me clued me in that I should focus not only on academic support but also on social support. I was also struck by differences between the experiences of students of color and white students, which led me to focus more on racial differences in academic and social life and how friends provided support for students' race-based experiences on campus. In 2006, when I wrote my dissertation using some of these data, the project was about how students manage racial and ethnic identities on a predominantly white campus and create academic and social communities, including by founding a chapter of a multicultural sorority. As I continued to reread transcripts and field notes, I realized, however, that the story of how students' friends support them differently according to the connections among their friends was still untold and that it would be a more complete story if I continued to follow these students into young adulthood. This book is where I chose to tell this story.

In this appendix, I elaborate on the data collection and analysis. I do not repeat information from earlier chapters here: see the introduction for details about MU, the college where I conducted my research; chapter 1 for information about the network data; and chapter 6 for information about the follow-up interviews.

## Sample

My decisions about who to include in the study were shaped by my goals: to better understand the experiences and perceptions of a diverse range of students. In line with a case study approach, I focused on how to best identify patterns in students' experiences rather than the goal of making causal claims (Small 2009). I did not construct my sample, therefore, to be generalizable to MU students or youth as a whole or to compare students across institutions. While one campus is not representative of the undergraduate experience, MU is an ideal place to begin such an investigation because it is the type of college attended by most students who attend four-year institutions.[1] Once we understand the strategies students use and the networks they form, future research should explore how common certain patterns are among students in a range of institutional environments.

Because I wanted to capture a range of experiences but planned to interview only about 80 students out of a population of 30,000, I recruited students using theoretical and snowball sampling. Using theoretical sampling, I oversampled black and Latino students so that they made up half my sample; the other half was white students.[2] I chose to focus on black and Latino students rather than other marginalized groups because of educational inequalities impacting these groups and because they make up a large enough population on campus to discuss group differences in my sample. I also theoretically sampled students who were not members of any student organizations and students who belonged to some of the over 400 student organizations, recruiting from four types: identity-based clubs for women and racial groups, residential living-learning centers, academic clubs, and Greek organizations (i.e., sororities and fraternities). To supplement these recruitment efforts, I asked participants to suggest people for me to speak with, interviewing those who fit into my theoretical sampling strategy. For approximately half of the participants, I interviewed one or more of their friends, which provided another window into the participants' lives and their friendship groups, similar to the approach used by Lilian Rubin (1985). Along with diversity in race and type of organizational memberships, I tried to recruit students from a range of points in their college career. Because much research, dating back to Theodore Newcomb (1961), finds that friendships become more stable over time, I did not interview students during their first term of classes at MU.[3] As shown in table A.1, I ended up with a sample diverse in many ways, including race, class, year in college, and organizational memberships. Table A.1 also provides a clear and comprehensive summary of the similarities and differences across the three network types—tight-knitters, compartmentalizers, and samplers—to supplement the in-depth portraits offered in chapters 3–5.

**Table A.1** Characteristics of participants by network type

| | Tight-Knitters | Compart-mentalizers | Samplers | Overall Sample* | Range |
|---|---|---|---|---|---|
| **Friendships during college:** | | | | | |
| Number of friends | 13 | 20 | 20 | 18 | 3–60 |
| MU friends (%) | 57 | 66 | 60 | 65 | 15–100 |
| Friends from home (%) | 45 | 36 | 33 | 38 | 0–100 |
| Friends from home who also attend MU (%) | 14 | 13 | 7 | 12 | 0–58 |
| Friends who are family members (%) | 0 | 2 | 5 | 2 | 0–25 |
| Same-race friends (%) | 77 | 80 | 60 | 75 | 0–100 |
| Same-gender friends (%) | 70 | 68 | 66 | 68 | 20–100 |
| Friends' majors named (%)[†] | 87 | 88 | 83 | 86 | 45–100 |
| Density | 0.86 | 0.48 | 0.24 | 0.56 | 0.08–1 |
| Density of first 10 friends | 0.88 | 0.63 | 0.38 | 0.67 | 0.14–1 |
| Betweenness centrality (normalized) | 0.04 | 0.25 | 0.62 | 0.25 | 0–0.89 |
| **Friendships after college:[‡]** | | | | | |
| Number of friends | 21 | 25 | 17 | 24 | 7–87 |
| MU friends (%) | 50 | 31 | 33 | 39 | 8–80 |
| Friends from 2004–5 (%) | 30 | 23 | 23 | 25 | 0–88 |
| Friends who are family members (%) | 10 | 6 | 5 | 6 | 0–47 |
| Same-race friends (%) | 81 | 75 | 53 | 73 | 11–100 |
| Same-gender friends (%) | 70 | 73 | 56 | 71 | 31–96 |
| Density score | 0.50 | 0.42 | 0.50 | 0.46 | 0.21–0.90 |
| Betweenness centrality (normalized) | 0.25 | 0.32 | 0.26 | 0.28 | 0.01–0.56 |
| **Background:** | | | | | |
| Race: | | | | | |
| White (%) | 9 | 85 | 33 | 51 | — |
| Black (%) | 55 | 6 | 33 | 28 | — |
| Latina/o (%) | 32 | 9 | 17 | 16 | — |
| Asian (%) | 5 | 0 | 17 | 4 | — |
| Gender (% female) | 63 | 79 | 50 | 73 | — |
| Age (years) | 20 | 20 | 20 | 20 | 18–22 |
| In-state resident | 86 | 67 | 75 | 76 | — |
| Lesbian, gay, or bisexual (%) | 9 | 3 | 8 | 6 | — |
| First-generation (%) | 73 | 36 | 42 | 46 | — |
| Class: | | | | | |
| Upper (%) | 23 | 27 | 33 | 28 | — |
| Middle (%) | 36 | 55 | 33 | 44 | — |
| Lower (%) | 41 | 18 | 33 | 28 | — |
| **Campus experiences:** | | | | | |
| Years at MU | 2.9 | 2.6 | 2.0 | 2.7 | 1–5 |
| Years at any college | 3.0 | 2.7 | 2.5 | 2.8 | 1–5 |
| Living on campus (%) | 55 | 48 | 75 | 48 | — |
| Number of clubs | 4.6 | 4.2 | 4.3 | 4.4 | 0–11 |

*(continued)*

**Table A.1** (*continued*)

| | Tight-Knitters | Compart-mentalizers | Samplers | Overall Sample* | Range |
|---|---|---|---|---|---|
| Greek affiliated (in sorority or fraternity) (%) | 32 | 48 | 17 | 45 | — |
| Employed (%) | 68 | 36 | 42 | 50 | — |
| Hours/week, if employed | 17.7 | 19.4 | 24.5 | 17.8 | 3–40 |
| In a romantic relationship (%) | 50 | 39 | 8 | 38 | — |
| Academic-social scale | 5.0 | 5.0 | 4.9 | 5.2 | 1–9 |
| Academic characteristics: | | | | | |
| GPA at first interview | 3.0 | 3.3 | 3.3 | 3.2 | 1.9–4.0 |
| Overall GPA§ | 2.9 | 3.3 | 3.3 | 3.2 | 1.9–4.0 |
| Graduated from MU (%)** | 77 | 91 | 92 | 87 | — |
| ACT score | 22 | 26 | 25 | 24 | 15–34 |
| N | 22 | 33 | 12 | 38–82# | — |

*Note*: See table I.2 notes for discussion of class and first-generation college student background along with ACT scores.

* This column includes participants who were not in any of the three network types because they participated only in a focus group, where I did not collect network data.

† This row indicates the percentage of friends whose majors the participant named out of the number of friends attending MU. I am not able to verify whether participants were correct, only that they firmly named a major. I separately calculated (1) "unsure" and "maybe" responses (e.g., "maybe chemistry"), which was higher (95% overall), and (2) majors named for friends attending any college or university, which was similar (87% overall). Patterns across network types and other background, campus, and academic variables were similar across these three measures.

‡ Number of friends was collected in the follow-up survey, and the N is 14 for tight-knitters, 23 for compartmentalizers, 5 for samplers, and 42 for the overall sample. The other items were collected in the follow-up telephone interview, and the N is 10 for tight-knitters, 18 for compartmentalizers, 4 for samplers, and 38 for the overall sample (which includes 6 respondents for whom I did not have network data during college).

§ Overall GPA is the final college GPA for the 46 participants providing this information on the web survey; for the others, I used GPA at first interview since it was the best available measure. Patterns across the two measures are similar; final college GPA was 3.0 for tight-knitters, 3.3 for compartmentalizers, and 3.4 for samplers.

** I used graduation lists from MU to determine whether students graduated. I collected these data through 2011 so that students would have six years to graduate (this corresponds to 150% of the time to degree, which is standard in higher education reporting and research). I cross-checked these institutional data with participants' self-reports in the 2009 web surveys; they matched in every case. No participants self-reported graduating from another institution, although 2 participants were attending branch campuses of MU in 2009 but had not graduated by 2011.

# The N indicates sample size and varies by measure: 42 for number of friends in 2009; 38 for other postcollege friendship measures; 65 for percentage of friends whose majors were named; 67 for density-related measures; 68 for other friendship measures; 78 for ACT scores; and 82 for all other measures.

## Interviews

In 2004–5, I conducted 68 in-depth one-on-one interviews with current MU students, encouraging the participants to tell stories about their identities by asking them about themselves, their friends, what brought them to MU, and how they envisioned their futures. In-depth interviews are particularly useful for developing a broad understanding of students' experiences in various aspects of college life and for exploring the meanings students attach to these experiences (Denzin and Lincoln 2000). I used a semistructured design, meaning that I had a list of topics to cover so that I could compare responses across interviews, but I used a conversational tone and let participants bring up topics of interest. The topics covered during the interviews appeared to be relevant to students and their lives, as evidenced by their comments at the end of the interview, which ranged from "That was really nice because that gave me a lot of room to talk and say what I wanted to say" to "I've learned a lot from this." I used pilot interviews to try out topics and questions with MU undergraduates, refining my approach and using language that was more common to the respondents' worlds.

I conducted the interviews in settings chosen by the participants, most often the MU library, my on-campus office, or participants' dorm rooms or apartments. For participating in the interview, students received ten dollars. Interviews lasted two hours on average and were tape-recorded and transcribed.

Following each interview and focus group, during and after college, the interviewer recorded ethnographic field notes to capture aspects of the participants and our interactions that are unlikely to be captured in the interview transcripts. When constructing field notes, I used the recording conventions presented by William Corsaro (1985), noting the central points of each participant's comments, emerging theoretical ideas, and possible changes to the interview questions.

## Focus Group Interviews

Toward the end of my original time in the field, I conducted four focus group interviews with 23 participants (2–10 per group) to explore points of interest and test out some ideas that emerged from the one-on-one interviews and observations. Nine focus group participants also participated in one-on-one interviews. As part of the case study design, each focus group was composed of members of an organization: the multicultural sorority, a historically white sorority, the African American interest living-learning center, and the Team Up scholarship program. The group format allowed

me to observe collective discourses, group behavior, and interactions occurring among peers. This design, in addition to the questions regarding
friends' involvements in academic life, provided additional evidence for
how friends discuss academic matters. For example, my questions about
the ways friends are involved in students' academics elicited lively and collaborative discussions from members of the multicultural sorority, while
they received only a sprinkling of tentative responses from members of
the historically white sorority. This suggests that it is not merely being in
a more socially focused group, such as a sorority, that may deter students
from discussing academic matters with friends. I later figured out that network type plays a much larger role.

I conducted the focus groups in a room that was centrally located on
campus. They lasted approximately 90 minutes. Focus groups were video-
taped, as well as audiotaped, to facilitate their transcription. Students received ten dollars along with snacks for attending a focus group.

## Surveys

At the beginning of each interview and focus group, participants completed
a survey that included background information (such as age, race, parents'
occupation, and membership in campus organizations) and identity scales
(such as the academic-social scale discussed in chapter 2). Students also indicated their willingness to participate in a follow-up interview two to five
years later, and 80 of the 82 students consented and provided additional
contact information. I used some survey questions, such as self-identified
race and the academic-social scale, as probes during the interview to get
students to talk concretely about issues that can be abstract and difficult
to discuss. In the course of these discussions, a few students changed their
survey responses. For example, a few students apologized for circling the
wrong number on an identity scale, saying that they misunderstood the
question or, as Julia put it, "Wow, I really wasn't even paying attention. I'm
sorry." These experiences show the strength of multiple methods, such as
increased validity and reliability through using qualitative data to add rich-
ness to and greater accuracy in quantitative responses.

## Ethnographic Observations

As another way to get to know MU campus life, I observed meetings and
events of seven campus clubs and organizations over an 11-month period.
I attended formal meetings, where I introduced myself and the study, in-

viting students to participate. I also attended other events that members invited me to, including campus-wide programs, recruitment efforts, community service activities, social events, and "study tables." During these events, I was able to informally follow up with some participants, finding out about changes in their lives since our interview. I jotted notes during events, expanding them into full field notes as soon as possible. Although only a few of my ethnographic observations appear in this book, they greatly informed my understandings of student life at MU.

## Friendship Networks

During the one-on-one interviews, I kept a list of the friends respondents mentioned. Toward the end of the interviews, I would review the list with them and ask them if they had any additions or deletions to the list. They almost always did. In contrast to a design that artificially constrains network size—an important concern for network analysis (Marsden 1990)—I used a more open approach for the number of friends and their definition.[4] I used the participants' self-definition of the term "friend," asking what the term meant to them. I also systematically collected information about the gender, race, major, and location of each friend (e.g., MU, another college, home) and details about how they met and how long they had been friends.[5] From this information, I am able to contextualize students' friendships and provide homophily measures of the similarity of students' friends along these dimensions.

It is possible that my figures for the racial composition of students' friendship networks may overestimate the number of participants' friends of a different race. During the first few interviews, I noticed that white students added nonwhite friends to their lists after I began asking for the race of their friends. For example, Greg, a white student, was listing his friends, "Hailey, Abi, Leslie [all white]. . . . [L]et's get some diversity in here, um, Ty [black] . . ." Therefore, after the initial interviews, I altered my data-gathering techniques so that I first asked for a list of students' friends and then asked for details about their friends. Some students still added nonwhite friends to the list after I started asking about race, but I think my approach decreased this tendency. It is, therefore, possible that the racial patterns in racial homophily of students' friendships discussed in chapter 1 may be even starker than what I present. I find less diversity than Mary Fischer (2008) and similar patterns to those found by Elizabeth Stearns and colleagues (2009), suggesting that my naturalistic approach may overestimate diversity less than other network techniques.

After I collected all this information about participants' friends, I used a density matrix to gather data about the relationships among their friends. Specifically, I asked students if their friends knew each other or not. Although this seems straightforward, I often had to clarify that what I meant was whether they had met, typically more than one time (unless it was an extended event, like a weekend-long wedding), although they did not have to consider each other friends. If participants indicated that they did not know or were unsure whether their friends knew each other, the friends were coded as not knowing each other. I was worried that answering this question would be tedious for students, but all but one completed this part of the interview, often very excitedly, despite the length of time that it took (sometimes as much as 20 minutes, for a student with 45 friends).[6] Therefore, between three and 990 relationships were assessed for each participant: three for the smallest network of three friends and 990 for the largest network of 45 friends. As discussed in chapter 1, the information in this density matrix enabled me to calculate density, modularity, and betweenness centrality.

## Archival Documents

From 2004 on, I have been collecting documents that provide a window into MU and the students there. These documents include articles from the campus and the local newspaper, articles written about MU in the national media, statewide and national reports, MU's official website, and pamphlets and flyers from and about MU and student organizations there. Although MU did not allow me access to records of individual students, I was able to use public sources, such as Commencement booklets produced each term, to determine if and when my participants graduated. As with the ethnographic observations, I only directly reference these archival documents a few times in this book, but they provided valuable background so that I could better understand student life and institutional culture.

## Follow-Up Surveys

In 2009, five years after I began interviewing students, I contacted participants to invite them to participate in a follow-up survey and interview. I used any available contact information to get in touch with the 80 participants who agreed to be contacted. I e-mailed, called, sent letters to their home addresses, and sent messages via Facebook and MySpace. While only two participants refused to participate, 29 did not respond to my attempts to contact them. Many young adults are highly mobile and I may have been unsuccessful in reaching them. Sixty percent of the original participants (49 students) completed the survey.

The survey asked participants about their remaining experiences at MU, educational and family changes, the importance of their racial identity in various settings, club and organizational memberships, and their friendships. Four students completed a pencil-and-paper version and the other 45 participants completed it online. It took 20 minutes on average to complete. The last question asked if they would be willing to participate in a telephone interview. All the participants agreed, although we were not able to schedule follow-up interviews with 11 of them.

## Follow-Up Interviews

Shortly after they completed the follow-up survey in 2009, almost half (38 students) of the original participants completed a telephone interview. Three graduate student research assistants helped me conduct the interviews. I designed the surveys and interviews to best use the interview time for questions that could not be asked in a survey format. We used several of the survey questions to open up a discussion about more sensitive or abstract issues, such as the biggest change in participants' lives since the first interview, what friendship means to them, their racial identity during college and currently, and their friends. The interviews lasted one hour on average. Participants were not paid for their participation, but those who completed a survey or interview were entered in a drawing for one of two fifty-dollar gift cards.

## Postcollege Friendship Networks

In the follow-up surveys, I asked participants to list their friends. During the follow-up interviews, the interviewers asked participants questions about each of their friends, similar to those asked during the original interviews. We asked about their friends' gender and race, whether they had attended MU, how long they had been friends, where and how they met, and how they usually stayed in contact with each other. We also asked which friends knew which other friends. This enabled me to calculate density, modularity, and betweenness centrality. It also enabled a methodological experiment in which I asked participants whether their friends knew each other (how I measured density in the original interviews) and whether their friends were friends with each other. Participants discussed how it was harder to decide whether their friends were friends than whether they knew each other. My original measure of density was not only less subjective but also showed the same patterns as "friendship density." The density scores I report, therefore, are based on participants' perceptions of whether their friends know each other.

During college, the three network types fit well using network density alone, with tight-knitters having a network density of 0.67–1.0; compartmentalizers, 0.34–0.64; and samplers, 0.08–0.32 (I also used measures of modularity and betweenness centrality, as discussed in chapters 1 and 3–5). As mentioned in chapter 6, after college, I supplemented density with modularity and betweenness centrality scores to place young adults into the three network types.

## Ethical Considerations

I use pseudonyms and disguise identifying information to protect participants' confidentiality. I had permission to use the university's name in research publications when I received permission to do the research from MU's Institutional Review Board for the protection of human subjects. However, as I continued in the research, I felt that using a pseudonym for the institution provided better confidentiality for my participants.

I carefully reflected on which details to include about participants in the book, particularly for those who are profiled at the beginning of chapters. If certain information was not essential, such as providing a hometown or a major, I did not include this or referred only to a region or a school rather than a specific major. Internal confidentiality—that is, preventing participants from finding out the identity of or other details about other participants (Tolich 2004)—was another concern. In general, I tried to provide enough rich description to contextualize participants within the university while not adding unnecessary details that might identify them to others.

I assigned pseudonyms not only to participants but to their friends. In assigning pseudonyms, I tried to capture the feel of a name without giving away too much. It was a delicate balance. I intended to encourage the participants' agency by allowing them to pick their own pseudonyms, and one-fourth of the participants suggested one. But because many participants chose pseudonyms that would have been identifiable to others (I determined this by asking participants why they chose that pseudonym), I used their suggestions only 58 percent of the time and only if their chosen names seemed likely to protect their confidentiality.[7]

Certainly, my identity as a relatively young[8] white[9] woman in a PhD program shaped the way that students related to me. Although I am from a working-class background, I most likely appeared middle class to the students because I was in graduate school. How a researcher's background facilitates connections with some participants and the meanings made in the course of the research is important in qualitative research. As Julie Bettie (2003, 22–23) put it, in reflexive ethnography, researchers "point to our own subjectivity, acknowledge that it undoubtedly shapes the story we tell, and—most importantly—recognize the fact of the power we wield, the power of interpretation." When we seemed to have a shared understanding in the interview, I asked participants to explain what they meant, similar to Allison Hurst's procedure (2010). When we did not seem to have a shared understanding, I would draw on this to get students to articulate taken-for-granted assumptions and to explain what they meant. Overall, students seemed to take the interviews and my questions seriously. Students seemed to sense that I was seeking to understand them, wherever they were, and their experiences, whatever they might be. I was pleasantly surprised by how willing students, particularly students of color, were to share their life experiences with me. These interactions seemed to be made easier by the fact that many of the students of color were referred by someone who at least implicitly vouched for me.

Social desirability is another ethical issue I considered, particularly as a graduate student talking to undergraduates about academic life. I strove to be nonjudgmental in the interviews, not reacting negatively to what participants told me. And I also frequently asked them if they or others had dissimilar views than what they initially discussed, in an effort to open up the possibility that they may have different experiences or opinions. The frequency with which students told me about friends distracting them from academics, for example, suggests that students felt free to present a self that would not impress someone who is academically serious, as they would likely perceive a PhD student.

## Analysis and Interpretation Techniques

I obtained descriptive statistics on the network and survey data using STATA 13. Pearson's chi-square test is used to compare means, and partial correlation coefficients are used to compare patterns among key variables in the analysis.

Using data from the friend list and density matrix, I constructed friendship networks, or sociograms, for each participant. I analyzed these data in both Gephi (Bastian, Heymann, and Jacomy 2009) and NetDraw (Borgatti

2002). I report scores for density, normalized betweenness centrality, and modularity from Gephi. The sociograms presented are those I constructed in NetDraw, placing the nodes using an algorithm that relies on network properties such as node repulsion and equal edge length (Hanneman and Riddle 2005). The nodes were not placed randomly but placed systematically and consistently across sociograms. In this way, differences in network structure can be attributed to actual differences in the networks rather than differences in how they were constructed.

I used a modified grounded theory approach (Charmaz 2006) to identify patterns from transcripts and field notes, creating theory from the data. I used Atlas.ti, a qualitative data analysis software package, to catalog and analyze excerpts that display emergent themes. Theory was further refined through the use of negative cases. After a pattern had been established in the coding, I searched through the interviews again looking for examples that confirmed or contradicted the emerging pattern. Emerging theories were refined or eliminated in order to explain these negative cases. As discussed in the introduction, I present the patterns that I found through profiling specific individuals and including quotations that both clearly illustrate patterns and do so in ways that engage the reader.

# NOTES

INTRODUCTION

1. This rate is almost three times higher at private institutions than public institutions (64% vs. 23.5%). Within five years, 56% of students graduate, and within six years, 61% of students graduate from four-year colleges (DeAngelo et al. 2011).

2. I use pseudonyms instead of proper names—including those for participants, their friends, campus organizations, and the campus itself—and disguise identifying information to protect participants' confidentiality. See the appendix for more detail.

3. I use the term "Latino" to refer to students who identified themselves as Latina, Latino, or Hispanic or by referencing a Latin American country, such as Mexico or Argentina. I use the term "black" to refer to students who identified themselves as black or African American. I use the term "students of color" to collectively refer to black and Latino students. None of my participants were immigrants. For simplicity, I use "race" to refer collectively to race and ethnicity, using "ethnicity" only when I refer to national or cultural background. As a sociologist, I view race as a socially constructed category that nonetheless shapes people's experiences.

4. Similar to Radford (2013), I determine social class on the basis of students' self-reports. Students are classified as lower class if they indicated that they were "poor" or "working class" on my survey, middle class if they chose "lower-middle class" or "middle class," and upper class if they chose "upper-middle class" or "upper class." I also cross-checked their responses to the class question with those corresponding to the occupation and education of their parents, stepparents, or guardians.

5. This is likely a conservative estimate, as it includes only the time students spend "socializing, recreating, and other," not the time they spend in fraternities/sororities and student clubs, which is probably also with friends (Arum and Roksa 2011, 97).

6. I track students' experiences of social and academic success and isolation. Throughout this book, I use "social marginality" and "isolation" to refer to extreme forms of loneliness and invisibility that students describe, often tied to race-based experiences on campus. I use "loneliness" to refer to this feeling in its less severe forms. "Social marginality" and "loneliness" both point to students who are not thriving socially or achieving the social success that they had hoped for and that the message that "college is the best years of your life" promises. Academic success is based on students' GPA (grade point average), whether they graduated, students' self-reports of academic engagement, and my interpretations of their experiences. Rather than

relying on a single measure, I use broad notions of academic and social success to capture whether students are thriving in college.

7. Later in the book, Chambliss and Takacs (2014, 89) argue that students need "at least one or two friends . . . for psychic survival at college" but that their "feeling of being 'at home,' as if this is 'my campus,'" is strengthened by having a "broader network of acquaintances." The conclusions from their network analysis, however, are based not on systematic collection of data about students' friendships but on students' involvement in campus organizations and general discussions of friends and acquaintances.

8. Procidano and Heller (1983) provide one well-cited example of this research. They measure perceived social support from both friends and family members, showing a range of levels of support and changes over time in the support from friends.

9. Derald Sue and colleagues (2007, 271) developed the following definition of microaggressions: "brief and commonplace daily verbal, behavioral, or environmental indignities, whether intentional or unintentional, that communicate hostile, derogatory, or negative racial slights and insults toward people of color."

10. For example, among the students who entered four-year public institutions in 2004—the first year of my study—61% of white women and 56% of white men, 51% of Latinas and 43% of Latinos, and 42% of black women and 33% of black men graduated within six years (NCES 2014).

11. In other words, most research that includes a qualitative component concentrates on only one or two groups. For example, researchers have focused on class differences among white undergraduates (Stuber 2011) or white women (Armstrong and Hamilton 2013) or on racial differences among women (Holland and Eisenhart 1990).

12. This number continues to rise—in 2013, 8.1 million students attended public four-year institutions.

13. Information in this table and in the text is from each school's Common Data Set, unless otherwise noted.

14. Among the schools in the Big Ten, four are more racially diverse than MU and three are less racially diverse than MU.

15. According to the latest NCES (2014) fall enrollment report, in 2005, whites made up 71% of students enrolled in public four-year institutions, declining to 64% in 2012. Most of this decline comes from 9%–13% increases in Latino students over this same period.

16. For example, a lower proportion of students receive Pell Grants, as well as other grants, scholarships, and federal loans, at MU than at some other large public universities, such as Florida State University, University of Kentucky, and University of New Hampshire, but MU is similar to many selective four-year public schools, such as University of California–Berkeley and University of North Carolina–Chapel Hill, on these financial aid measures. On the other hand, a higher proportion of students receive financial aid at MU than at some private schools, such as Georgetown, Harvard, and Princeton. The Big Ten alone display a large range, with 10%–43% of students per school receiving Pell Grants.

17. Many schools outside the Big Ten have similar rates of Greek participation, including Florida State University, University of Kentucky, and University of North Carolina–Chapel Hill.

18. For example, some public schools, such as University of California–Berkeley and University of New Hampshire, have Greek participation rates of around 10%. And

a small, but growing, number of small liberal arts colleges have no sororities or fraternities.

1. Most findings about students' networks come from the 68 students who completed individual interviews. I base my discussion of network types on the 67 students who completed the density matrix during this interview; one student never completed this portion of the interview.

2. A full 75% of students named between six and 24 friends, with the middle 50% naming between 11 and 23 friends. While the mean was 18, the median was 16, and the modal values were 11, 15, and 19 (with five students naming these numbers of friends).

3. More specifically, Stearns, Buchmann, and Bonneau's (2009, 179) survey used a "name generator" approach, asking respondents, "Other than your immediate family members, think about your closest friends or most important people in your life." Another survey (antonio 2004, 453) asked students to name "UCLA students with whom they spent most of their time and who they considered to be their 'best friends' on campus." In contrast, I did not restrict the number or type of friends whom students could name; for example, they could name friends from outside MU (which composed 35% of their networks, on average) and family members (which composed 2% of their networks, on average). See the appendix for more details about my methodology.

4. I found no difference in the proportion of friends made at MU between students in their third year and those who spent four or more years on campus.

5. Network analysis does not provide clear guidelines on what is considered a "dense" or "sparse" network. Network researchers occasionally refer to high-, medium-, and low-density networks, but they do not explain the construction or boundaries of these categories (C. Fischer 1982, 149; Haynie 2001, 1044). Therefore, although my categories are seemingly consistent with those in this previous research, I chose these cut points primarily based on their fit with the data. I tried a variety of other cut points as well; however, dividing density into thirds represented patterns I saw in the data (both quantitative and qualitative data) best. For example, few students have network densities near these cut points (i.e., 33%–34% and 66%–67%).

6. Claude Fischer (1982, 149) notes, "Although several studies have crudely estimated density, very few have done it well." By this, he means that they often use "global measures" to ask respondents to reflect on the proportion of their friends who know each other rather than systematically collecting such information.

7. As Freeman (1977, 35), who is generally credited with this measure, puts it, "a point in a communication network is central to the extent that it falls on the shortest path between pairs of other points." Or in more technical terms, "an actor is central if it lies between other actors on their geodesics, implying that to have a large 'between-ness' centrality, the actor must be between many of the actors via their geodesics" (Wasserman and Faust 1994, 189). Thanks to Scott Pauls for his suggestion to consider betweenness centrality and to Emmanuel Blankson for his work in the network analysis program Gephi.

8. These categories, however, are not simply a result of network size differences. When I use a restricted definition of friendship, these same three categories generally emerge, although the breakpoints were slightly higher. For example, considering only the first 10 friends mentioned by students, the average density is 0.88 for tight-

knitters, 0.63 for compartmentalizers, and 0.38 for samplers. Consequently, these network types remain distinct.

9. On average, tight-knitters have ACT scores of 22 and GPAs of 2.9, and 77% graduated from MU within six years. In contrast, compartmentalizers and samplers have ACT scores of 25–26 and GPAs of 3.3, and 91%–92% graduated.

10. In addition to similar overall density scores, they also have similar density scores when I restrict their friendships to the first 10 friends they mention or to their same-race friends. They also have similar modularity and betweenness centrality scores.

11. Women differed little: the 17 affiliated women have 75% same-gender friends, and the 29 unaffiliated women have 71% same-gender friends.

12. In her research on students at 28 selective colleges, Mary Fischer (2008) finds similar patterns but more friendship diversity. I expect this greater diversity is due to the methodology of the National Longitudinal Survey of Freshmen, which asks students to report the number of their 10 closest friends who are white, Asian, Hispanic, and black. As discussed in the appendix, I found that asking students who their friends are first, followed by asking about their race, resulted in less diversity and presumably more accuracy. Fischer reports that white students have the highest percentages of same-race friends (76%), followed by black (58%), Asian (36%), and Hispanic (19%) students, findings that are similar to mine and to those of other studies.

13. There are not enough Asian students in my sample to assess patterns.

14. For example, regarding network composition, both first-generation and non-first-generation students' networks contained 65% friends from MU and 2% family and similar numbers of friends (first-generation students named 18 friends; non-first-generation students named 19). Upper-class students had slightly fewer friends from MU (56% of their network vs. 63%–65% among lower- and middle-class students), and lower-class students had fewer friends from home (32% of their network vs. 40%–42% among middle- and upper-class students).

15. Although my sample size gets rather small, it is notable that no difference existed between the 13 middle-class students of color (who named 13.2 friends, on average) and the six upper-class students of color (who named 13.5 friends). Also, there was little difference in the number of friends students of color reported by whether they were the first in their families to attend college: first-generation college students reported 17 friends ($N = 26$), and non-first-generation students reported 14 ($N = 8$).

16. It does not differ between black and Latino men: the average is 24 for each group.

17. Only 17% of first-year students were in romantic relationships, whereas 60% of fourth-year students were.

CHAPTER TWO

1. Although researchers have shown that college friendships can be important and positive, rarely have studies centered on these relationships; e.g., see Astin 1993; Kuh et al. 2005; Moffatt 1989; Tinto 1993, 2012. Even Chambliss and Takacs's (2014) recent book on personal relationships in college is interested in more than student friendships and discusses other relationships, such as those with professors, and they examine these on a liberal arts campus, which is attended by far fewer youth than large public universities like MU.

2. These stories are "social products," created and re-created through people telling them. Firsthand accounts offer a powerful way to validate beliefs, and the shared aspect of these stories makes certain experiences seem normal. Bonilla-Silva (2014)

identified testimonies of color-blind racism and their rhetorical goals; for example, firsthand accounts of negative interactions with blacks or a racist grandparent work to uphold positive self-presentation and the belief that blacks use race as an excuse.

3. The Medical College Admission Test (MCAT) is typically required for admission into US medical schools. Most students take the multiple-choice test in the year before they apply and spend months preparing, sometimes with expensive preparation classes or tutoring.

4. Italics within a quotation indicate words that participants stressed, unless I note otherwise.

5. Students also described instances when they justifiably sacrificed their social lives for academics and those when they justifiably sacrificed their academic lives for friends. Even when students expressed regret, they did not focus on negative consequences, instead framing the sacrifice as justifiable. Some students framed spending less time with friends as a justifiable sacrifice for academic commitments, such as internships and immediately before big tests or assignments. On the other side of the balance, some students discussed situations that called for placing friends above academic commitments. Most often these situations involved friends who were "upset" or "sad," although some circumstances were clearly more serious, such as when a friend's sister had passed away. Whether the justifiable imbalance was toward the social or the academic, it showed students' recognition of specific instances where imbalance was necessary.

6. Chapters 3–5 discuss connections between students' friendship networks and balance. For example, as a low-achieving tight-knitter, Sean had social support from his friends but found his friends ill-equipped to provide him with instrumental help, and he did not find them to be a good source of intellectual discussions or emotional support for academics (see chapter 3). In contrast, Betsy segmented her sorority friends from academics friends, receiving social support, academic support, and instrumental help from different groups of friends (see chapter 4).

7. With a GPA of 2.2, Kim is an interesting exception. She differs considerably from the average and the other two students discussed here who rated themselves as more social: Jocelyn had a 3.7 GPA and Maddie had a 3.2 GPA. Chapter 3 discusses some reasons for Kim's low GPA.

8. In the methodological appendix, I reflect on the interview process and social desirability.

9. "Academic time" and "social time" may follow a more complicated pattern throughout terms at other schools. For example, students at Dartmouth College, where I currently teach, describe the middle and end of terms as more academic, coinciding with midterm and final exams and projects, and the beginning of terms and campus holidays as more social. (Each term, the college sponsors a weekend of social events that involve alumni and students: Homecoming in fall, Carnival in winter, and Green Key in spring.) The institutionally sanctioned holidays, higher academic selectivity, and short term (9–9.5 weeks, as opposed to a 15-week semester) may all play a role.

10. The next chapter discusses a variety of powerful ways that Alberto's friends were involved in his academic life, so it is particularly important that even he saw his friends as providing a break from academic pressure.

11. Examples of these strategies are sprinkled throughout many qualitative studies of undergraduates' experiences. For example, instances where students engaged in intellectual discussions can be found in Binder and Wood's (2013) research on

conservative students and alumni and Moffatt's (1989) research in residence halls; instances of instrumental assistance can be found in Willie's (2003) and Beasley's (2011) research on black students, Mullen's (2010) and Lareau's (2015) research on social class, and Chambliss and Takacs's (2014) research on students at Hamilton College; competition among peers encourages students' pursuit of grades in Becker, Geer, and Hughes's ([1968] 1995) study of the "grade point average perspective."

12.  Perhaps Brooks's (2007) findings are more limited because of the size of her sample (11 students) or because of cultural differences between higher education in the United Kingdom (where she conducted her research) and in the United States. A study comparing students' experiences in the two countries could best pinpoint the reason for these differences.

13.  While some social support researchers divide informational from instrumental support (e.g., Lazarus and Folkman 1984), others combine these types (e.g., Cutrona and Russell 1990; Wills and Shinar 2000). Separating tips or advice from friends (which would be informational) from other forms of instrumental support did not yield clear patterns between these groups, so I discuss them together.

14.  While Mullen (2010, 143–44) identifies differences in what she calls "practical help" across campuses, I focus on differences by network type. Students at both the campuses she studied reported actively helping each other, but students at Southern Connecticut State University mentioned learning from peers much less often than students at Yale University did.

15.  If the goal is exclusively academic—to improve the "critical thinking, analytical reasoning, problem solving, and writing" measured by the Collegiate Learning Assessment (CLA)—then students would do better to study alone than with peers, as shown by the positive association between CLA performance and time spent studying alone and the negative association between CLA performance and time spent studying with peers (Arum and Roksa 2011, 21). Arum and Roksa (2011, 2014) do not distinguish between studying with peers and studying with friends or delve into how this time is spent.

16.  This finding builds on research that looks at race and gender separately. The white students I studied follow the gendered pattern where women more frequently expressed feelings and managed their emotions through seeking social support (Simon and Nath 2004; Thoits 1989), and many of the students of color sought emotional support from other students to deal with race-based experiences on campus (Lasley Barajas and Pierce 2001; McCabe 2009; Willie 2003). As explained in the upcoming chapters, emotional support in tight-knit and compartmentalized networks helped combat racial isolation, and this support was missing from samplers' networks.

17.  I mention a student's major when she or he referred to intellectual discussions stemming from classes to give a sense of where this occurred. Such discussions did not occur with only one type of major.

18.  Perhaps this variation among participants explains the conclusions of researchers who have focused on small groups of students or one dorm floor. For example, Brooks (2007, 698) notes that "friends rarely played a very direct role in facilitating academic or intellectual learning." Nathan's (2005, 99) conclusion is even more dramatic: "Virtually none of the talk, aside from out-of-class meetings for a group project or joint homework session, concerned either the substantive content of a class or any other topic that might be labeled academic or intellectual."

19.  Other work on student development refers to social "involvement" with peers

(Astin 1993) or "integration" with the norms and values of peers and faculty (Tinto 1993, 2012). Peer effects research explores how peers indirectly affect students' preferences and beliefs by setting expectations and enforcing norms, what I term "implicit emotional support" (Davies and Kandel 1981; Hallinan and Williams 1990). Peer effects research also asserts that these impacts can be direct, such as when students ask each other for help (Hasan and Bagde 2013), although Brooks (2007, 699) notes that there is "scant evidence" of friends' direct involvement in academics. I find much evidence supporting direct involvement and the other roles Brooks identifies for friends: social support and "social learning" (the term Brooks uses to encompass learning about who they are, how they differ from others, and their interest in politics).

20. Researchers often study peer effects through performance in terms of grades or test scores, with a few considering college major, dropping out of college, and fraternity membership (Hasan and Bagde 2013; Lomi et al. 2011; Sacerdote 2001; Winston and Zimmerman 2004). Although scholarly interest in peer effects in higher education is growing—much of it in the field of economics—empirical findings are mixed, and scholars have focused greater attention on methodological issues than on understanding mechanisms. Sacerdote (2011) provides a recent review of this research.

CHAPTER THREE

1. Academic outcomes and social experiences were also often mismatched among samplers, as discussed in chapter 5. Unlike tight-knitters, however, samplers typically experienced academic success but not social success.

2. Some of Alberto's story appeared previously to illustrate friendships based on racial solidarity in McCabe 2015.

3. As discussed in the introduction, network diagrams can indicate specific attributes. In the sociograms, node shape indicates gender (women are circles; men are triangles), and color indicates race (black = black, white = white, gray = Latina/o, and light gray = Asian or multiracial, including Latino-white and Asian-black).

4. As explained in chapter 1, network density represents the proportion of ties present. It is calculated by dividing the number of present ties by the number of possible ties (Marsden 1990). In my study, it represents the participants' perspective of which friends know which other friends. Tight-knitters are participants with a network density of 0.67–1.0, meaning that at least two-thirds of their friends know each other. Alberto's friendship network had a density of 0.95.

5. In figure 3.1, friends from home are not clustered together as they are among compartmentalizers (see chapter 4) or, to a lesser extent, samplers (see chapter 5). If this was the case, figure 3.1 would display a division between Alberto's friends from home (Alejandroh, Melissa, Pedro, Raymond, Pilar, and Nadia) and his MU friends (Enrico, Esteban, Jose, and Teresa, who currently are at MU, and Sasha, Melissa, Miguel, and Ramon, who used to be MU students). Melissa appears in both categories because she was both a niece and friend from home who attended MU with Alberto before transferring.

6. I use the term "social support" to refer to nonacademic emotional or instrumental support that students described. If the support was specific to academics, I use "emotional support" to refer to expressing caring and understanding and "instrumental support" to refer to informational and tangible help. Although they have not been applied specifically to academics, these categories are regularly used in

research and theory on social support (see Cutrona and Russell 1990; Semmer et al. 2008; Wills and Shinar 2000).

7. On the 10-point scale described in chapter 2, Keisha placed herself as a "5," while Alberto placed himself as a "7," slightly more social, but both noted that they were "balanced."

8. The differences between their networks are not simply about network size. As discussed later, higher- and lower-achieving tight-knitters report similar numbers of friends (the mean numbers of friends were 11 and 14, respectively, and the median was 11 in both groups).

9. As explained in chapter 1, I let respondents define what "friend" meant to them. Some students included family members and romantic partners, while others did not.

10. The two white students' networks differed from those of other tight-knitters in important ways. While their friends provided general social support, they did not provide social support for race-based experiences on campus. They also spoke of their friends and what they did together in ways more similar to compartmentalizers, the network type most common among white students (discussed in the next chapter). For example, Ridge's friends were his high school friends who also attended MU, and Justin distinguished between his "party friends" and his "academic friends" and how he talked to them about different things.

11. Chapter 1 explains that some students of color formed homophilous networks, while others were diverse; also see McCabe 2015. Of the 19 black and Latino tight-knitters, 10 had more than 85% same-race friends, six had 67%–73% same-race friends, and three had fewer than 33% same-race friends. Students of color formed tight-knit networks, but not all of them did so with same-race friends.

12. Chapter 5 explains how black and Latino samplers also discuss race-based experiences, but they do not use their friendship network to cope, instead relying on one-on-one friendships.

13. As detailed in the appendix, I used graduation lists from MU to determine whether students graduated within six years.

14. The five black students who did not graduate were all tight-knitters. And the average GPA among the black tight-knitters was 2.7, whereas it was 3.0 among black samplers and compartmentalizers.

15. Future research with larger and representative samples could test these claims. As shown in table 3.1, although higher-achieving and lower-achieving tight-knitters came from all class backgrounds and had a range of ACT scores, fewer of the higher-achieving students came from lower-class backgrounds or were first-generation students, and they had a slightly higher average ACT score (22.5 vs. 21.1). These differences also are not related to network size. Despite the differences in number of friends reported by Alberto and Keisha, higher- and lower-achieving tight knitters are similar (the mean number of friends was 11 for the former group and 14 for the latter, and the median was 11 in both groups).

16. I did not ask this question because pilot interviews indicated that students frequently did not know their friends' class backgrounds, which would result in too much missing data.

17. Also striking is the concentration of black women among lower-achieving tight-knitters. It is unclear, however, how the intersection of race and class shapes the experiences and networks of these seven black women, who differ significantly from each other, for example, in terms of organizations they belong to and characteristics

of their networks, including size (four to 23 friends), percentage of friends from home (30%–86%), MU friends (0%–74%), same-race friends (67%–100%), and same-gender friends (56%–100%).

18. And they received *specific types* of instrumental help from friends, as discussed later.

19. As with social capital, researchers typically focus on the benefits of multiplex ties but occasionally mention their drawbacks; research finds, for example, that "highly multiplex ties" (e.g., having a friend who is also a coworker and a neighbor) are "very demanding," but people prefer these types of relationships (Verbrugge 1979, 1306; also see review in Kuwabara, Luo, and Sheldon 2010). Researchers have called for more studies containing multiplex ties, particularly research measuring multiple relations over time (McPherson, Smith-Lovin, and Cook 2001). The analysis here, where emotional support, instrumental help, and intellectual engagement among friends are assessed during and after college, provides insight into multiplex relations over time.

20. Although most theoretical work suggests that dense networks should be more supportive, empirical work on this question is mixed. Some studies find more support within dense networks (Carter and Feld 2004; Pescosolido 1991; Ueno 2005; Wellman and Gulia 1999). Other research finds positive outcomes for people in less dense networks. For example, C. Fischer (1982, 149) found better mental health among less affluent adults when they had less dense networks, and Hirsch (1980) found low network density associated with greater satisfaction with socializing and emotional support. However, these latter studies are dated and based solely on adults; thus, we have no way to know if they apply to contemporary college-age youth.

21. This finding differs from the "weakness of strong ties" argument regarding social control, which asserts that because people in relationships involving "strong ties," such as friends in tightly knit networks, want to be liked and have few outside sources of social support, they might not be effective in forcing other people in the group to comply with group obligations (D. Anthony 2005; Flache 2002; Flache and Macy 1996). I find that tight-knitters generally complied with group obligations, although the obligations differed: in higher-achievers' networks, friends provided instrumental help, emotional support, and intellectual engagement, and higher-achievers redirected friends who were academic distractions; whereas lower-achievers' networks were not expected to provide these resources, and lower-achievers tolerated friends distracting one another academically.

22. Tight-knitters' normalized betweenness centrality score is 0.04, on average, whereas it is 0.25 for compartmentalizers and 0.62 for samplers.

23. Tight-knitters' modularity score is 0.02, on average, whereas it is 0.19 for compartmentalizers and 0.25 for samplers. As mentioned in chapters 4 and 5, compartmentalizers and samplers have similar scores.

24. Of the higher-achieving tight-knitters, seven regularly engaged in intellectual discussions with friends, three engaged less frequently (meaning their engagement was "limited"), and only one did not engage at all. In contrast, the lower-achieving tight-knitters engaged in limited ways (six students) or not at all (five students), and none regularly engaged friends in intellectual discussions.

25. Among higher-achievers, eight reported regular emotional support regarding academics and three reported limited support; none of the lower-achievers reported regular support, 10 reported limited support, and one reported no support.

26. Chapter 5 also discusses social costs. Samplers discussed feeling different from their

peers, not specifically their friends. More generally, the social cost of low-density networks was lack of social support.

27. Five lower-achieving tight-knitters were in the same living-learning center for students interested in African American culture, and at least four of those students knew each other (the four who attended my focus group with members of this organization); however, four other black students who were lower-achieving tight-knitters were not members of this organization, which suggests that it is not only this organization driving particular behaviors and lower achievement.

28. Seeing academics as "all on me" is not always associated with negative academic outcomes. As discussed in chapter 5, most of the samplers view academics as their personal responsibility, and all of them graduated from MU.

29. Team Up is a scholarship program aimed at students who are members of "underrepresented" groups, particularly first-generation college students and students of color. Participants in Team Up take part in the summer bridge program, living on campus the summer before their first year to prepare them academically and socially for college, receive scholarships if they maintain a certain GPA, and have access to tutoring and advising.

30. Although Ana attributed her dense network to the racial distribution at MU, this does not fit with the experience of samplers, the second most common network type for Latino students, as discussed in chapter 5.

31. It is notable that the three higher-achieving tight-knitters who received only limited emotional support from friends were white or Asian. All black and Latino higher-achieving tight-knitters received strong emotional support from their friends. In addition, the only higher-achieving tight-knitter who did not have an academic multiplex tie was Ridge, one of the two white students.

32. Warren Buffett, CEO of Berkshire Hathaway, gave this advice at a Berkshire Hathaway annual meeting (Zweig 2004). In 2012 *Time* magazine placed Buffett on its list of the world's one hundred most influential people, with President Barack Obama describing him as "not just one of the world's richest men, but also one of the most admired and respected."

33. This strategy aligns with common network interventions identified by Valente (2012)—specifically, altering the network by adding nodes. Valente (2012, 51) notes that "node-addition interventions often create connections randomly, yet it is probably preferable to add nodes to a network selectively on the basis of network position . . . to bridge disconnected or loosely connected groups." My advice to seek out friends who can connect you to their group is consistent with Valente's argument, although students often would not know the types of connections held by a new friend.

CHAPTER FOUR

1. In chapter 3, I introduced the term *"academic multiplex tie"* to refer to a relationship providing at least two of the three types of academic involvement: emotional support, instrumental help, and intellectual engagement.

2. This is the scholarship program, first mentioned by Julio in chapter 3, that is aimed at students who are members of "underrepresented" groups, particularly first-generation college students and students of color.

3. Using normalized betweenness centrality measures, I find that compartmentalizers had betweenness centrality scores between 0.07 and 0.56, with an average of 0.25. While a few of these scores overlapped with those of samplers (who had scores

between 0.42 and 0.89) and tight-knitters (who had scores between 0 and 0.28), most scores differed substantially, as reflected in the means of samplers, at 0.62, and tight-knitters, at 0.04. Interestingly, modularity scores, another network measure, distinguished tight-knitters from the other two groups but had a large degree of overlap between samplers and compartmentalizers.

4. For example, research finds that sorority and fraternity members have lower levels of academic achievement (Astin 1993; Blimling 1989; Charles et al. 2009; Pike and Askew 1990), have lower cognitive outcomes (Arum and Roksa 2011; Pascarella, Edison, and Whitt 1996; Pike 2003; but also see Hernandez et al. 1999; Pike 2000), and are less likely to express enjoying challenging academic activities than non-Greek students (Inkelas and Weisman 2003). This research, however, leaves open the question of *how* these effects occur.

5. I previously discussed support from peers in broad strokes (see McCabe 2009). Here, I expand on this theme by showing how it differs by network type.

CHAPTER FIVE

1. As discussed in chapter 1, fewer than one-third of samplers' friends know each other. The density of their friendship networks ranges from 0.08 to 0.32.

2. The only exception is Jocelyn, who did not belong to any campus clubs or organizations. Other samplers belonged to between three and nine clubs, with an average of 4.3.

3. For example, Chickering and Reisser's (1993, 209) notion of "developing purpose" proved the most relevant, complete, and measurable way to define goal orientation because it focuses specifically on college students and employs a holistic measurement of purpose, which requires "an increasing ability to be intentional, to assess interests and options, to clarify goals, to make plans, and to persist despite obstacles" in terms of the student's purpose for going to college and for future plans. However, I found no significant difference among network types in either aspect of purpose. I am grateful to a former Dartmouth student, Gina Greenwalt, for bringing Chickering and Reisser's concept to my attention and for coding the interview transcripts.

4. Five of the 12 samplers had friends who also participated in the study; all five had at least one friend who was a compartmentalizer, one sampler included two tight-knitters in his network, and two samplers named each other. Although the sample size is small, these findings do not suggest that samplers are only (or even primarily) friends with other samplers.

5. See chapter 1 for a fuller discussion of density and betweenness centrality.

6. As discussed in chapter 4, using normalized betweenness centrality measures, I find that samplers had the highest betweenness centrality scores (0.42–0.89 vs. 0.07–0.56 for compartmentalizers and 0–0.28 for tight-knitters).

7. Modularity scores may not distinguish well between compartmentalizers and samplers in my sample for three reasons: (1) my networks are smaller than most networks used to distinguish communities (e.g., see Newman 2006); (2) modularity is computed by subtracting the expected number of edges in the network from the observed number of edges, and many of my networks have nodes that are either bridges between cluster or outside any clusters, and the modularity algorithms place everyone in a community, which does not fit my data; (3) relatedly, some networks have one (or two) tightly knit community along with smaller groups that could or could not be characterized as communities. Supporting the value of these modu-

larity scores, however, is that the two samplers with the highest modularity scores (Deb at 0.39 and Javier at 0.40) are the only two with multiple academic multiplex ties.

8. This is a two-week program where students take an intensive class and live in the dorms prior to their first semester. It differs from the Team Up program discussed in chapter 3 because it is not a scholarship program, it is open to all students, and it lasts for only two weeks of the summer.

9. This last recommendation would work because samplers' friends are not necessarily other samplers.

10. For example, although education scholars generally believe that institutions should "support their students, academically and socially" (Kuh et al. 2005, 241), they tend to measure social "involvement" (Astin 1993) and "integration" (Tinto 1993) using scales of peer group relations and out-of-class interactions with faculty. Samplers may have scored highly on these scales, despite experiencing isolation and feeling disappointed with their friendships.

CHAPTER SIX

1. As explained in the methodological appendix, 60% of the original participants (49 students) completed the web-based survey in 2009, with almost half (38 students) completing a telephone interview. I supplemented this information with college records for all participants.

2. As in the first interviews, I did not limit the number or type of people they could name as friends. I left the definition of "friend" up to participants but asked for their definition. However, rather than compiling a list of friends throughout the interview, I asked participants for a list of their friends in the online survey. During the interview, I asked if there were friends they wished to add or remove from this list. I also collected background information about their friends and determined which friends knew which other friends, which enabled me to calculate measures of homophily, density, modularity, and betweenness centrality. This design allowed me to elicit rich descriptions of each friendship in shorter interviews. See the methodological appendix for more detail.

3. Regarding romantic relationships, 27% described themselves as single, 14% as dating, 31% as in a committed relationship, 12% as cohabiting, 12% as engaged, and 22% as married. Numbers total to more than 100% because some participants identified with more than one category.

4. Of these three participants, one was married.

5. In terms of education, the six-year graduation rate among my participants was higher than MU's overall rate: 87% of my participants graduated, compared with 73% overall. Because I did not interview students during their first term at MU, which is when students are most likely to drop out of college, this group may be underrepresented in my sample, which may account for the higher graduation rate.

6. The median was $20,000–$25,000, and the mode was $25,000–$30,000.

7. The census figures for 25- to 34-year-olds and the results of the Baccalaureate and Beyond Longitudinal Study (Cataldi et al. 2014) both average $45,000–$50,000 but are based on full-time, year-round workers who have, on average, been out of college longer than 1–4 years. My figures also could differ because my sample is not representative and black and Latino students, who have lower incomes on average, make up half of it.

8. Although I cannot be certain of the reasons for this discrepancy, I suspect it occurred because (1) I asked about "student loans," and my participants used a broader definition than "federal student loans"; and (2) my sample is not representative, with black and Latino students making up half my sample, and first-generation college students also making up half—both groups have higher rates of student loan usage in my sample and in general.

9. Arum and Roksa (2014, 72–73) note that 20% of their sample found a job through a personal tie and that "less than half" of these used college friends, with the rest relying on relatives or "other personal contacts."

10. This is the range for the middle 50%; 75% of participants listed between 10 and 33 friends. The mean and mode was 24, while the median was 20. The only difference by group was by gender, and when I excluded the two men with the most friends (who reported 77 and 87), the gender difference disappeared.

11. Among 29- to 33-year-olds, 9% of ties remained "intimate" and another 11% "became significant" 10 years into the study; these numbers were lower than the 40%–42% of ties that remained intimate or significant over time among 34- to 66-year-olds (Wellman et al. 1997).

12. The other important factor was the number of relatives living nearby (C. Fischer 1982).

13. For example, the standard deviation for network density during college was 0.249, and the standard deviation after college was 0.158.

14. Although their sample size is small, this finding about marriage disrupting ties attracted attention; it appeared, for example, in their abstract and in reviews of friendship research, such as Crosnoe 2000.

15. See the note to table 6.2 for more information about the criteria I used to assign network types after college. After college, Alberto's overall network density was 0.46, and the density of his MU subgroup was 0.89. The low betweenness centrality (0.25) and modularity (0.13) scores of his postcollege network were also more consistent with the networks of tight-knitters than compartmentalizers during college.

16. Rather than being one cohesive group, Erica's friendship group consisted of four clusters, with only a few ties between them. As discussed in chapter 3, she lost her entire tight-knit network through a falling out with one friend. It is unsurprising, therefore, that her network would differ from those of other tight-knitters. Her network also differed in two other ways. First, Erica kept only four friends (17%) over time, all of whom were friends she had made prior to attending MU. This is much lower than the 30% average for tight-knitters. Second, her after-college network included only two friends (8%) who had attended MU, one of whom was a friend she had made prior to MU and the other was someone she met after they had both left MU. This also is much lower than the 50% average for tight-knitters.

17. Alberto's after-college network contained 62% MU friends, which is much higher than the average among my sample (39%) and also higher than the average for tight-knitters (50%).

18. He kept 19% of his friends, compared with 30% among tight-knitters and 25% overall.

19. Her relatively high centrality (0.45) and modularity (0.34) scores confirm her network as fitting into the compartmentalizer type.

20. After college, Mary had 45% MU friends (compared with 31% among compartmentalizers) and 35% of the same friends (compared with 23% among compartmentalizers).

21. Martin stayed in touch with friends in a variety of ways. He tried to see most of his friends in person at least once a year. It was easier to see those who attended law school with him and those who lived near his home, so those contacts occurred multiple times in a year. He stayed in touch with others primarily through Facebook, e-mail, or phone.

22. My findings are tentative because my after-college sample is too small to discern meaningful patterns in relationship and employment types by network structure.

23. These students do different things with different groups and get different types of support from them, similar to the mothers Small (2009b) studied.

CHAPTER SEVEN

1. Residence Life staff match roommates based on multiple factors, including interests and hobbies, sleep schedule, roommate preferences, study habits, and Myers-Briggs Type. One marker of their success is that 35%–40% choose the same roommate for sophomore year, with a rate as high as 80% one year. See http://www.davidson.edu/student-life/residence-life/new-students.

2. Jayakumar (2008) finds that these effects specifically apply to whites from segregated precollege neighborhoods who are attending a diverse college.

3. As mentioned earlier, I speculate that more black, Latino, and Asian students might be compartmentalizers on more diverse campuses; there may be fewer samplers at smaller campuses, particularly in smaller schools in rural areas; and there may be more samplers on commuter campuses.

4. Although pedagogical sources refer to these techniques by a range of names—including collaborative learning, team-based learning, and project-based learning—and there are some differences in approach, they share a focus on designing meaningful group work.

5. Faculty can consult many great sources that describe the steps needed to successfully implement meaningful group work. For example, see Johnson, Johnson, and Smith 1998 on cooperative learning and Michaelsen, Knight, and Fink 2004 on team-based learning.

6. In a study of students' discussion networks rather than friendships, Thomas (2000, 609) reaches a similar conclusion: "a broader discussion network is better. Those students with a greater proportion of ties outside of their peer group perform better academically and are more likely to persist." In my data, such cautions fit most closely with Erica's experience of being ostracized from her tight-knit network.

7. Erica, the tight-knitter discussed in chapter 3 who had a falling out with one friend and lost all her friends as a result, illustrates this pattern. The other network types have more options when a friendship tie ends; even if other friendship ties dissolve as a result, they do not lose their full network. Theoretically, this shows how these two negative effects of social capital are most closely tied with "bounded solidarity" as a source of social capital. Portes and Sensenbrenner (1993, 1345) show that "bounded solidarity" comes from a "blockage of exit options" and "outside discrimination" (similar to what happens to tight-knitters who are students of color), but they do not tie these sources or antecedents to particular negative effects. Compartmentalizers, on the other hand, do not typically bond based on outside discrimination and have more freedom to leave the group; thus, the negative effects they experience typically concern what Portes and Sensenbrenner (1993, 1342) call downward leveling norms that keep particular groups "in the same situation." For

compartmentalizers who segment their types of support, this might involve focusing on social life rather than academics.

1.  NCES (2014) reports that more students attend public than private four-year institutions: in 2005, 6.8 million students attended public and 4.2 million attended private four-year institutions.

2.  Nine students in my sample indicated that they were multiracial. All but one of these students primarily identified with one racial group—three black, two Latino, two white, and one Asian—which is how I classify them in this study. The remaining student identified as multiracial.

3.  I did interview one student (Akira) during the final-exam period following her first semester.

4.  As mentioned in chapter 1, most academic studies restrict the number of friends that people can mention, for example, by asking people to name their 10 closest friends. Many also restrict other features of the friends people can mention, for example, allowing students to name only friends who attend the same school or asking them for their five closest female friends and five closest male friends. The most commonly used data set on young people's friendships, the National Longitudinal Study of Adolescent Health (Add Health), uses such a format, asking students to report their five closest female friends and five closest male friends who attend their school.

5.  Due to the logistics of getting reliable network data of this depth, this information is not available for the 14 students who participated only in focus groups. Consequently, the sample including network data is 68 students.

6.  The one student who did not complete it offered to do a second interview because we had already been talking for two hours, but given his busy schedule of classes, extracurricular activities, and paid work, we were not able to schedule it. He had the largest friendship network (60 friends).

7.  Two participants chose their own name. Others chose a nickname or their "bar name" or "fake name," often a variant of their first name, which anyone who partied with them would know. For example, one day as I was walking near the campus library, one of my participants waved to me. As the sidewalk curved and she turned her back to me, I saw her pseudonym written across the back of her sweatshirt.

8.  From some students' reactions, they viewed me as just slightly older. For example, at one of the study tables I was observing, a student asked me about my boyfriend. When I revealed that we had been together for 10 years, her eyes widened and she excitedly told everyone else at the table. She asked when we had met and seemed surprised that it was in college.

9.  I expect that not all the students knew that I was white when they agreed to be interviewed. If they were part of the snowball sample, they may have found out from their friend. When meeting in a public place, I described myself to students so that we could find each other, usually including that I had "blonde hair," which may have implicitly signaled my racial identity. Given the racial composition of campus, it seems reasonable that students would assume I was white.

# REFERENCES

ACHA. 2010. *American College Health Association–National College Health Assessment II: Reference Group Executive Summary, Spring 2010.* Linthicum, MD: American College Health Association.

Adler, Patricia A., and Peter Adler. 1998. *Peer Power: Preadolescent Culture and Identity.* New Brunswick, NJ: Rutgers University Press.

Akom, A. A. 2003. "Reexamining Resistance as Oppositional Behavior: The Nation of Islam and the Creation of a Black Achievement Ideology." *Sociology of Education* 76: 305–325.

Allen, I. Elaine, and Jeff Seaman. 2013. *Changing Course: Ten Years of Tracking Online Education in the United States.* Newburyport, MA: Online Learning Consortium.

Allen, Walter R., Edgar G. Epps, and Nesha Z. Haniff, eds. 1991. *College in Black and White: African American Students in Predominantly White and in Historically Black Public Universities.* Albany: State University of New York Press.

Altman, Anna. 2014. "A College Education Should Include Rooming with a Stranger." *New York Times,* September 7. http://op-talk.blogs.nytimes.com//2014/09/07/a-college-education-should-include-rooming-with-a-stranger/.

Alwin, Duane F., Ronald L. Cohen, and Theodore M. Newcomb. 1991. *Political Attitudes over the Life Span: The Bennington Women after Fifty Years.* Madison: University of Wisconsin Press.

Anthony, Amanda Koontz, and Janice McCabe. 2015. "Friendship Talk as Identity Work: Defining the Self through Friend Relationships." *Symbolic Interaction* 38 (1): 64–82.

Anthony, Denise A. 2005. "Cooperation in Microcredit Borrowing Groups: Identity, Sanctions, and Reciprocity in the Production of Collective Goods." *American Sociological Review* 70:496–515.

antonio, anthony lising. 2001. "Diversity and the Influence of Friendship Groups in College." *Review of Higher Education* 25 (1): 63–89.

———. 2004. "The Influence of Friendship Groups on Intellectual Self-Confidence and Educational Aspirations in College." *Journal of Higher Education* 75 (4): 446–71.

Aries, Elizabeth. 2008. *Race and Class Matters at an Elite College.* Philadelphia: Temple University Press.

Armstrong, Elizabeth A., and Laura T. Hamilton. 2013. *Paying for the Party: How College Maintains Inequality.* Cambridge, MA: Harvard University Press.

Armstrong, Elizabeth A., Laura Hamilton, and Brian Sweeney. 2006. "Sexual Assault on

Campus: A Multilevel, Integrative Approach to Party Rape." *Social Problems* 53 (4): 483–99.

Armstrong, Elizabeth A., with Johanna C. Massé. 2014. "The Sociology of Higher Education: Contributions and New Directions." *Contemporary Sociology* 43 (6): 801–11.

Arnett, Jeffrey Jensen. 2004. *Emerging Adulthood: The Winding Road from the Late Teens through the Twenties.* New York: Oxford University Press.

Arnett, Jeffrey Jensen, Marion Kloep, Leo B. Hendry, and Jennifer L. Tanner. 2011. *Debating Emerging Adulthood: Stage or Process.* New York: Oxford University Press.

Arum, Richard, and Josipa Roksa. 2011. *Academically Adrift: Limited Learning on College Campuses.* Chicago: University of Chicago Press.

———. 2014. *Aspiring Adults Adrift: Tentative Transitions of College Graduates.* Chicago: University of Chicago Press.

Astin, Alexander W. 1993. *What Matters in College? Four Critical Years Revisited.* San Francisco: Jossey-Bass.

Baker, Therese L., and William Vélez. 1996. "Access to and Opportunity in Postsecondary Education in the United States: A Review." *Sociology of Education* 69:82–101.

Bastian, Mathieu, Sebastien Heymann, and Mathieu Jacomy. 2009. "Gephi: An Open Source Software for Exploring and Manipulating Networks." Paper presented at Third International AAAI Conference on Weblogs and Social Media, https://gephi.org/publications/gephi-bastian-feb09.pdf.

Beasley, Mya A. 2011. *Opting Out: Losing the Potential of America's Young Black Elite.* Chicago: University of Chicago Press.

Becker, Howard S., Blanche Geer, and Everett C. Hughes. (1968) 1995. *Making the Grade: The Academic Side of College Life.* New Brunswick, NJ: Transaction.

Berkowitz, Alexandra, and Irene Padavic. 1999. "'Getting a Man or Getting Ahead': A Comparison of Black and White Sororities." *Journal of Contemporary Ethnography* 27: 530–57.

Bettie, Julie. 2003. *Women without Class: Girls, Race, and Identity.* Berkeley: University of California Press.

Binder, Amy J., and Kate Wood. 2013. *Becoming Right: How Campuses Shape Young Conservatives.* Princeton, NJ: Princeton University Press.

Blimling, Gregory S. 1989. "A Meta-analysis of the Influence of College Residence Halls on Academic Performance." *Journal of College Student Development* 30:298–308.

Bonilla-Silva, Eduardo. 2014. *Racism without Racists: Color-Blind Racism and the Persistence of Racial Inequality in America.* 4th ed. Lanham, MD: Rowman and Littlefield.

Borgatti, Stephen P. 2002. *NetDraw: Graph Visualization Software.* Harvard, MA: Analytic Technologies.

Bourdieu, Pierre. 1986. "The Forms of Capital." In *Handbook of Theory and Research for the Sociology of Education,* edited by John Richardson, 241–58. New York: Greenwood.

boyd, dana. 2014. *It's Complicated: The Social Lives of Networked Teens.* New Haven, CT: Yale University Press.

Brooks, Rachel. 2007. "Friends, Peers, and Higher Education." *British Journal of Sociology of Education* 28:693–707.

Burt, Ronald S. 2004. "Structural Holes and Good Ideas." *American Journal of Sociology* 110:349–99.

Cacioppo, John T., James H. Fowler, and Nicholas A. Christakis. 2009. "Alone in the Crowd: The Structure and Spread of Loneliness in a Large Social Network." *Journal of Personality and Social Psychology* 97 (6): 977–91.

Carter, W. Craig, and Scott L. Feld. 2004. "Principles Relating Social Regard to Size and

Density of Personal Networks, with Applications to Stigma." *Social Networks* 26: 323–29.

Cataldi, Emily Forrest, Peter Siegel, Bryan Shepherd, and Jennifer Cooney. 2014. *Baccalaureate and Beyond: A First Look at the Employment Experiences and Lives of College Graduates, 4 Years On (B&B:08/12)*. Washington, DC: US Department of Education.

Chambliss, Daniel F., and Christopher G. Takacs. 2014. *How College Works*. Cambridge, MA: Harvard University Press.

Charles, Camille Z., Mary J. Fischer, Margarita A. Mooney, and Douglas S. Massey. 2009. *Taming the River: Negotiating the Academic, Financial, and Social Currents in Selective Colleges and Universities*. Princeton, NJ: Princeton University Press.

Charmaz, Kathy. 2006. *Constructing Grounded Theory: A Practical Guide through Qualitative Analysis*. Thousand Oaks, CA: Sage.

Cherng, Hua-Yu Sebastian, Jessica McCrory Calarco, and Grace Kao. 2013. "Along for the Ride: Best Friends' Resources and Adolescents' College Completion." *American Educational Research Journal* 50 (1):76–106.

Chickering, Arthur W., and Linda Reisser. 1993. *Education and Identity*. 2nd ed. San Francisco: Jossey-Bass.

Christakis, Nicholas A., and James H. Fowler. 2009. *Connected: The Surprising Power of Our Social Networks and How They Shape Our Lives*. New York: Little, Brown.

Clydesdale, Tim 2007. *The First Year Out: Understanding American Teens after High School*. Chicago: University of Chicago Press.

Coleman, James. 1961. *The Adolescent Society: The Social Life of the Teenager and Its Impact on Education*. New York: Free Press.

———. 1990. *Equality and Achievement in Education*. Boulder, CO: Westview Press.

Collins, Patricia Hill. 1990. *Black Feminist Thought: Knowledge, Consciousness, and the Politics of Empowerment*. New York: Routledge.

Corsaro, William A. 1985. *Friendship and Peer Culture in the Early Years*. Norwood, NJ: Ablex.

Crosnoe, Robert. 2000. "Friendships in Childhood and Adolescence: The Life Course and New Directions." *Social Psychology Quarterly* 63 (4): 377–91.

Crosnoe, Robert, Shannon Cavanagh, and Glen H. Elder Jr. 2003. "Adolescent Friendships as Academic Resources: The Intersection of Friendship, Race, and School Disadvantage." *Sociological Perspectives* 46:331–52.

Cutrona, Carolyn E., and Daniel W. Russell. 1990. "Type of Social Support and Specific Stress: Toward a Theory of Optimal Matching." In *Social Support: An Interactional View*, edited by B. R Sarason, I. G. Sarason, and G. R. Pierce, 319–66. New York: Wiley.

Datnow, Amanda, and Robert Cooper. 1997. "Peer Networks of African American Students in Independent Schools: Affirming Academic Success and Racial Identity." *Journal of Negro Education* 66 (1): 56–72.

Davies, Mark, and Denise B. Kandel. 1981. "Parental and Peer Influences on Adolescents' Educational Plans: Some Further Evidence." *American Journal of Sociology* 87:363–87.

DeAngelo, Linda, Ray Franke, Sylvia Hurtado, John H. Pryor, and Serge Tran. 2011. *Completing College: Assessing Graduation Rates at Four-Year Institutions*. Los Angeles: HERI.

DeFrancesco, Vincent. 2014. "Police Investigate Racist Fliers at 2 California Universities." *Chronicle of Higher Education*, February 11. http://chronicle.com/blogs/ticker/police-investigate-racist-fliers-at-two-california-universities/72633.

Delbanco, Andrew. 2012. *College: What It Was, Is, and Should Be*. Princeton, NJ: Princeton University Press.

Denzin, Norman K., and Yvonna S. Lincoln. 2000. "The Discipline and Practice of Qualitative Research." In *Handbook of Qualitative Research*, 2nd ed., edited by Norman K. Denzin and Yvonna S. Lincoln, 1–28. Thousand Oaks, CA: Sage.

DePaulo, Bella M., and Jeffrey D. Fisher. 1980. "The Costs of Asking for Help." *Basic and Applied Social Psychology* 1:23–35.

DiPrete, Thomas A., and Claudia Buchmann. 2013. *The Rise of Women: The Growing Gender Gap in Education and What It Means for American Schools.* New York: Russell Sage Foundation.

Eder, Donna, with Cathy C. Evans and Stephen Parker. 1995. *School Talk: Gender and Adolescent Culture.* New Brunswick, NJ: Rutgers University Press.

Emirbayer, Mustafa. 1997. "Manifesto for a Relational Sociology." *American Journal of Sociology* 103 (2): 281–317.

Epstein, Joyce Levy. 1983. "School Environment and Student Friendships: Issues, Implications, and Interventions." In *Friends in School: Patterns of Selection and Influence in Secondary Schools*, edited by Joyce L. Epstein and Nancy Karweit, 235–54. New York: Academic Press.

Feagin, Joe R., Hernan Vera, and Mikitah Imani. 1996. *The Agony of Education: Black Students at White Colleges and Universities.* New York: Routledge.

Feld, Scott. 1981. "The Focused Organization of Organizational Ties." *American Journal of Sociology* 86:1015–35.

———. 1997. "Structural Embeddedness and Stability of Interpersonal Relations." *Social Networks* 19:91–95.

Feld, Scott, and William C. Carter. 1998. "Foci of Activity as Changing Contexts for Friendship." In *Placing Friendship in Context*, edited by Rebecca G. Adams and Graham Allan, 136–52. New York: Cambridge University Press.

Felmlee, Diane, Elizabeth Sweet, and H. Colleen Sinclair. 2012. "Gender Rules: Same- and Cross-Gender Friendships Norms." *Sex Roles* 66:518–29.

Fischer, Claude S. 1982. *To Dwell among Friends: Personal Networks in Town and City.* Chicago: University of Chicago Press.

Fischer, Claude S., and Yossi Shavit. 1995. "National Differences in Network Density: Israel and the United States." *Social Networks* 17 (2): 129–45.

Fischer, Mary J. 2008. "Does Campus Diversity Promote Friendship Diversity? A Look at Interracial Friendships in College." *Social Science Quarterly* 89 (3): 631–55.

Flache, Andreas. 2002. "The Rational Weakness of Strong Ties: Failure of Group Solidarity in a Highly Cohesive Group of Rational Agents." *Journal of Mathematical Sociology* 26:189–216.

Flache, Andreas, and Michael Macy. 1996. "The Weakness of Strong Ties: Collective Action Failure in a Highly Cohesive Group." *Journal of Mathematical Sociology* 21:3–28.

Flashman, Jennifer. 2012. "Academic Achievement and Its Impact on Friend Dynamics." *Sociology of Education* 85:61–80.

———. 2014. "Friend Effects and Racial Disparities in Academic Achievement." *Sociological Science* 1:260–76.

Flora, Carlin. 2013. *Friendfluence: The Surprising Ways Friends Make Us Who We Are.* New York: Doubleday.

Flores-Gonzalez, Nilda. 2002. *School Kids / Street Kids: Identity Development in Latino Students.* New York: Teachers College Press.

Frank, Kenneth A., Chandra Muller, and Anna S. Mueller. 2013. "The Embeddedness of Adolescent Friendship Nominations: The Formation of Social Capital in Emergent Network Structures." *American Journal of Sociology* 119 (1): 216–53.

Freeman, Linton C. 1977. "A Set of Measures of Centrality Based on Betweenness." *Sociometry* 40:35–41.

Gouldner, Alvin W. 1960. "The Norm of Reciprocity: A Preliminary Statement." *American Sociological Review* 25 (2): 161–78.

Granovetter, Mark S. 1973. "The Strength of Weak Ties." *American Journal of Sociology* 78 (6): 1360–80.

Grigsby, Mary. 2009. *College Life through the Eyes of Students*. Albany: State University of New York Press.

Gurin, Patricia. 1999. "Expert Report of Patricia Gurin: *Gratz, et al. v. Bollinger, et al.*, No. 97–75321 (E.D. Mich.), *Grutter, et al. v. Bollinger, et al.*, No. 97–75928 (E.D. Mich.)." In *The Compelling Need for Diversity in Higher Education*. http://www.umich.edu/~urel/admissions/legal/expert/qual.html.

Gurin, Patricia, Eric Dey, Sylvia Hurtado, and Gerald Gurin. 2002. "Diversity and Higher Education: Theory and Impact on Educational Outcomes." *Harvard Educational Review* 72 (3): 330–66.

Hall, Wendell D., Alberto F. Cabrera, and Jeffrey F. Milem. 2011. "A Tale of Two Groups: Differences between Minority Students and Non-minority Students in Their Predispositions to and Engagement with Diverse Peers at a Predominantly White Institution." *Research in Higher Education* 52:420–39.

Hallinan, Maureen T., and Richard A. Williams. 1990. "Students' Characteristics and the Peer-Influence Process." *Sociology of Education* 63:122–32.

Hanneman, Robert, and Mark Riddle. 2005. "Chapter 4: Working with NetDraw to Visualize Graphs." In *Introduction to Social Network Methods*. Riverside: University of California–Riverside. http://faculty.ucr.edu/~hanneman/.

Harper, Casandra E., and Fanny Yeung. 2013. "Perceptions of Institutional Commitment to Diversity as a Predictor of College Students' Openness to Diverse Perspectives." *Review of Higher Education* 37:25–44.

Hasan, Sharique, and Surendrakumar Bagde. 2013. "The Mechanics of Social Capital and Academic Performance in an Indian College." *American Sociological Review* 78 (6): 1009–32.

Haynie, Dana. 2001. "Delinquent Peers Revisited: Does Network Structure Matter?" *American Journal of Sociology* 106 (4): 1013–57.

Hefner, David. 2002. "Black Cultural Centers: Standing on Shaky Ground?" *Black Issues in Higher Education* 18 (26): 22–29.

Hernandez, Karen, Stacey Hogan, Cynthia Hathaway, and Cheryl D. Lovell. 1999. "Analysis of the Literature on the Impact of Student Involvement on Student Development and Learning: More Questions than Answers?" *National Association of Student Personnel Administrators (NASPA) Journal* 36:184–97.

Hirsch, Barton J. 1980. "Natural Support Systems and Coping with Major Life Changes." *American Journal of Community Psychology* 8 (2): 159–72.

Holland, Dorothy C., and Margaret A. Eisenhart. 1990. *Educated in Romance: Women, Achievement, and College Culture*. Chicago: University of Chicago Press.

Homans, George C. 1958. "Social Behavior as Exchange." *American Journal of Sociology* 63 (6): 597–606.

Horowitz, Helen Lefkowitz. 1987. *Campus Life: Undergraduate Cultures from the End of the Eighteenth Century to the Present*. New York: A. A. Knopf.

Horvat, Erin McNamara, and Kristine S. Lewis. 2003. "Reassessing the 'Burden of Acting White': The Importance of Peer Groups in Managing Academic Success." *Sociology of Education* 76:265–80.

Howe, Neil, and William Strauss. 2007. *Millennials Go to College: Strategies for a New Generation on Campus*. 2nd ed. Great Falls, VA: LifeCourse Associates.

Hurst, Allison L. 2010. *The Burden of Academic Success: Loyalists, Renegades, and Double Agents*. Lanham, MD: Lexington.

Hurtado, Sylvia. 2007. "Linking Diversity with the Educational and Civic Missions of Higher Education." *Review of Higher Education* 30 (2): 185–96.

Hurtado, Sylvia, and Deborah Faye Carter. 1997. "Effects of College Transition and Perceptions of the Campus Racial Climate on Latino Students' Sense of Belonging." *Sociology of Education* 70 (4): 324–45.

Hurtado, Sylvia, and Adriana Ruiz. 2012. "The Climate for Underrepresented Groups and Diversity on Campus." In *HERI Research Brief*. Los Angeles, CA: Higher Education Research Institution at UCLA.

Inkelas, Karen Kurotsuchi, and Jennifer L. Weisman. 2003. "Different by Design: An Examination of Student Outcomes among Participants in Three Types of Living-Learning Programs." *Journal of College Student Development* 44 (3): 335–68.

Jayakumar, Uma M. 2008. "Can Higher Education Meet the Needs of an Increasingly Diverse and Global Society?" *Harvard Education Review* 78 (4): 615–51.

Johnson, David W., Roger T. Johnson, and Karl. A. Smith. 1998. "Cooperative Learning Returns to College: What Evidence Is There That It Works?" *Change* 30 (4): 6–35.

Jones, Lee, Jeanett Castellanos, and Darnell Cole. 2002. "Examining the Ethnic Minority Student Experience at Predominantly White Institutions: A Case Study." *Journal of Hispanic Higher Education* 1:19–39.

Kao, Grace, and Kara Joyner. 2004. "Do Race and Ethnicity Matter among Friends? Activities among Interracial, Interethnic, and Intraethnic Adolescent Friends." *Sociological Quarterly* 45 (3): 557–73.

Kaufman, Peter. 2003. "Learning to Not Labor: How Working-Class Individuals Construct Middle-Class Identities." *Sociological Quarterly* 44 (3): 481–504.

Kimmel, Michael. 2008. *Guyland: The Perilous World Where Boys Become Men*. New York: HarperCollins.

Kuh, George D., Jillian Kinzie, John H. Schuh, Elizabeth J. Whitt, and Associates. 2005. *Student Success in College: Creating Conditions That Matter*. San Francisco: Jossey-Bass.

Kuwabara, Ko, Jiao Luo, and Oliver Sheldon. 2010. "Multiplex Exchange Relations." In *Advances in Group Processes*, vol. 27, edited by Shane R. Thye and Edward J. Lawler, 239–68. Bellevue, WA: Emerald.

Lareau, Annette. 2003. *Unequal Childhoods: Class, Race, and Family Life*. Berkeley: University of California Press.

———. 2015. "Cultural Knowledge and Social Inequality." *American Sociological Review* 80:1–27.

Lasley Barajas, Heidi, and Jennifer L. Pierce. 2001. "The Significance of Race and Gender in School Success among Latinas and Latinos in College." *Gender and Society* 15:859–78.

Lazarus, Richard S., and Susan Folkman. 1984. *Stress, Appraisal, and Coping*. New York: Springer.

Lewis, James L., Robert K. Ream, Kathleen M. Bocian, Richard A. Cardullo, Kimberly A. Hammond, and Lisa A. Fast. 2012. "Con Cariño: Teacher Caring, Math Self-Efficacy, and Math Achievement among Hispanic English Learners." *Teachers College Record* 114 (7): 1–42.

Locks, Angela M., Sylvia Hurtado, Nicholas A. Bowman, and Laticia Oseguera. 2008. "Extending Notions of Campus Climate and Diversity to Students' Transition to College." *Review of Higher Education* 31:257–85.

Loes, Chad, Ernest Pascarella, and Paul Umbach. 2012. "Effects of Diversity Experiences on Critical Thinking Skills: Who Benefits?" *Journal of Higher Education* 83 (1): 1–25.

Lohse, Andrew. 2014. *Confessions of an Ivy League Frat Boy: A Memoir.* New York: St. Martin's Press.

Lomi, Alessandro, Tom A. B. Snijders, Christian E. G. Steglich, and Vanina Jasmine Torló. 2011. "Why Are Some More Peer than Others? Evidence from a Longitudinal Study of Social Networks and Individual Academic Performance." *Social Science Research* 40:1506–20.

Lounsbury, John W, and Daniel L. DeNeui. 1995. "Psychological Sense of Community on Campus." *College Student Journal* 29:170–77.

Maines, David R. 1993. "Narrative's Moment and Sociology's Phenomena: Toward a Narrative Sociology." *Sociological Quarterly* 34 (1): 17–38.

Marmaros, David, and Bruce Sacerdote. 2006. "How Do Friendships Form?" *Quarterly Journal of Economics* 121 (1): 79–119.

Marsden, Peter V. 1987. "Core Discussion Networks of Americans." *American Sociological Review* 52 (1): 122–31.

———. 1990. "Network Data and Measurement." *Annual Review of Sociology* 16:435–63.

———. 2000. "Social Networks." In *Encyclopedia of Sociology*, 2nd ed., edited by Edgar F. Borgatta and Rhonda J. V. Montgomery, 2727–35. New York: Macmillan Reference.

Martinez Alemán, Ana M. 1997. "Understanding and Investigating Female Friendship's Educative Value." *Journal of Higher Education* 68:119–59.

———. 2000. "Race Talks: Undergraduate Women of Color and Female Friendships." *Review of Higher Education* 23:133–52.

———. 2010. "College Women's Friendships: The Longitudinal View." *Journal of Higher Education* 81 (5): 553–82.

Massey, Douglas S., Camille Z. Charles, Garvey F. Lundy, and Mary J. Fischer. 2003. *The Source of the River: The Social Origins of Freshmen at America's Selective Colleges and Universities.* Princeton, NJ: Princeton University Press.

McCabe, Janice. 2009. "Racial and Gender Microaggressions on a Predominantly-White Campus: Experiences of Black, Latina/o and White Undergraduates." *Race, Gender and Class* 16:133–51.

———. 2011. "Doing Multiculturalism: An Interactionist Analysis of the Practices of a Multicultural Sorority." *Journal of Contemporary Ethnography* 40:521–49.

———. 2015. "'That's What Makes Our Friendships Stronger': Supportive Friendships Based on Racial Solidarity and Racial Diversity." In *Sharing Space, Negotiating Difference: Contemporary Ethnographies of Power and Marginality on Campus*, edited by Elizabeth M. Lee and Chaise LaDousa, 64–79. New York: Routledge.

McPherson, J. Miller, Pamela A. Popielarz, and Sonja Drobnic. 1992. "Social Networks and Organizational Dynamics." *American Sociological Review* 57:153–70.

McPherson, Miller, and Lynn Smith-Lovin. 1987. "Homophily in Voluntary Organizations: Status Distance and the Composition of Face-to-Face Groups." *American Sociological Review* 52:370–79.

McPherson, Miller, Lynn Smith-Lovin, and James M. Cook. 2001. "Birds of a Feather: Homophily in Social Networks." *Annual Review of Sociology* 27:415–44.

Mehan, Hugh, Lea Hubbard, and Irene Villanueva. 1994. "Forming Academic Identities: Accommodation with Assimilation among Involuntary Minorities." *Anthropology and Education Quarterly* 25:91–117.

Mettler, Suzanne. 2014. *Degrees of Inequality: How the Politics of Higher Education Sabotaged the American Dream.* New York: Basic.

Michaelsen, Larry K., Arletta Bauman Knight, and L. Dee Fink, eds. 2004. *Team-Based Learning: A Transformative Use of Small Groups in College Teaching*. Sterling, VA: Stylus.

Milem, Jeffrey F., Mitchell J. Chang, and anthony lising antonio. 2005. *Making Diversity Work on Campus: A Research-Based Perspective*. Washington, DC: American Association of Colleges and Universities.

Milner, Murray, Jr. 2006. *Freaks, Geeks and Cool Kids: American Teenagers, Schools, and the Culture of Consumption*. New York: Routledge.

Moffatt, Michael. 1989. *Coming of Age in New Jersey: College and American Culture*. New Brunswick, NJ: Rutgers University Press.

Moody, James. 2001. "Race, School Integration, and Friendship Segregation in America." *American Journal of Sociology* 107 (3): 679–716.

Mullen, Ann L. 2010. *Degrees of Inequality: Culture, Class, and Gender in American Higher Education*. Baltimore: Johns Hopkins University Press.

Myers, Kristen. 2005. *Racetalk: Racism Hiding in Plain Sight*. Lanham, MD: Rowman and Littlefield.

Nathan, Rebekah [aka Cathy Small]. 2005. *My Freshman Year: What a Professor Learned by Becoming a Student*. Ithaca, NY: Cornell University Press.

NCES (National Center for Education Statistics). 2014. *Digest of Education Statistics*. Washington, DC: US Department of Education Institute of Education Sciences.

Newcomb, Theodore M. 1961. *The Acquaintance Process*. New York: Holt, Rinehart and Winston.

———. 1967. *Persistence and Change: Bennington College and Its Students after Twenty-Five Years*. New York: Wiley.

Newcomb, Theodore M., and Everett K. Wilson. 1966. *College Peer Groups: Problems and Prospects for Research*. Chicago: Aldine.

Newman, M. E. J. 2006. "Modularity and Community Structure in Networks." *PNAS* 103: 8577–82.

Pascarella, Earnest, Marcia Edison, Amuary Nora, Linda Hagedorn, and Patrick Terenzini. 1996. "Influences on Students' Openness to Diversity and Challenge in the First Year of College." *Journal of Higher Education* 67:174–95.

Pascarella, Ernest T., Marcia I. Edison, and E. J. Whitt. 1996. "Cognitive Effects of Greek Affiliation during the First Year of College." *National Association of Student Personnel Administrators (NASPA) Journal* 33: 242–59.

Pascarella, Ernest T., and Patrick T. Terenzini. 2005. *How College Affects Students*, vol. 2, *A Third Decade of Research*. San Francisco: Jossey-Bass.

Pescosolido, Bernice A. 1991. "Illness Careers and Network Ties: A Conceptual Model of Utilization and Compliance." In *Advances in Medical Sociology*, vol. 2, edited by Gary Albrecht and Judith Levy, 161–84. Greenwich, CT: JAI.

Pike, Gary R. 1999. "The Effects of Residential Learning Communities and Traditional Residential Living Arrangements on Educational Gains during the First Year of College." *Journal of College Student Development* 40 (3): 269–84.

———. 2000. "The Influence of Fraternity or Sorority Membership on Students' College Experiences and Cognitive Development." *Research in Higher Education* 41 (1): 117–39.

———. 2003. "Membership in a Fraternity or Sorority, Student Engagement, and Educational Outcomes at AAU Public Research Universities." *Journal of College Student Development* 44 (3): 369–82.

Pike, Gary R., and Jerry W. Askew. 1990. "The Impact of Fraternity or Sorority Membership on Academic Involvement and Learning Outcomes." *National Association of Student Personnel Administrators (NASPA) Journal* 28 (1): 13–19.

Pollack, William, with Todd Shuster. 2000. *Real Boys' Voices*. New York: Penguin.

Portes, Alejandro. 1998. "Social Capital: Its Origins and Applications in Modern Sociology." *Annual Review of Sociology* 24:1–24.

Portes, Alejandro, and Julia Sensenbrenner. 1993. "Embeddedness and Immigration: Notes on the Social Determinants of Economic Action." *American Journal of Sociology* 98:1320–50.

Procidano, Mary E., and Kenneth Heller. 1983. "Measures of Perceived Social Support from Friends and from Family: Three Validation Studies." *American Journal of Community Psychology* 11 (1): 1–24.

Putnam, Robert D. 2000. *Bowling Alone: The Collapse and Revival of American Community*. New York: Simon and Schuster.

Radford, Alexandria Walton. 2013. *Top Student, Top School? How Social Class Shapes Where Valedictorians Go to College*. Chicago: University of Chicago Press.

Rawlins, William K. 1992. *Friendship Matters: Communication, Dialectics, and the Life Course*. New Brunswick, NJ: Transaction Publishers.

Ray, Rashawn, and Jason A. Rosow. 2012. "Two Different Worlds of Black and White Fraternity Men: Visibility and Accountability as Mechanisms of Privilege." *Journal of Contemporary Ethnography* 41:66–95.

Ream, Robert K. 2005. *Uprooting Children: Mobility, Social Capital, and Mexican American Underachievement*. New York: LFB Scholarly Publishing.

Reed, Matthew. 2008. *Student Debt and the Class of 2007*. Project on Student Debt. projectonstudentdebt.org/files/pub/classof2007.pdf.

Riegle-Crumb, Catherine, and Rebecca Callahan. 2009. "Exploring the Academic Benefits of Friendship Ties for Latino Boys and Girls." *Social Science Quarterly* 90:611–31.

Robbins, Alexandra. 2004. *Pledged: The Secret Life of Sororities*. New York: Hyperion.

Roksa, Josipa, Eric Grodsky, Richard Arum, and Adam Gamoran. 2007. "Changes in Higher Education and Social Stratification in the United States." In *Stratification in Higher Education: A Comparative Study*, edited by Yossi Shavit, Richard Arum, and Adam Gamoran, 164–91. Palo Alto, CA: Stanford University Press.

Rubin, Lilian B. 1985. *Just Friends: The Role of Friendship in Our Lives*. New York: Harper and Row.

Sacerdote, Bruce. 2001. "Peer Effects with Random Assignment: Results for Dartmouth Roommates." *Quarterly Journal of Economics* 2:681–704.

———. 2011. "Peer Effects in Education: How Might They Work, How Big Are They and How Much Do We Know Thus Far?" In *Handbook of the Economics of Education*, vol. 3, edited by Eric A. Hanushek, Stephen Machin, and Ludger Woessmann, 249–77. Waltham, MA: Elsevier.

Schlossberg, Nancy K. 1989. "Marginality and Mattering: Key Issues in Building Community." *New Directions for Student Services* 48:5–15.

Schreck, Christopher J., Bonnie S. Fisher, and J. Mitchell Miller. 2004. "The Social Context of Violent Victimization: A Study of the Delinquent Peer Effect." *Justice Quarterly* 21 (1): 23–47.

Schweizer, Thomas, Michael Schnegg, and Suzanne Berzborn. 1998. "Personal Networks and Social Support in a Multiethnic Community of Southern California." *Social Networks* 20:1–21.

Semmer, Norbert K., Achim Elfering, Nicola Jacobshagen, Tanja Perrot, Terry A. Beehr, and Norbert Boos. 2008. "The Emotional Meaning of Instrumental Social Support." *International Journal of Stress Management* 15 (3): 235–51.

Sheets, Virgil L., and Robyn Lugar. 2005. "Friendship and Gender in Russia and the United States." *Sex Roles* 52:131–40.

Simmel, Georg. 1906. "The Sociology of Secrecy and Secret Societies." *American Journal of Sociology* 11 (4): 441–98.

———. (1908) 1971. "Group Expansion and the Development of Individuality." In *George Simmel: On Individuality and Social Forms*, edited by Donald N. Levine, 251–93. Chicago: University of Chicago Press.

———. 1955. *"Conflict" and "The Web of Group-Affiliations."* New York: Free Press.

Simon, Robin W., and Leda K. Nath. 2004. "Gender and Emotion in the U.S.: Do Men and Women Differ in Self-Reports of Feelings and Expressive Behavior?" *American Journal of Sociology* 109:1137–76.

Small, Mario. 2009a. "'How Many Cases Do I Need?' On Science and the Logic of Case Selection in Field-Based Research." *Ethnography* 10:5–38.

———. 2009b. *Unanticipated Gains: Origins of Network Inequality in Everyday Life.* New York: Oxford University Press.

Smith, William A., Walter R. Allen, and Lynette L. Danley. 2007. "'Assume the Position, You Fit the Description': Psychosocial Experiences and Racial Battle Fatigue among African American Male College Students." *American Behavioral Scientist* 51:551–78.

Solórzano, Daniel G. 1998. "Critical Race Theory, Race and Gender Microaggressions, and the Experience of Chicana and Chicano Scholars." *International Journal of Qualitative Studies in Education* 11:121–36.

Solórzano, Daniel G., Miguel Ceja, and Tara Yosso. 2000. "Critical Race Theory, Racial Microaggressions, and Campus Racial Climate: The Experiences of African American College Students." *Journal of Negro Education* 69:60–73.

Spencer, Liz, and Ray Pahl. 2006. *Rethinking Friendship: Hidden Solidarities Today.* Princeton, NJ: Princeton University Press.

Sperber, Murray. 2000. *Beer and Circus: How Big-Time College Sports Is Crippling Undergraduate Education.* New York: Henry Holt.

Stanton-Salazar, Ricardo D. 2001. *Manufacturing Hope and Despair: The School and Kin Support Networks of U.S.-Mexican Youth.* New York: Teachers College Press.

Stearns, Elizabeth, Claudia Buchmann, and Kara Bonneau. 2009. "Interracial Friendships in the Transition to College: Do Birds of a Feather Flock Together once They Leave the Nest?" *Sociology of Education* 82:173–95.

Stevens, Mitchell L., Elizabeth A. Armstrong, and Richard Arum. 2008. "Sieve, Incubator, Temple, Hub: Empirical and Theoretical Advances in the Sociology of Higher Education." *Annual Review of Sociology* 34:127–51.

Stinebrickner, Ralph, and Todd R. Stinebrickner. 2006. "What Can Be Learned about Peer Effects Using College Roommates? Evidence from New Survey Data and Students from Disadvantaged Backgrounds." *Journal of Public Economics* 90:1435–54.

Stuber, Jenny M. 2011. *Inside the College Gates: How Class and Culture Matter in Higher Education.* Lanham, MD: Lexington.

Sue, Derald Wing, Christina M. Capodilupo, Gina C. Torino, Jennifer Bucceri, Aisha M. B. Holder, Kevin L. Nadal, and Marta Esquilin. 2007. "Racial Microaggressions in Everyday Life: Implications for Clinical Practice." *American Psychologist* 62 (4): 271–86.

Tatum, Beverly Daniel. 1997. *"Why Are All the Black Kids Sitting Together in the Cafeteria?" and Other Conversations about Race.* New York: Basic.

Terenzini, Patrick, Laura Rendon, M. Lee Upcraft, Susan Millar, Kevin Allison, Patricia

Gregg, and Romero Jalomo. 1994. "The Transition to College: Diverse Students, Diverse Stories." *Research in Higher Education* 35 (1): 57–73.

Thoits, Peggy A. 1989. "The Sociology of Emotions." *Annual Review of Sociology* 61: 837–57.

Thomas, Scott L. 2000. "Ties That Bind: A Social Network Approach to Understanding Student Integration and Persistence." *Journal of Higher Education* 71 (5): 591–615.

Tinto, Vincent. 1993. *Leaving College: Rethinking the Causes and Cures of Student Attrition*. 2nd ed. Chicago: University of Chicago Press.

———. 2012. *Completing College: Rethinking Institutional Action*. Chicago: University of Chicago Press.

Tolich, Martin. 2004 "Internal Confidentiality: When Confidentiality Assurances Fail Relational Informants." *Qualitative Sociology* 27 (1): 101–6.

Torbenson, Craig LaRon, and Gregory S. Parks. 2009. *Brothers and Sisters: Diversity in College Fraternities and Sororities*. Cranbury, NJ: Associated University Presses.

Ueno, Koji. 2005. "The Effects of Friendship Networks on Adolescent Depressive Symptoms." *Social Science Research* 34:484–510.

Valente, Thomas W. 2012. "Network Interventions." *Science* 337 (6090): 49–53.

Valenzuela, Angela. 1999. *Subtractive Schooling: U.S.-Mexican Youth and the Politics of Caring*. Albany: State University of New York Press.

Vedres, Balázs, and David Stark. 2010. "Structural Folds: Generative Disruption in Overlapping Groups." *American Journal of Sociology* 115 (4): 1150–90.

Vega, Tanzina. 2014. "Students See Many Slights as Racial 'Microaggressions.'" *New York Times*, March 21. http://www.nytimes.com/2014/03/22/us/as-diversity-increases -slights-get-subtler-but-still-sting.html?_r=0.

Verbrugge, Lois M. 1979. "Multiplexity in Adult Friendships." *Social Forces* 57 (4): 1286–1309.

Vesely, Pam, Lisa Bloom, and John Sherlock. 2007. "Key Elements of Building Online Community: Comparing Faculty and Student Perceptions." *Journal of Online Learning and Teaching* 3 (3): 234–46.

Wasserman, Stanley, and Katherine Faust. 1994. *Social Network Analysis: Methods and Applications*. New York: Cambridge University Press.

Way, Niobe. 2013. *Deep Secrets: Boys' Friendships and the Crisis of Connection*. Cambridge, MA: Harvard University Press.

Weiss, Karen G. 2013. *Party School: Crime, Campus, and Community*. Boston: Northeastern University Press.

Wellman, Barry. 1979. "The Community Question: The Intimate Networks of East Yorkers." *American Journal of Sociology* 84 (5): 1201–31.

Wellman, Barry, and Milena Gulia. 1999. "The Network Basis of Social Support: A Network Is More than the Sum of Its Ties." In *Networks in the Global Village: Life in Contemporary Communities*, edited by Barry Wellman, 83–118. Boulder, CO: Westview Press.

Wellman, Barry, Renita Yuk-lin Wong, David Tindall, and Nancy Nazer. 1997. "A Decade of Network Change: Turnover, Persistence and Stability in Personal Communities." *Social Networks* 19:27–50.

Wilkins, Amy C. 2014. "Race, Age, and Identity Transformations in the Transition from High School to College for Black and First-Generation White Men." *Sociology of Education* 87 (3): 171–87.

Willie, Sarah S. 2003. *Acting Black: College, Identity, and the Performance of Race*. New York: Routledge.

Willis, Paul. 1977. *Learning to Labour: How Working Class Kids Get Working Class Jobs*. New York: Columbia University Press.

Wills, Thomas A., and Ori Shinar. 2000. "Measuring Perceived and Received Social Support." In *Social Support Measurement and Intervention*, edited by S. Cohen, L. G. Underwood, and B. H. Gottlieb, 85–135. New York: Oxford University Press.

Winkle-Wagner, Rachelle. 2009. *The Unchosen Me: Race, Gender, and Identity among Black Women in College*. Baltimore, MD: Johns Hopkins University Press.

Winston, Gordon C., and David J. Zimmerman. 2004. "Peer Effects in Higher Education." In *College Choices: The Economics of Where to Go, When to Go, and How to Pay for It*, edited by Caroline M. Hoxby, 395–423. Chicago: University of Chicago Press.

Zimmerman, David J. 2003. "Peer Effects in Academic Outcomes: Evidence from a Natural Experiment." *Review of Economics and Statistics* 85:9–23.

Zweig, Jason. 2004. "The Higher Wisdom of Warren." *Money* 33 (7): 37–39.

Page numbers followed by the letter *f* indicate a figure; those followed by the letter *t* indicate a table.